ROUTLEDGE LIBRARY EDITIONS: LIBRARY AND INFORMATION SCIENCE

Volume 72

READING AND THE ART OF LIBRARIANSHIP

READING AND THE ART OF LIBRARIANSHIP
Selected Essays of John B. Nicholson, Jr.

JOHN B. NICHOLSON, JR.

Guest editors
Paul Z. DuBois and Dean H. Keller

LONDON AND NEW YORK

First published in 1986 by The Haworth Press, Inc.

This edition first published in 2020
by Routledge
2 Park Square, Milton Park, Abingdon, Oxon OX14 4RN

and by Routledge
52 Vanderbilt Avenue, New York, NY 10017

Routledge is an imprint of the Taylor & Francis Group, an informa business

© 1986 The Haworth Press, Inc.

All rights reserved. No part of this book may be reprinted or reproduced or utilised in any form or by any electronic, mechanical, or other means, now known or hereafter invented, including photocopying and recording, or in any information storage or retrieval system, without permission in writing from the publishers.

Trademark notice: Product or corporate names may be trademarks or registered trademarks, and are used only for identification and explanation without intent to infringe.

British Library Cataloguing in Publication Data
A catalogue record for this book is available from the British Library

ISBN: 978-0-367-34616-4 (Set)
ISBN: 978-0-429-34352-0 (Set) (ebk)
ISBN: 978-0-367-40808-4 (Volume 72) (hbk)
ISBN: 978-0-367-40849-7 (Volume 72) (pbk)
ISBN: 978-0-367-80941-6 (Volume 72) (ebk)

Publisher's Note
The publisher has gone to great lengths to ensure the quality of this reprint but points out that some imperfections in the original copies may be apparent.

Disclaimer
The publisher has made every effort to trace copyright holders and would welcome correspondence from those they have been unable to trace.

PLEASE NOTE THE FOLLOWING CORRECTIONS ON PAGES XIII AND XVI OF <u>READING AND THE ART OF LIBRARIANSHIP: SELECTED ESSAYS OF JOHN B. NICHOLSON, JR.</u>

THE THIRD SENTENCE OF THE THIRD PARAGRAPH ON PAGE XIII SHOULD READ: ORIGINALLY THESE ESSAYS APPEARED IN <u>PRINTER'S MARK</u>, A PUBLICATION OF THE KENT STATE UNIVERSITY LIBRARY, AND IN <u>LETTERS FROM ANAGNOSTES SOLITARIUM</u>, A PUBLICATION OF THE UNIVERSITY OF BALTIMORE.

THE FIRST SENTENCE OF THE THIRD PARAGRAPH ON PAGE XVI SHOULD READ: FINALLY THERE IS THE LAST ESSAY IN THE COLLECTION, "THE FREEDOM TO READ," ON A SUBJECT THAT ONE MIGHT FEEL HAS BEEN OVERLY ATTENDED TO BY LIBRARIANS BUT ONE WHICH JOHN NICKOLSON BRINGS A SPECIAL ELOQUENCE BECAUSE FOR HIM BOOKS REPRESENT MORE THAN AN OUTLET FOR UNPOPULAR IDEAS THAT SHOULD BE PERMITTED A HEARING.

Reading and the Art of Librarianship: Selected Essays of John B. Nicholson, Jr.

John B. Nicholson, Jr.

Paul Z. DuBois and Dean H. Keller
Guest Editors

The Haworth Press
New York • London

Reading and the Art of Librarianship: Selected Essays of John B. Nicholson, Jr. has also been published as *Collection Management*, Volume 8, Numbers 3/4, Fall/Winter 1986.

© 1986 by The Haworth Press, Inc. All rights reserved. No part of this book may be reproduced or utilized in any form or by any means, electronic or mechanical, including photocopying, microfilm and recording, or by any information storage and retrieval system, without permission in writing from the publisher. Printed in the United States of America.

The Haworth Press, Inc., 12 West 32 Street, New York, NY 10001
EUROSPAN/Haworth, 3 Henrietta Street, London WC2E 8LU England

Library of Congress Cataloging in Publication Data

Nicholson, John B.
  Reading and the art of librarianship.

  "Has also been published as Collection management, volume 8, numbers 3/4, fall/winter 1986"—
  Includes index.
  1. Books and reading. 2. Book collecting. 3. Library science. 4. Literature.
I. DuBois, Paul Z., 1936-   . II. Keller, Dean H. III. Title.
Z1003.N428 1986   028'.9   86-18442
ISBN 0-86656-585-X

We regret to inform the readers of this book that John B. Nicholson, Jr. died on October 14, 1986 in Baltimore, Maryland. This book becomes a memorial to a man whose life was devoted to the world of books, reading, and librarianship.

Paul Z. DuBois
Dean H. Keller

Reading and the Art of Librarianship: Selected Essays of John B. Nicholson, Jr.

Collection Management
Volume 8, Numbers 3/4

CONTENTS

Preface *Paul Z. DuBois*	xiii
Acknowledgements *Paul Z. DuBois* *Dean H. Keller*	xix
SECTION I—THE NATURE OF READING: JOYS, PLEASURES, AND FEARS	1
Of the Pleasure of Rereading	3
A Disease Known as Bibliophobia	7
Power of the Unread	11
A Matter of Taste	15
Jam for Today	19
Good Books	23
A Desert Island Test	27
The Act of Reading	31

Unexpected Pleasures	35
Friends	39
The Power of Books	43
Surprised by Joy	45
A Long Dinner	49
Dialogue With the Author	53
SECTION II—LITERARY CREATION AND TYPES OF LITERATURE	57
Exceptional Pleasures	59
Books to Live Without	63
Christmas Packages	69
Counting Cats in Zanzibar	73
Books and Winter	79
Books About Books	83
Family Sagas	87
John Drinkwater and T. H. White on England and America	91
Literary Creation	95
The Familiar Essay	97
Books and Journeys	101
What Makes a Good Book?	105
Bibliographic Ghosts	109

Too Many Books?	113
Literary Criticism	117
Across Canada	121
Alone	125
Classics and Bestsellers	129
Secret Worlds	133
The Debonaire	135
Springboard Books	139
Fairy Tales	143
SECTION III—ELEVEN AUTHORS	147
A Succeeding Pleasure: Constance Holme	149
Last of the Procounsuls: John Buchan	153
A Murderous Love Affair	159
An Enemy of the Devil	163
The Jewel Naulakha	167
Charles Dickens	171
Austin Tappan Wright	175
Charles Williams	179
Stephen R. Donaldson	181
His People, His Country	185
Edwin Way Teale	189

SECTION IV—BOOK COLLECTING	191
Disreputable Scholarship	193
Treasure Hunt	197
Books as Treasures	201
From Bibliomania to Bibliophobia	205
Book Shops	209
Book Hunting	211
What Collectors Collect	215
Disposing of Collections	217
A Book Mystery	221
When Is a Book Not a Book?	225
SECTION V—LIBRARIES, LIBRARIANSHIP, AND THE FREEDOM TO READ	229
Information Retrieval	231
Books in Unexpected Places	235
Computers	239
Libraries and Technology	241
Humor in the Library	245
The Coonskin Library	249
Edwin W. Willoughby	253
The Pierpont Morgan Library	257

Conversations and the Freedom to Read	261
Blanche McCrum	263
Carnegie Libraries	265
The Bookish Empire	267
The Freedom to Read	269
Index	273

John B. Nicholson, Jr.

Preface

Paul Z. DuBois

John B. Nicholson's essays offer a window into the mind of a librarian who believes that reading is one of the most precious of our freedoms and that no calling is more worthy than sharing the fruits of that experience with other readers. At a time when the censor stalks the land with renewed purpose and when competing forms of media regularly announce the imminent "death of the book," the editors hope that these remarkable essays will find a new and appreciative audience.

It may well be that prefaces to such collections are superfluous, but at a minimum a preface can serve the worthy purpose of warning the reader of what will not be found in a book. Those seeking formal literary criticism, statistical or formulary approaches to collection development, or an "objective" discussion of the course that academic librarianship has taken over the last half century will be disappointed. These are familiar essays—personal, intimate, and informal, dealing, occasionally humorously, with one man's opinions and prejudices on the world of books. Readers will find an older form of criticism—what an earlier age called "appreciations." They will also find a highly spirited defense of those librarians who have championed books and reading as the central core of librarianship. At the same time they will discover a mind open to the revolutionary changes that have transformed librarianship, an approach to books and writers that can sing praise or, as in "Books to Live Without," can offer a view of the emperors without clothes in the world of literature.

The editors, both former students of the author, have selected a representative sampling from the almost three hundred essays available to them. Originally, these essays appeared in *Printer's Mark,* a publication of the Kent state University Library, and in *Letters From Anagnostes Solitarium,* a publication of the University of Baltimore. The titles of these publications offer more than a little insight into their author's particular enthusiasms. The first issue of *Printer's Mark* (1959) and each subsequent issue offered as a masthead a different printer's mark—those distinctive devices that identified the great European printers of the early centuries of printing. Printing, publishing, the beauty and delight in books as physical objects join to form one strand in the librarianship of John B. Nicholson. The other strand, and the one more dominant in this particular collection, is the experience of Anagnostes Solitarium—a rather dubious, as the author himself admits, Latinized version of The Lonely Reader. It is the whole point of these essays that for the genuinely alive and sensitive reader (and for John Nicholson this means one who is constantly re-reading) there can be no loneliness, for the world of literature offers friends, Samuel Pickwick, Stalky, Almira Todd, Soames Forsyte, Roger Mifflin, Peter Wimsey, who become even better friends with each re-reading. He describes these book friends who do not change and the curious and often delightful tension that comes from re-discovering them when they have not changed but the reader has.

The paradox of the lonely reader is that the world commonly assigns loneliness to reading when as every reader knows one is never less alone than when reading. And yet the world is not entirely wrong. It seldom is. There is something terribly lonely about reading for during the act of reading the reader is in his or her own world. The outsider cannot enter into the lively dialogue taking place between author and reader. Much touted communal pleasures from watching plays to attending sporting events seem obvious and showy by comparison. All of this is better expressed by John Nicholson in his essays which have been divided, somewhat arbitrarily, into five sections: "The Nature of Reading," "Literary Creation and Types of Literature," "Eleven Authors," "Book Collecting," and "Libraries, Librarianship, and the Freedom to Read."

The editors believe that the author is best revealed in his own words, but perhaps a few biographical notes are in order for those not satisfied with the skeleton sketch in *Who's Who In America*. John Nicholson was born in Chicago (1912), grew up in Lakewood, Ohio, and was graduated in 1935 from Washington and Lee University. Two years later he received a graduate degree from the Columbia School of Library Service. Over the years he pursued additional graduate study at Washington and Lee, the University of Chicago and Western Reserve University.

The formative influences, however, were not degrees or even courses but rather friends, teachers, and bookmen. He had the rare privilege of working closely with such educators as Blanche McCrum at Washington and Lee, Pierce Butler at Chicago, and in a humble but unforgettable capacity with Douglas Southall Freeman in the latter's writing of the classic Robert E. Lee biography. His friendships with great bookmen such as Harry Korner of the old Korner & Wood Book Store in Cleveland, John Kohn and Michael Papantonio of the Seven Gables Book Shop, Geoffrey Steele and many others extended over a lifetime and helped to make him a genuine bookman as well as a great librarian and teacher. And yet the most decisive influence in his life-long love affair with reading was a grandmother who first introduced him to the world of books, encouraged his wide ranging reading habits and helped to form his standards of taste and his determination to share his own reading pleasures with others.

Of these special people John Nicholson has written, "A group of loving, wise people opened a series of doors for me, and each of the doors led out into a brightly lit, easily followed road, that has led me, through . . . a landscape that has always given me the greatest kind of joy, and satisfaction, and, yes, wonderment." G. K. Chesterton observed, "The world will never starve for wonders; but only want of wonder." It is this sense of wonder that lifts John Nicholson's essays, written as they were, hastily, and often under a deadline, well above the ordinary "reviews" of the library world. It is this quest of wonder that led him to explore the islands, utopias and imaginary lands of literature: Islandia, Perelandra, Narnia, Middle Earth, and others. His discoveries on these sensitive explorations await the reader of these essays.

The last section in this collection deals more directly with the world of libraries, the world in which John Nicholson played a significant part for almost half a century. His first professional positions were in reference at Duke University and later at Dickinson College. In 1943 he became Chief Librarian at Fenn College in Cleveland. Two years later he moved to Kent State University where he served as Library Director from 1945 to 1966. During his years at Kent he was an instrumental force in building the collection into a major research facility to support a variety of doctoral programs. He also founded the department of library science there and led it to its present status as Ohio's only ALA accredited school. He played an influential role in the early library networking programs in Ohio and in fact was one of the key figures in founding what was to become OCLC, the nation's largest bibliographical utility. He later served as the Library Director at the University of Baltimore where he retired in 1981 after again playing a key role in both collection building and in helping to extend and transform academic library cooperation in Maryland.

It is this wealth of experience that informs the essays on what John Nicholson is careful to call the art, rather than the science, of librarianship. They represent a variety of interests ranging from humor in the library to an essay on Ohio's most fascinating collection of books, the Coonskin Library. There is a tribute to Blanche McCrum who, perhaps more than any other librarian, served for John Nicholson as a model of the most demanding and professional standards offered by academic librarianship.

Finally, there is the last essay in the collection, "The Freedom to Read," on a subject that one might feel has been overly attended to by librarians but one which John Nickolson brings a special eloquence because for him books represent more than an outlet for unpopular ideas that should be permitted a hearing. He sees reading itself, in a world increasingly devoted to information that has been filtered, processed, and managed, as one of the last and most precious freedoms left to individuals. As he notes, "Only so long as such freedom is possible, will the kind of society we live in survive."

Among the many strong preferences of John Nicholson is one that champions a French translation of the most famous of the Biblical Beatitudes: "The debonaire shall inherit the earth." He argues that this is truer to the spirit of the faith than the word "meek" which in modern parlance, to the young at least, connotes wimpishness.

> To be debonaire is to be care-less! Just so, the inheritor of the earth in the French mind is one who simply could care less about himself, yielding up his body and spirit with absolute freedom, knowing full well that his mind, his body, his spirit, his soul, are safe in the hands of his Creator, thus making it a simple, obvious matter to offer his entire faith in his Creator, with no other thought than confidently giving himself in that faith.

It is in this same debonaire spirit that these essays are now offered. They are presented as they came to their readers originally and not revised or "updated" for a new audience. They are free of "care" and thus the essayist is happy to step to the background for a moment and let his friends Richard Hannay, John Lang, Arthur Pendennis and Robinson of England speak to the reader. You will find some old friends, some that are new, more than a few rascals and at least one devil. So browse (lovely bovine word) among them and for a few moments leave the world of computers and flow-charts and join the debonaire.

Acknowledgements

The editors wish to acknowledge, with gratitude, the office of Research and Sponsored Programs at Kent State University for a grant to enable us to prepare the final manuscript of this collection, Alberta Adolph and Judith Conley for secretarial assistance, and our wives, Carol DuBois and Patricia Keller, for helping to proofread and index the essays. Peter Gellatly, Senior Editor, and William M. Cohen, Publisher, of The Haworth Press, Inc. were enthusiastic about the project from the outset and were supportive at every stage of its development.

Finally, we are grateful to John B. Nicholson, Jr. for allowing us to select and publish these essays which were originally intended only for colleagues and friends within the institutions he served.

Paul Z. DuBois
Dean H. Keller

SECTION I
THE NATURE OF READING: JOYS, PLEASURES, AND FEARS

These essays speak, in a fundamental way, to the theme of collection development. The literature of librarianship today contains much on the subject, most of it concerned with objectifying the activity. We are encouraged to conduct shelflist counts, perform citation studies, check holdings against standard bibliographies and indexes, engage in cooperative agreements, etc. Few would deny the value of these activities, but reason dictates that the individuals performing them, or at least those who interpret the results, should have a strong academic background, know how books are used, be aware of what is happening in education, research, and in the book trade, and be able to communicate the strengths, weaknesses, and value of books and collections of books to the readers who will use them now and in the future. The essays in this first section assume that those engaged in collection development read at least some of the books they collect and offer insights into that most important act of reading.

Of the Pleasure of Rereading

As a librarian I have spent most of my life glancing with a rather jaundiced eye at the ranges upon ranges of books which have passed by my door on their way to the library shelves. It is one of the frustrations, of course, of any librarian's life that most of these books must remain unread, or at the most must be glimpsed in the kaleidoscope of bibliographic wonder which makes up a library's book collection. Again, a commonplace in the academic conversation is the complaint that no scholar can possibly have more than a passing acquaintance with the enormous number of books which appear in his field of academic interest. It is my opinion, however, that much of this complaint of a surfeit of reading materials, this frustration because of quantity, is a matter of posturing rather than actuality. It is somehow fashionable for the scholar, the librarian, to feel sorry for himself because of the vast quantity of material he must survey. This attitude, as a matter of fact, represents in a way the sort of thing defined by Benedictine monks as "over-scrupulosity," as a conscious form of humility, which when it is examined carefully, may be found not to represent humility at all, but instead a variety of pride.

Whatever the truth of this matter, as a librarian I would like to suggest that there are different kinds of reading, and that there are some forms of reading which no one, whether scholar or layman, can afford to live without. There is, of course, the kind of reading which is accomplished in the tension of study, in which the reader scans page after page in search of those bits of literary gold which go into the mint of scholarship. There is that kind of reading in which the reader finds himself caught up in an experience of excitement and wonder, inspired by the revelation which the printed pages unfold before him. There is the kind of reading which is probably not reading at all, when the eye seeks a single word, a phrase, an exposition of a meaning, a simple fact. There is the kind of reading which is best described as an exercise, perhaps, in which the reading becomes a mechanical act followed only occasionally by the process of mental understanding. There are these and many other kinds of reading, but none of them, to me, seems to represent the kind of experience which returns to the reader the greatest degree of intellectual and spiritual gain.

Perhaps it was Chaucer's Clerk of Oxenford who first knew the meaning of the kind of reading which I feel represents almost the finest aspect of the art of reading. He it was, you will remember, about whom Chaucer wrote, "For him was levere have at his beddes hedde, Twenty bookes, clad in blak or reed . . . " Those "twenty bookes" represented, no doubt, for the clerk a careful, painstaking selection, from those he might have possessed. They were the books which represented for him a winnowing of the knowledge and wisdom of his Oxford world. If one could have slipped quietly into the room where dwelled this clerk, he would have discovered, beyond the shadow of a doubt, those twenty books to be well worn, well read, well cared for, much written in, and of course much loved. In those twenty books there would have hardly been a page which was not indeed a part of the clerk's awareness, of his being. The books "clad in blak" would probably have been those dealing with the clerk's own discipline, law perhaps. Those "in reed" would have been more apt to represent his religious interests. But no matter what their subject, one thing may be assumed as certain—that these books were part of the very life of the "clerk of Oxenford."

Now I must confess that included in my own "twenty bookes," there are two different kinds. There are those like Pierce Butler's *Introduction to Library Science*, the only truly philosophical book written about the work of the librarian; and there is, of course, Holbrook Jackson's *Fear of Books*, a kind of book that clears the librarian's mind of the romantic cobwebs about the nobility of the thing we are sometimes in danger of endowing with too great powers; there is a copy of Georg Schneider's great German classic, *Handbuch der Bibliographie*, a caustic and incisive analysis of the problems of the bibliographer; and there are a dozen or more professional texts, not the least of which is the remarkable *Estimate of Standards for a College Library*, by Blanche P. McCrum.

There is another shelf, however, of books which are of the very essence of the kind about which I most like to talk. Of my "twenty bookes" there are some ten or twelve which have nothing to do with professional reading at all, but consist of those special friends among my books who have become a part of personal reading in a special way. It is my firm conviction that one does not gain a friend by seeing him once. A one-time acquaintance is but a passing thing.

A friend must be cultivated, with care, with understanding, with affection. Just so, a book which is glanced at hurriedly and put away has certainly not been read, nor has it been given a chance to find a place for itself in one's consciousness. If on the second reading it still has appeal, it has a chance to become a long-time friend. The second reading will reveal a whole new perspective for the reader, for passages hastily skimmed over will be seen to hold new and exciting provocation. And on the third reading the book begins to assume a whole new character, becomes a personality, with facets of temperament hardly seen in the first acquaintance. Christopher Morley's *Parnassus on Wheels* was such a book for me. On first reading it was a joyous book of common sense and laughter. A second reading revealed its hero's dedication to the world of books in a whole new light. A third and fourth reading found none of the laughter gone, but brought into focus some fascinating and delightful prejudices in favor of some kinds of books, and against some others. Today there are still passages which shine through their merriment with the honesty and beauty, too, that make this a minor classic for all bookmen.

Another volume that comes often from my shelf is John Muir's *Yosemite*, and there are some twelve pages in that volume which are darkened by the fingers that have turned those pages countless times. These twelve pages tell of the young John Muir, hypnotized by the thunder of the downward pouring torrent of Yosemite Fall; of his creeping to the very brink of the fall, and clinging to the dripping stones where the foaming stream leaps out above the valley in its suicidal plunge. This passage has made this book a friend because of the revelation of the terror of the man who wrote the lines, the fascination he felt in the mysterious thunder of the raging torrent; the compulsion to find a place as close to the brink of the fall as he could reach. It is a spine-chilling description that makes the reader restless and tense as he reads, but which draws him back over and over again to sense vicariously the experience of the man who wrote of his own fearful compulsion. A first reading of these pages swept the reader along in the sudden flood of Muir's prose, almost onomatopoetic in its rush of adjectives and phrases. A second reading brought out the echo of the hypnotic drawing power of the river's mad rush to the brink; third and fourth readings revealed a whole new symphony of emotion and nerve-tingling responses to the terrifying downward thrust of boiling white water.

To read a book, then, is one thing, when this reading is accomplished in the first clash of the author's mind and spirit with the reader's. To savor a book, on second reading, is to sense that odd mixture of memory and anticipation that children know as they await Christmas. To *know* a book, to possess and be possessed by a book, is an amalgam of these things, and much more, and when this miracle occurs, the reader has gained a friend who will never betray, a friend who will always be waiting in time of need, a friend who will become a part of the reader himself.

The Printer's Mark,
February, 1962

A Disease Known as Bibliophobia

Bibliophobia, as may be deduced from the word itself, is "the fear of books." It is a disease which may be found among the most literate of peoples, and at the same time it may be discovered among those who know nothing of books at all. Indeed, there is to be found a most virulent form of it among those who have never read a book, since among people who suffer from this unfortunate lack of experience there are many who look upon the printed page as an instrument of the blackest of black magic. A paradox may be seen in the fact that the disease of bibliophobia takes on an equally violent face among those who have learned to recognize the power of books to disturb men's minds, and provoke them to creative thought. The disease is a popular disease, in many senses of that word. It is extremely popular in that it is prevalent among such a high proportion of the population. It is popular, too, in the sense that it is a disease thought fashionable among certain types of intellectuals, as I will demonstrate, to decry the value of books. But let us look at some of the aspects of the disease in such a way as to make clear in our own minds the dangers of its ravages.

To begin with, books have in their very nature a peculiar quality of magic. There are those of us who feel this quality is of the essence of white magic, blessed as we have been by the wonder of reading, and delighted as we have been by the joy of the world which books have created for us. There are those unfortunate souls who look with fear upon the miracle of reading, being afraid of what that reading may accomplish. I remember very well, for example, a young student who flatly refused to read a book about a religion other than her own, and when asked why she refused she said, "Because I don't want to be changed." There are others, of course, who are deeply concerned that books shall not be read, because of their fear of the effect which the reading may produce. And oddly enough, there are those who transfer this fear of the effect of books to a fear of the books themselves. When this last occurs we find books becoming such symbols of fear that they suffer grievous fates of mutilation, of burning, and destruction.

Bibliophobia may be shown to take on many forms as a disease. It may appear in a violent form among so-called practical business men, who often suffer from a delusion that wisdom, and even knowledge, are only gained through hard experience. Sufferers from this particular form of the disease are actively suspicious of "book learning," and openly distrustful of the theories which they are certain germinate only in the pages of print which make up the "impractical" training of the scholar. The man of great physical vigor and vitality, who prides himself on being a "man of action," is often scornful of the reader of books because he fears that this apparently sedentary activity, if he were to indulge in it, would first soften and weaken him, and second label him as somehow effeminate and afraid of the challenge of physical action. It takes still a different form in the person who actually fears the labor of reading, and the possibility as well that such an arduous activity will demand the painful process of thought which may result from the activity. Still another aspect of the disease is to be found in the desire of some not to be changed, and these poor souls remain content within the safe harbors of their ignorance rather than test themselves against the chancy winds of freshly stirring ideas.

The passive bibliophobe hates rather than fears books, and hates them so consistently as to make a strong effort to avoid any contact with them whatever. Do you not remember M. Chrysale, Moliere's woman-ridden character in *Les Femmes Savantes*, who, harassed by his lady scholars fought shy of all books, saying,

> . . . your everlasting books
> Don't suit me. Just save out a big old Plutarch
> To press my neck-bands in, and burn the rest.

A pitiable figure, is he not? Thus cutting off his miserable, quaking self from all hope of betterment, surrendering all to his enemies who, foolish though they were, at least kept touch with ideas in their books.

A most unhappy form taken by this disease is that cynical, and indeed preposterous type which leads its victims to assume the sleazy pose of hating books. "What do I care for first or last editions," cried D. H. Lawrence, "I have never read one of my own published works." This comment might well call forth the criticism that a reading of his own works might have brought revisions which would have improved some of their more lurid passages, either by elimination or revision. Richard Jeffries revealed himself a victim of an advanced form of this hateful pose as he wrote that he "would destroy the deadening influence of tradition," especially that part of it enshrined in books. "Take a broom and sweep the papyri into the dust," he scrawls, and he would do the same with the classics for "certainly nothing could be less valuable," despite the fact that these very harborers of tradition gave him the standards which he applied in his rasping criticisms of his literary contemporaries. And hear how one of the greatest among the creators of books, Theophile Gautier, raves in the fever of the disease, "Je vois protest, afin que vous le sachiez, je haïs de tout mon coeur ce qui ressemble, de près ou de loin, à un livre; je ne conçois pas a quoi cela sert." Such posturing, for sole effect alone, is not only the mark of the most unwarranted of conceits, but is the mark of the fop, whose purpose is to gain attention like the bawling child.

There is another irrational fearsomeness, symptomatic of this all but incurable disease, which does seem to warrant sympathy, even while at the same time its cars should draw forth something less than pity. This form of the disease is seen in those poor, fearful minds who see in knowledge power, and in power nothing but daunting selfishness, and in that selfishness only enslavement. This sufferer, who would doubtless seek power in reading for himself if he had but the wit to recognize the elements of power to be found in his reading, cries out against the book as a tool for those who would use others. He sees each thoughtful volume as an oracle before whose wisdom he must prostrate himself, and yet he would destroy the shrine lest some other seek to use its prophecies to gain control of even his own poor mind.

I must confess my own fear of books, yet I feel it is a fear more justified than some of these I have already mentioned. I have a desperate fear of those books which are inadequate for their own purpose. I fear, for example, the books which defend or explain some of our basic democratic concepts with sentimental, half thought out reasons, instead of the hard, clear reasoning which alone throws down the gauntlet to those enemies of freedom whose well tempered blades of argument thrust toward us constantly. I fear those books whose elements so lack both polish and good taste that they become even for the sophisticated reader, cancerous misstatements, overstatements of the idiosyncrasies of life, and so present only warped and tortured, astigmatic portrayals of humanity. I fear those books which are written so untruly, with so little concern for the common good that they offer only salaciousness, and panting scenes of overheated sensation, all presented under the guise of adventure. This is no plea for censorship, in truth, but rather an appeal for honesty among writers, and for a renewal of that conspiratorial agreement among men of good will against the common and too familiar evils which beset the world of the common and unsuspecting reader.

But to be *afraid* of books!!! What a tragic illness bibliophobia is! To be afraid of good companions, to ward off their always ready offers of comfort in a world so lonely and so cruel as this? To refuse their warmth, their laughter, and their joy, in a world where these commodities in their wealth are rare enough indeed, to turn away from that rarest of all opportunities, that chance to face another mind across the measured spaces of black and white, where the contests of the mind may be fought in full equality by little men against the giants . . . to turn away from this is to turn from a chance to touch a peculiar facet of immortality. Few men write a book, a poem, an essay, because they are told to do so. Rather, a poem or a piece of prose is written because its author is somehow called, deep from the deep, to create a fresh new thing, to yield a little of himself, to see that bit of himself somehow transmuted from its nature of common self into a new lovely thing beyond his dreams because it has risen from them. To be afraid of this, to be shaken fearfully by this new created thing that has been called forth from the mind can only mark with ineradicable stain the lesser mind.

The Printer's Mark,
February, 1963

Power of the Unread

I have spoken on occasion of books which have sought me out and forced themselves upon me with an insistence which was not to be denied. These books must always remain for me among my choicest treasures, for invariably when their battle has been won and I have succumbed to their pressing ideas of good, I have found that they have become my most beloved friends, to whom I have continued to turn year after year, for comfort and for wisdom and for joy.

There are other books, however, which have managed to win their battle without this final victory over an individual. Their victory has been more oblique, yet no less complete. This is the victory won by the books which for many reasons have not been read, and yet continue to exert their force most subtly. These are the books perhaps of other times, which yet continue to exert their powers on the world about them. I have never met a person who in the course of a normal conversation has admitted to having read *Uncle Tom's Cabin* in its entirety. It is a book which I must confess I found most dull in my first and only reading. It was not that its ideas were unapparent, not at all. But rather that for me it seemed a book entirely out of fashion. Its overpowering sentiment, its overt appeals for sympathy, its obvious conviction, were lost, on me at least, probably because in some measure its victory had been won too long before I first felt its impact. Even today, with the problem of the minority still as real in many ways as it was in the troubled day of Harriet Beecher Stowe, the poignancy of Uncle Tom's tragedy lacks something for our day. And yet, there is no doubt whatever in any thoughtful person's mind that Mrs. Stowe's little sermon still lives today and has an influence. It certainly is one of the iron nails which men have used to nail the charter of freedom on the door of each man's house.

I suppose that among my friends there is hardly one who would admit to having read all, or even most, of Milton's *Areopagitica*, yet every schoolboy, every man even of the least education in its broadest sense, will hear that word and sense somehow the pride of Englishmen and of men of the western world in the freedom of the press. Written as it was in the mid-seventeenth century, the heavy prose of Milton's "speech for the liberty of unlicensed printing" was in its day upon the lips of his countrymen. Today its measured phrases and classic cadences lie encased in text books, to be read by those who subject themselves to the minor disciplines of survey courses of literature, and hardly with a sense of the blazing power which those words once bore. I have even heard graduate students lay a claim of "old hat traditional" against its sentences. And yet, though not read so often as it should be, indeed hardly read at all save under the duress of class assignment, the very existence of this splendid prose has kept alive through the centuries the ideas of freedom, and especially the freedom of men to express themselves publicly.

There are other great books which live not so much in their own presence as in the impact they have had on other men's words. The writings of John Donne, as a whole, are hardly known to general readers. His sermons, his poems, indeed his prose, save for the scholar or the specialist drawn to him for his impact on his own time, have gathered dust on library shelves through countless years. And yet the phrases turned by him, the solid thoughtful words which ring out from the dusty volumes which bear his name have filled the world with sound and meaning, now soft and gentle as he speaks to lovers on their marriage day, now sonorous and mindful of the littleness of men as the bell tolls his deathly memorial. These words, so often unread, and yet always in the consciousness of reading men, even in the mouths of men who seldom read, are a measure of the power of unread books to touch the world, and shape its ways.

The reader of today, greatly to his loss, is seldom trained in the vocabulary of classic allusion, and so he is often brought up hard against some phrase of loveliness and beauty which for him holds little meaning. Yet, once touched by the miracle of allusion, the reader becomes aware of the power of books that remain unread, and indeed may continue so, to move one toward better things and greater hopes. How often have you met Dante across the pages of a work less mighty than his own *Inferno*, which has called upon his precious wisdom to make its point more firm? How often have you been touched by Emerson's cool sentences and transcendental views? Have you not heard Chaucer's laughter ringing down the ages as you have read some more modern and less graceful tale? Yet how many times have you read the sources of these sounds of greatness? Dante, Emerson, Chaucer, a fair motley trio, all too often unread, and when read, too often not understood. Yet they touch men today through the power of their words, through the music of ideas which filled their own minds so fully that their flood of greatness was too much even for them and they had to share the wonders they knew. They are still sharing, they are still intruding themselves upon us, unread though they may be by littler men.

A book could be written on the effect of books not read upon our populations. The authors of such books would certainly include Montesquieu, Voltaire, and Pascal, among the French. John Locke, Dryden, Pope, and Blackstone, to mould another strange crew all unlike each other, are bound together in the likeness of having their books too often stand together and unmoved upon our shelves. This is not to say, I hasten to add, that the authors of these books are utterly ignored, but rather that their renown depends too much, if not entirely, upon the words of others than themselves, for our modern reader is often prone to acceptance of ideas at second hand.

What an odd paradox this is. Young people are dependent upon their elders to learn of great books, great ideas. Great teachers, then, hold tremendous power in their hands to lead the young to read well and fully. And while these things are true, the young too often seek to learn only from the lips of their teachers of the words, the ideas, and the beliefs of writers of the past. And in so doing they miss the greatest of experiences, that in which free minds of today face with absolute equality the free mind of another across the pages of a great book. The young person of today may sense the impact of Pascal's mind, of Montesquieu's, of Locke's, of Dryden's, of any other writer's, and may accept the other's ideas or reject them, may glory in them, or may seek to prove them wrong. This is one of the last and greatest of the freedoms, and one which the young must defend and make always possible. Retaining the freedom to reject, yet insisting on the right of the author to say what he or she feels must be said, the reader discovers some of the deeper values of true freedom, and cannot help but recognize that only in such freedom can wisdom hope to operate for good.

So let us not be sad that some books are unread. Rather, let us be sure that even though such books may not be opened over long spans of years, they have nonetheless their effect on us. Let us make certain that they are well cared for and kept ready for the moment when they will be read. And let us look for every opportunity to push them into action, knowing that even though we may fail to urge them on another reader, they nonetheless are accomplishing a mission in their very existence. I once heard a great librarian say, "An unread

book is like a time bomb, set to explode at some moment of time.''
Yes, an unread book is like a time bomb, and any time that one chooses to enter a great library where the books lie in ranges side by side, one hears the subtle sound of that bomb, whispering on the moment of its destiny. Good books, great books, wise books, are often unread for days, months, and years. But those same books, explosive in their power, will somehow succeed in their secret mission and will be read. And even while they lie in wait, they are doing their splendid task, for having been read once, they send the echoes of their own greatness into the writings of others and into the speech of great men, so that though seeming dead, they live and prosper and eventually have their way.

The Printer's Mark,
June, 1963

A Matter of Taste

It is Edmund Fuller who has, in recent years, expressed very strongly the idea that great books, good books, are books which have great and good people behind them. Now his thesis is convincing, and there is small argument to be brought against it, for it is only those with sound ideas, sound beliefs, and more than this, that rare form of creative goodness who can discuss the problems of life in such a manner as to endow these problems with sufficient universality that they become good and indeed worthwhile reading.

I would like to extend this idea along a somewhat different line which will, I trust, leave open the opportunity for reading to more of us than might be implied by Fuller, who would, I am sure, suggest that good men make the best readers. The line I will pursue is inherent in the suggestion first that people of intellectual curiosity and of some inner statute are people who read. But how they read is another question. It is a personal philosophy of my own which leads me to suggest that the best reading occurs when the reader manages to participate himself or herself in the matter being read. Now this sounds like utter nonsense to many, and its achievement, even for those who may find themselves somehow in agreement with the idea, is hardly a matter either of ease or, for that matter, consistency. I do not achieve it myself on many occasions, and yet I am convinced that when I do achieve this vicarious participation, my reading at once becomes a thing of purpose and delight.

Now how can one best "enter into" a book as one reads it? There is the rub. There is the question. It can be done, first of all, rather mechanically, by going through a certain procedure. For example, one might well do that thing which is so seldom done by the casual reader, one might read the introduction of the book as a means of placing the book in some sort of perspective, allotting it to its proper segment of the literary spectrum. This is at least a first step. A second step might involve some effort to determine the author's own personal background, as a means of comprehending that bias, if you will, from which he or she approaches problems. This is in itself a somewhat precarious procedure, since it may well so prejudice the reader against the posture and position of the writer as to make it difficult to join with him or her in whatever literary effort follows. If this last is true it is perhaps too much to expect the reader to enter into the writer's effort, and therefore he or she may wish to channel whatever reading is done along some other more congenial path. I am not suggesting that the reader should read only those works which are in complete agreement with the reader's own taste, but rather I am admitting that this is what the reader will most often do. And since I am endeavoring to suggest means by which the reader may best enjoy his or her reading, I must preclude the kind of self discipline involved in reading "what one must read" as opposed to what one would enjoy reading.

Another means of enjoying most what one is reading, or is about to read, lies in a most difficult feat, that of preparing oneself to enjoy what is about to be offered by the author. How is this done? There are two ways. First, in my own case, I do a considerable amount of rereading, it being part of my philosophy that one does not learn to know a book or its characters nor to make them part of one's own consciousness save by meeting them more than once. And having found a particular book a satisfying personal experience, it is easy, or at least easier, to prepare myself for enjoyment, knowing that I am on somewhat familiar ground. Second, and more difficult, one must prepare one's attitude to read a new book. I like, for example, to open a book, seen for the first time, at its opening page, there to scan quickly the first few paragraphs. If these paragraphs strike some special response, then a quick sampling of some random pages in later chapters, will reveal at once whether or not the author's style has pervaded the entire work, or, as so often happens, those first paragraphs represent a solitary high point from which he has leapt off into a generally mediocre narrative. This is, in fact, merely the accentuation of the sort of failure which occurs when a playwright develops a fine second act, and then slides swiftly into oblivion in a third act with no strong scene for a climax. But having discovered a well-formed style and a consistent narrative form that are congenial to one's taste, it is easier to anticipate the pleasure one shall have in reading on.

For my part, I find it very difficult indeed to enter into a book if that book has been "recommended" or urged upon me by another. This paradox, for a librarian, is a sadly difficult one, for friends continually ask for recommendations, and yet I cannot honestly make such recommendations, save in a few particular instances. A book that is "good," whatever that may mean, for me, certainly may not be good for another, for many reasons, and I have known a thousand examples of books much admired by others, which to me were hardly worth the opening of the covers. There are ways, however, in which a book may be introduced, and not "recommended" which leave me eager to taste the suggested title for myself. And these ways are more apt to be suggestive of the place in which a book is held by its critics, or the place it holds itself in the body of literature to which it belongs. A brief paragraph suggesting half a dozen titles described as "spring board books" led me to read Kipling's *Puck of Pook's Hill*, to my everlasting satisfaction. A footnote in an essay by Sir William Osler, led me to seek Edmund Gosse's *Father and Son*, as a personal footnote to the tragedy of the great conflict which raged between the two ages separated by Darwin's *Origin of Species* when it was published in 1859. A passing mention by John Drinkwater in *Robinson of England* of Gilbert White's *Natural History of Selbourne* resulted in years of pleasureful rereading of this lovely little volume, and has made collecting its innumerable editions a joyous and all but endless hobby.

What is it that leads a reader to choose a book from the hundreds on library shelves? Let us admit that in all probability it is what causes a young lady to choose a dress of one color as opposed to another; it is what persuades a person to select one entree instead of another from a menu; it is what leads one individual to choose a friend from the group when another would certainly choose differently. It is a subtle combination of taste, in its literary sense and mood; of knowledge, and desire for knowledge; of desire for adventure and wishfulness for the comfort of familiar things. I happen to like books, or at least tend to like books whose opening paragraphs have to do with winter and its mixture of cold and comfort. I like books, too, about English inns and utopias. Such eclecticism is startling to some of my friends, but a taste which offers at least the virtue of variety. Just what it is that sets these moods and choices, I cannot well explain, but that they are present in my daily choosing cannot be denied.

I suppose that if I were to offer any sort of advice in this matter of choosing books for reading, I would have to suggest first of all that whatever one chooses should, at the least, be encompassed by those things in which one has an interest. The individual enamored of steam engines is hardly likely to find joy in reading of Japanese gardens; and far subtler differences of taste have bearing on whether or not a book will serve its purpose. Beyond this, there are those momentary differences occurring in each individual reader to be taken into account. There are weary evenings, when a taste of Arthur Guiterman's *Antiseptic Baby and the Prophylactic Pup* are just the answer for a mood that needs a pick-me-up and a hearty laugh; but there are at least as many evenings when the incisiveness of Pope's *Essay on Criticism* meets the need. If these differences seem too far and widely spread, it can only be explained that such divergence does occur. Suffice it to say that the reader must satisfy himself or herself, and what makes this so difficult is that one must take into account in choosing two special elements—first, knowledge of one's self and one's need, and, second, awareness of books which hold within them some special ingredient that meets these special individual needs.

The Printer's Mark,
August, 1964

Jam for Today

"The law is," said the White Queen, "jam for yesterday, jam for tomorrow, but never jam for today." She was very firm in her opinion that this sort of mad economy was the simple and only way of things, and a way which was not to be disturbed or even considered further.

But for the reader, the White Queen's philosophy is merely a delightful impossibility. Very few among the hobbies and occupations of people can make a claim of existence not alone in the brightly lighted present moment, but in the past and the future too. For the reader can relive the pleasures of past discoveries, even as he or she indulges in this hobby in the immediate present, and, having done so, can anticipate the pleasures to be had in the future.

Not long ago I picked up a nicely printed copy of W. M. Thackeray's *Pendennis*, and as I turned the first pages, skipping over the long paragraphs of mannered prose which make up the introduction, I could not help but remember, and with pleasure, the first time this book came to me. It was one of those discoveries that a young reader makes in a library when he or she has been turned loose to mine the rich veins that lie along the shelves. In those days long sets of volumes had a peculiar appeal to me, for each new battalion of an author's works that I discovered promised the sheer, drunken pleasure of starting with the first volume and reading through the entire set, assured that there were more ahead as each new volume was finished. I like to look back to those exciting days and remember the satisfactions they brought. I remember that I developed a habit of opening a book new to me to read at least the first paragraph or so, to catch a glimpse of what there was in store for me. And then the book would be tucked under an arm, along with a companion or two, and all the way home I would wonder, recalling the taste of those first paragraphs, just how the tale would unfold itself. The most painful anticipation which would then ensue was at times breathless, almost painful in its intensity. *Pendennis*, as I now recall that first reading, was of special wonder, for the foibles and youthful misdeed of its hero seemed so natural and so lifelike that the book held warmth and the shock that recognition of reality creates.

Perhaps it is only fair to say that today the book seems to hold less of this wonder of which I speak. This fact is one of the things for which I shall forever be ungrateful to the scholars and critics who tore away some of the happy veil of romance, as I was forced to "study" Thackeray, and hear his "significance" discussed by teachers and scholars who had themselves lost much of that wondrous taste for meeting another mind across the pages of a book, and saw only the desperate need for judgment in its place.

I can still look back across the years, however, to glimpse those shining milestones of reading which, in memory at least, have lost none of their glistening excitement. It may not be amiss, therefore, to suggest here that the "jam for today" is a tasty snack which should not be denied the young or the not so young, and should become a vital part of the diet of every individual with the taste for reading. As a reader I am perhaps guilty of indulging in the sin of gluttony at least in my eagerness to seek out in each day's reading some of those things which are worth the storing up in memory. In my current reading I cast about continually, looking here and looking there for those opening paragraphs, or those whole volumes which I can make my own with a certainty that I can later remember them with the same kind of joy which I felt on first reading them. And it is this business of forever seeking which leads me to reread at least one book for every current title that I choose from the shelves.

At the risk of bringing down the wrath of those who are forever crying out in favor of more and more "practical experience" for our young people today, I would like to suggest that much of the hope that these youngsters have for having memories in the future is being destroyed by this everlasting insistence upon "reality," whatever that may truly mean. Recently I glanced along the shelves of a rather well stocked book store, to see what books there were for children of any age, and I must confess that I was left with little enthusiasm when I was through. There were so many books of science, which in some respects I suppose has become the romance and fairy story of our day, that I wondered if there could be any child in the community of children who was not steeped in astronomical lore or the new mathematics or the new biology or the new science, or about the practical things of community life like fire engines or trains or airplanes, or whatever else you might name. There were no books to be seen which could lift a child out of the solid, physical facts of daily existence (and it must be admitted that even space exploration has become for children a matter of daily acceptance) and into the world where children can live on the sunnier planes of romance and imagination. It is a pity, is it not, that knights, and princesses in need of assistance, and dragons, and elves and gnomes, and even sea roving pirates, to say nothing of friendly talking animals, have so disappeared?

Jam for every day should not be sickeningly sweet, but at least a little sweet. Jam for today should possess the rich colors of the fruits of imagination. Jam for today or any day, should reek a little of the scents which, in later years, will be brought back in flooding memories as the older child catches the heady odor of baking bread in passing a bakery door or as the warm musky scent of the bolts of cloth in a dry goods store will recall some moment out of yesterday. Jam for today, if it is worth the eating, should call up those recollections which may well be for years on end forgotten, but which, in the remembering will be rich and filled with the happiest tastes of satisfaction.

Now this is no plea for a return to some of the silly and sentimental books which had no sense of reality in themselves. But it is plea, a crying out in the wilderness of practicality, for those good things, those richly rewarding, everlasting things, those blessed things which every human being needs, as a cloak against the winds and storms of every day's experience, for warmth, and comfort, and simply for joy. We cannot afford to deprive young people of these things. The child who cannot see in the whirling cyclones of fall leaves the dance of elves and oriental dervishes has lost something which the age of science cannot provide a substitute for. The man who, watching the swift boiling of summer cumulus, has no recollections of the stately frigates which once sailed across his youthful skies, the woman who passes a ring of brown-capped mushrooms and has no recollection of the moonlit dances of the elven horde, and the scientist who hears the first sparkling cries of the spring peepers and has no memory of the mystery which they evoked in years past . . . these are people whose minds and hearts have been starved and are exposed to all the hurtful loneliness which a too real world has in plenitude.

A woman once asked me to prepare a list of suggested books for her daughter to read on a long holiday abroad. I suggested that before they reached England, and indeed while there, that it might be interesting to read some of the legends of Arthur, the noblest of kings, that before they reached France, the *Song of Roland*, in even a prose version, and some of the legends of Charlemagne would suffice, and that for Spain, or for even the whole world, that at least some part of *Don Quixote* would offer both amusement and wisdom. She looked at me aghast. "I wanted you to suggest something which she could read which would do her good," she said. I later learned that she gave the child a book of history to read, and I am happy to say it was lost overboard at sea.

I would not suggest that all reading should be for entertainment, nor for joy alone, for these in an excessive diet soon become cloying and of little purpose. But let us have at least a little jam for each day, jam which will sharpen the taste buds for the everlasting pleasures.

The Printer's Mark,
November, 1965

Good Books

"Go with mean people and you think life is mean. Then read Plutarch, and the world is a proud place, peopled with men of positive quality, with heroes and demigods standing around us, who will not let us sleep." So said Emerson in his essay on books. What a splendid kind of optimism this holds out to the reader! And how truly it reveals the opportunities which are to be found by any person, rich or poor, who will yield himself or herself up to the pleasure and excitement of good reading.

To paraphrase Emerson, to read a mean book is to think all books are mean, and what could be further from the truth than to think that all books are useless things? Great books, good books, books with body and heart and character, can show the way for the reader into such wondrous countries and such splendid palaces of the mind that there can be no denying that in those palaces the reader will meet "heroes and demigods" who will not let him sleep. A few nights ago I settled down in my study with a new book which I opened without suspecting what it would do to me. Almost from the opening paragraph I was caught up in a swiftly moving narrative which so stirred my mind and so caught my whole consciousness up into its quickening pace that when I finally closed the book my clock was pointing its narrow hands at a morning hour which would discourage any early wakening.

Yet there is another aspect of the great book, of any great book, which must be considered. No book of any worth can ever safely be said to be neutral. No good book ever stands straddling the line of compromise. If the serious reader will only admit it, he must agree that every good book actually is an aggressive kind of opponent that waits only for the opportunity to intrude itself upon the mind of the reader who falls into its grasp. You do not believe me? Let me explain what it is I speak of. Books lie quietly enough upon their shelves, it is true, but their quietness is most misleading. Good books, in fact, plot and plan ways to draw the reader they have chosen into a dialogue of reading and response. They are quiet, until the moment arises when the unsuspecting reader first looks upon the opening pages, and then the triumphant lines of print march boldly across the page, and the battle is won.

Once years ago a less favorite aunt gave me a dark-faced copy of *The Education of Henry Adams*. A proper note of thanks for the gift was written which only barely hid the lack of interest. The book, which was bound in dark brown buckram, was allowed to stand for a day or so on the bedside table, but other volumes soon were present which pushed it to the rear until finally in a moment when there was not room for more enjoyable reading on that table, the *Education* was put on a high shelf in a bookcase where it could look down on its more favored brothers as they were opened and read and given more favorable attention. But this was not the end, and barely the beginning of the battle. It was placed on its high shelf in December. Three times before the end of the following summer that book either fell from its shelf, and at least on one other occasion somehow appeared on the table by the bed. It would not be ignored. I am not saying that it managed these perambulations of its own accord, although I would not say that it had not so managed. But the fact remains that in some mysterious way it managed to keep itself within my reluctant consciousness. I fought back with an irritability that should have discouraged even the self assertive Henry Adams, and for a while I thought I was successful. Finally a long journey suggested that some reading would be appropriate for several days of railroad travel. I am quite certain that I put two books in my suitcase, for I remember having chosen them. Still, when I opened that suitcase on the first evening of the trip, with the clicking of the rails making their pleasant rhythm beneath me, there were not two books, but a single one, and its binding of dark brown buckram. Its gold lettered title looked up at me, and there was Henry Adams, bent upon victory whether I would or not.

Two days I spent with Henry, and by the end of the first I had capitulated. First his self conscious and, at first glance, supercilious attitude angered me, and I tried more than once to push him aside. But slowly the greatness of the mind behind the lines of print, the knowledgability and the wisdom began to shine through. It is a book of such density, as Justice Oliver Wendell Holmes once said, that one finds upon every page and in every sentence some clearly defined observation which must be hesitated over, reread, and then agreed with in wonder. Its passages are possessed of a strange abrasiveness, which strikes against the reader's mind, honing the surface, sharpening and making keen the reader's thought. Its prose is elegant and graceful, free from vulgarity or rudeness, and yet those long paragraphs are sharp and probing, and quite sufficiently disturbing and provocative. It is a book which has since lived on a shelf close by my regular reading place, and it has been turned to so often that its dark cover is still darker and its pages show the signs of the wear they have experienced.

Now the persistence of this book may seem to some to be sheer fantasy, and if it were the only example I could give of having been tantalized and cornered by a book until I had to yield and give it serious attention, I would agree. But I could tell of a dozen other books, each of which has managed somehow to force itself into my awareness, and stand between me and other reading or other duties until I gave myself to the experience. John Buchan's splendid *Montrose*, a classic of biographical writing was one to which I yielded only after a long struggle, to find that its pages were so richly accoutred with great thoughts that it stands almost alone in modern biographical works. For years I stubbornly resisted *Walden*, and almost won the battle, until by accident I picked up *A Week on the Concord and Merrimack*, and became so delighted and charmed that I finally could not hold out against the challenge of *Walden*. I once found a copy of Washington Irving's *Astoria*, and bought it only because it was a collector's item at a reasonable price. But here again, a book forced its way onto my reading table and became a favorite in spite of me.

If my friends will forgive me, it is this kind of experience which makes me feel quite certain that books with great men behind them are in fact extensions of those men, and are endowed with a peculiar and quite special kind of liveliness. They have particular powers, first to entice, sometimes to bully the reader, always to change him or her subtly, sometimes to lead toward good things. I never enter a large library when it is quiet and deserted that I am not aware of a restless vitality which seems to permeate its atmosphere, and I am convinced that this restlessness is nothing more or less than the spirited will of great books to draw the reader into the marvelous world of the printed page, where there are no prisons for the mind but only great expanses of a brightly lighted kingdom, where the riches of the Indies are laid out for any who would seek them.

Letters from Anagnostes Solitarium,
November, 1968

A Desert Island Test

If you knew that you were to be marooned in a comfortable but remote mountain inn for the better part of a winter season, what books would you choose to have with you for that imprisonment? The question was asked after a discussion of the foolishness of choosing the ten books one would best choose to be left with on a desert island. The latter proposition carries with it a sense of permanency and so would require a different kind of selection. But a temporary imprisonment brings about the need for less concern with the giants, demanding only that one find amusement or comfort or general interest. A list of the best things for all time would sound pompous and overdone if it were to be offered for "a long winter's night" of reading. So, on the evening when two of us were playing this little game of "books for a desert island," we prepared our lists and then prepared to defend them.

For myself, I would have no choice but to take, first of all, the one book which has been a preoccupation of mine for more than twenty years, *Islandia*, by Austin Tappan Wright. A long, leisurely, but intense novel, it is the sort of book which can be reread with pleasure time and time again, each time resulting in new discoveries of its beauty, depth, and creative thought. The country of Islandia, which existed for forty years in Austin Tappan Wright's mind, is a fantastically convincing dream world, so convincing that when one has finished reading the novel he knows for certain that there *is* an Islandia and that he could be content with its simple and satisfying ways and customs. Its hero is perhaps a little too introspective, but he is himself the kind of person one would care to know, and his companions in Islandia are so free of the tensions and violent energy of our own tempestuous world that they seem to draw the reader to them and offer only their friendliness and whatever their country has to offer in the way of peace and the good life. *Islandia* must go into my packet of winter reading.

Another book, perhaps as utopian in its way as Wright's *Islandia*, even though it is drawn from nineteenth century reality, is the strikingly beautiful series of vignettes and short stories published by Sarah Orne Jewett in *The Country of the Pointed Firs*. Miss Jewett, entranced by the quietly sturdy character of her Maine coast acquaintances, wrote, in the latter half of the nineteenth century, this book and others equally as splendid, stories which without any question will stand very close to the top of American writings for all time. Willa Cather has said that of all American works only *Huckleberry Finn* and *The Country of the Pointed Firs* can be assured of standing the test of the centuries. One of the leading figures in the work, Mrs. Todd, and her utterly satisfying mother, Mrs. Blackett, along with her silent and understandably shy brother William, are human characters of such fineness, such charm, and such interest that they must stand among American literary creations of the centuries.

As a means of stirring up one's interest in further reading and as a means as well of making for argument across the pages of a book, who could ask for more than the two books which should be required reading for every librarian, for every teacher, than Christopher Morley's pair, *Parnassus on Wheels*, and *The Haunted Bookshop*? No character in American literature has more enthusiasm, has more opinions, or is more willing to talk about books and reading than Roger Mifflin, Morley's inimitable mouthpiece. His impatience with the lazy-minded is a breath of fresh air in a world which sorely needs his vast capacity for idealism.

There are some long winter evenings, of course, when nothing but a mystery story is required, but there are too few of this particular genre which can bear rereading. One mystery writer, however, who lifted the mystery story above the common ruck was Dorothy Sayers, and even though her stories may at first glance seem somewhat dated they nonetheless withstand the erosion of the years and hold themselves much more than a cut above the general run. Miss Sayers once wrote that in her later works she was struggling with problems inherent in the writing of a detective yarn as a true novel instead of merely a patterned puzzle. Four of her works would suffice to entertain and even on second reading provide a puzzling enjoyment. The best title for a mystery in the opinion of many is her *Murder Must Advertise*, an excellent tale of a murder in an advertising agency, an agency, incidentally, in which Miss Sayers herself served her apprenticeship. Two fine "love stories with murderous interruptions" (to quote Miss Sayers) that must perforce be included in a winter's reading are *Strong Poison* and *Busman's Honeymoon*. Telling, in part, the story of the developing love affair between Lord Peter Wimsey and Harriet Vane, Miss Sayers's leading figures, they provide both excellent mystery puzzles and altogether amusing character studies of the Wimsey family. And for one of the most intriguing settings for murder ever designed, one must include Dorothy Sayers's *The Nine Tailors*, in which the great bells of a country cathedral in the English fen country serve as both villains and heroes of the story.

For a traditional long English novel with all of the wit and biting satire one can wish for, almost no English author surpassed Anthony Trollope and his splendid Barchester series. The best of these, and without any question the best for a cold evening before a comfortable fire, is *The Eustace Diamonds*, replete with all its entangled subplots which delighted Trollope and intrigue the reader and with all the incisively developed characters, not one of which fails to appear as a reality nor is less than well rounded, from the least of the fawning servants to the most insipid of the suitors to the naughtiest of the ladies of the ecclesiastical court.

And finally, for the solid reading which permits one both the pleasure of seeing the far horizons glitter with ideas and with perceptive understanding both of nature and of man, what better book could one tuck into the bookman's baggage than Henry David Thoreau's *Week on the Concord and Merrimack*? Reading this lovely work, second only to *Walden* for its revelation of the author's mind and thoughts, is like floating down those two New England streams, watching the scene change with every hour, listening in the cool evening to the sounds which mark the closing of the day, and wakening in the darkness to listen to the beating of a village drum calling the volunteers to their gathering place.

These ten books are of sufficient variance to provide for most moods; they are of sufficient worth to stir the reader's mind with pleasure or with provocation. Going into a winter's seclusion, they could keep the mind alert, alive and entertained, and serve the purpose which all general reading serves, to whet the taste for more, yet comfort the spirit in loneliness.

Letters from Anagnostes Solitarium,
June, 1970

The Act of Reading

The act of reading is truly an astonishing thing. It is a kind of miracle. The mere contemplation of the magical act of gazing at a page, filled with odd and, in many ways, meaningless symbols, with the resultant experience of thought, is almost frightening. Stop to consider it for a moment. An adult reader opens a book which he holds before him. On the shining white page of paper someone has imprinted in English, twenty-six symbols, arranged in curious patterns and sequences. Sometimes one of the symbols will stand alone. On other occasions it may be seen that two symbols are set together; or three may appear, or four, or five, or seven, or ten, or any number may be arranged in a seemingly endless variety of arrangements. This is the first part of the miracle of reading. Still something else occurs, however, which is even more startling.

The reader gazes at these curiously arranged symbols, and immediately his mind is flooded with an astonishing series of reactions. And these reactions differ even from reader to reader. Let us say, for example, that the little group of symbols is made up of three separate symbols, as a "t," plus an "r," plus two identical symbols, an "e" and then another "e." When they have been arranged together, they form the pattern "tree." The mind of one reader, seeing this particular combination of symbols, will at once envision a vast spreading oak. Another reader's mind, on seeing this combination of symbols, will conjure up a splendid wine glass elm. Still another will picture in his mind another kind of tree altogether. So this particular arrangement of symbols does not, apparently, mean exactly the same thing to every reader. Of course if the combination of symbols in "tree" is preceded by another set of symbols, as "oak tree," or "elm tree," then each reader will see the same kind of "tree."

Carry this miracle one step further. Let us say that five of these magical symbols are arranged to form the combination "running." But when this set of symbols, so arranged, is placed in proper context with several other groups of symbols, a startling number of images or ideas will flood the mind of the reader whose eye falls upon the group. Notice how these images for ideas change in the following:

> The man is running.
> The stream was running rapidly down hill.
> The water was running from the faucet.
> The motor was running.
> The leaves were running before the wind.
> The quarterback was running the team well.
> The running of the tide.

Now, once again, set the five symbols, arranged in this particular order, aside and by themselves, and notice that meaning seems to drop away immediately:

> running

It provides the same kind of experience or sensation that one often encounters when asked to sign one's name five hundred times. After the two hundredth the peculiar combination of letters which make up one's own symbol or name are apt to become meaningless, and one must force the mind to put them in the order that forms the symbol of one's self.

An astonishing thing about the act or art of reading, then, is that we really know very little about what transpires in this miraculous act. We can only be grateful, be delighted, be amused, by the fact that it provides us with so many opportunities to experience good things, to meet the challenge of another human being's ideas, to experience innumerable things vicariously that we can never hope to experience in our own lives. The art of reading permits us to meet the high experiences and expressions which only the genius, the poet, the great literary mind can express in words. Stop for a moment more to consider what the literary mind can do by arranging these strangely drawn symbols in a different pattern from the pattern set forth by others. Perhaps most of us might say: "I stood for a long while today at a fork in the road and before taking one road stared down the other to where it disappeared in the low bushes." Now listen as Robert Frost takes most of the same words and exactly the same idea and turns them into a haunting melody:

> Two roads diverged in a yellow wood

And sorry I could not travel both
And be one traveller, long I stood
And gazed down one to where it bent in the
   undergrowth.

The words of these two samples are, in themselves, not too different. The number of symbols making up the words and lines are not too different. But somehow the arrangement of these symbols in Frost's version has wrought a miracle. And equally miraculous is the difference in the impact of Robert Frost's poem upon the eye, the ear, the mind of different readers. One reader is appealed to by the utter simplicity of the verse. Another is repulsed by the same simple arrangement of symbols. One reader sees in the mind's eye the golden yellow of New England's fall colors against an October sky. Another sees the same yellow against the drab gray of late fall.

There are strange reactions to the symbols occurring to different people. A friend has told me that the reading experience for him is a kind of psychedelic adventure: That particular words, when his eye touches them, are always in special colors. For my own part, the symbols which represent numbers always appear to me, when I think of them, in a range of color. The word eight is always deep red. The word seven is always forest green. The word four is always deep yellow . . . not orange, but deep golden yellow. The word two is always dark blue.

The act of reading, it seems to me, can in a way be compared to the experience one has when walking down a familiar street in one's home community. Pass the bakery shop, with its door standing invitingly open, and the smell of baking bread calls up a host of images. Pass the dry goods store, and the warm, inimitable scene of the bolts of cloth stir up a hundred fleeting pictures. Stand for a moment in the door of the local candy shop, and the sweet-acrid scent of chocolate brings back all kinds of recollections. Just so, when the reader's eye glides along the marching lines of printed symbols a thousand times, a thousand images are called up to flood the mind with meaning, and with pleasure, and with thought.

Letters from Anagnostes Solitarium,
July, 1971

Unexpected Pleasures

Henry D. Thoreau, in that volume of his printed works entitled *The Maine Woods*, wrote both simply and with profundity of his observations on three separate journeys into the Maine woods in the mid-nineteenth century. The essays, while perhaps lacking some of the angry depth of his political tracts and some of the perceptivity of *Walden*, are nonetheless blessed with a keen sense of the wonder of the natural world through which he travelled. One particularly poignant sketch of this series occurs in the final essay, "The Allegash and East Branch," in which he narrates his adventures on a journey northward through lovely Moosehead Lake and back toward Bangor along the East Branch River.

Thoreau recounts how one evening, after the camp had slept, he was wakened in the night and arose to stir the fire and gather the dying embers in the darkness. He was startled to see a ring of glowing light in the depths of the blackened embers, and upon closer examination he found it to be phosphorescent glow from a tree whose inner bark had so entered into decay as to form this ring of cold light, mysteriously glowing in the dark as though to mark in its macabre fashion a place of special natural wonder. Closer examination led him to tear away a portion of the decaying stump to reveal a whole length of the mysterious light, and he broke off chips of the bright phosphorescence and held them in his hand to see even the swirling lines of his palm revealed in the trembling light. He kept the chips until the next night and dampened them when it became dark, hoping to restore them to their glowing beauty, but in the day the chips had lost their magic and could never regain their glowing enchantment. As the essay proceeds, Thoreau comments in an aside that this little event made the entire journey worth its trouble, and he goes on to say that it was a continual surprise and delight to him that no matter how many days he spent in the forest or in wild country, nature seemed always to have some new excitement, some fresh message to impart.

It is not too farfetched certainly to suggest that this sort of new and ever exciting kind of fresh experience for the naturalist is one

35

which the reader too can experience, throughout a lifetime, if he or she is willing to explore the highways and the byways of reading with patience and a willingness to seek out at some pain the wonders of the quiet worlds that lie beneath the covers of the books on almost any library's shelves. These surprises and excitements come to one's attention wherever books may be found, and often the inviting paths to such experience open up in most unlikely places.

The very essay by Thoreau, which has been mentioned, was called to one reader's attention by a brief pictorial essay in a conservation magazine, a somewhat unlikely source for literary inspiration. But the pictures of those Maine forests and quiet streams caught so the mood of the Thoreau essay that this reader, who had not taken the trouble before to explore the particular series of sketches by Thoreau of which this essay is one, was led to seek the book and then spent an exalted hour or two following him through those northern forests and along the Allegash and East rivers in company with his Indian guide and friend.

A chance remark by a colleague mentioning a title with an unusual sound and taste, *Bitter Lemons*, by Lawrence Durrell, resulted in amusement and delight in that writer's pungent prose and somewhat heady descriptions of his adventures on Cyprus in the difficult years of the mid-fifties. It was a byway which opened up by accident, and yet brought pleasure and the joy of exploration to the reader.

A passing comment by John Drinkwater, in a little volume, intended to be an introduction to the fascination of English history and literature, spoke of the odd quality of light, sunniness and warm breezes which flow out of the pages of William Morris's *News from Nowhere*. It is a volume often enough passed over by the casual reader, and yet, upon introduction, it is a narrative so filled with both beauty and wisdom as to delight the most critical reader of this astonishing nineteenth century eclectic.

Like the experience known by Thoreau, there are times when one is brought to full attention by some surprising or delightful manifestation in the magic forest of reading. In these moments of surprise it often happens that the reader will pause in sheer delight to savor the beauty of what he or she has come upon and, in the enjoyment, will find a peculiar pleasure in repeating that phrase or passage, as one glances back at some newly discovered painting or replays some musical passage in delight. Just so, even as Thoreau discovered, the next day's rereading, or the next year's, may find the passage dull and even meaningless.

Yet if the reader finds some literary gold, and if that gold is *real*, and not fool's gold, compacted of sentiment or careless artistry or worse, it will shine clear and bright, will echo in a thoughtful re-reading the full beauty and excitement found in its first reading. And the reader, caught up in this miracle, will treasure it once again and will know, as the New England naturalist and philosopher discovered, the wonder of finding ever new things in the forest and of sensing new meanings in the light and color of other men's minds and wisdom.

There are some books which are best held safe in fond memory and, once read, never read again. There are those books, read in youth, which hold about them a delightful aura of sheer pleasure. To reread them in the context of maturity is but to destroy them forever. A few years ago I mistakenly decided to gather a shelf full of the books which I remembered having most enjoyed as a child and to keep these books against the day when my young son might enjoy them too. The idea was not really a bad one and gave me some pleasure for a year as I sought out the titles that I had remembered, and bought them, now in used copies, now in newly printed editions. The mistake occurred when I sat down to reread them. Like the chips of phosphorescent wood which Thoreau tried to reawaken into magic glow the second time, these books burned but dully, and in some cases refused to glow at all. One or two, of course, still held their charm, but reading them again, in this new and obviously less receptive mood, brought for the most part disappointment and chagrin.

Now this need not always be the case. There are some books which I can reread once a year and find within their covers great contentment. I have tried now and then to determine what the elements are in such books which make them thus forever acceptable. I find that these mysterious qualities are not to be defined completely. Some of them, I suspect, hold their delight because of associations connected with their first reading. Others reflect without a doubt personal philosophies which need some reassuring or rededication. Still others are possessed of those timeless qualities which make the classics reach above their fellows to shoulder against the literary sky and block out lesser horizons.

It has amused me to discover that perspectives change with time, as I recall youthful reading delights. Speaking recently concerning the life of Rudyard Kipling in the United States, I seemed to remember that the portion of his intriguing *Captains Courageous* which describes the exciting train journey across America which brought Harvey Cheyne's mother and father to Boston to meet their long-lost son was at least a half-hundred pages in length. Rereading the book in preparation for my talk, I discovered, to my surprise, that this portion of the book barely required a dozen pages. And in the last reading they were too quickly covered, too soon read through. Another foreshortening or forelengthening, perhaps, occurred in a recollection of the length of the fabulous journey down through the Eastern gorges made by *The African Queen*, C. S. Forester's steam-powered mistress of the jungle rivers. The journey, even including the long delays for repairs at the base of the tumbling cascades, covers far fewer pages of reading than memory recalled. But the pages, few though they may be, still glow with excitement and with each return for another downstream voyage recall the breathless first reading.

An evening's pleasure reading seems a far cry from adventure in the Maine woods with Thoreau, and yet his firelit experience carries with it the same touch of miracle that the reading of a great book produces.

Letters from Anagnostes Solitarium,
November, 1971

Friends

One of the most exciting things one can ever experience is that hushed pause in the theater when the lights dim and the audience settles into expectant attention as the curtain lifts to reveal the lighted stage. There is in that moment a fraction of an instant when each character on stage is held in breathless anticipation before a quick movement sets the stage alive and enlists the vicarious participation of each watcher. It truly is a magical moment, one which never ceases to astonish me no matter how many plays I see. There is only one regretful aspect of that exciting instant for the playgoers. Regardless of the theater buff's eagerness to see the play, to see any play, there are enough badly written plays to bring disappointment. In that disappointment the author of each bad play has betrayed his audience's faith and trust. There are too few moments of wonder in each individual's life to warrant carelessness in the author's work or in the stage director's interpretation of it.

Another happy moment comes for me whenever a favorite author appears with a new offering. It is a pleasant thing for one of my reading generation to be able to look back into those years when such delightful juvenile journals as *St. Nicholas Magazine, The American Boy,* and *Boy's Life* appeared with regularity to introduce their readers to writers both new and old. I remember waiting impatiently for the arrival of each of those juvenile magazines, especially when a preceding issue had promised that Ralph Henry Barbour or Augusta Hulell Seaman or Percy Reese Fitzhugh would be featured in the succeeding issue in a new story of school life or a teasing mystery or a piece of hilarious nonsense involving one of Mr. Fitzhugh's amusing Boy Scout troops. I remember the amusement of starting out with one of Clarence Buddington Kelland's serialized adventures of Catty Atkins. Looking back, I can see clearly that the pleasures which were found in such literary contrivances were compounded of several things. There was, to begin with, the happy experience of meeting once again an author in whom one trusted for pleasure. There was, too, the happiness of remeeting characters who were old friends, friends who never failed to meet one's expectations of good fellowship. There was the tantalizing satisfaction of reaching the closing paragraphs of one segment of the story and wishing most impatiently that there were another page to read, instead of a dangling bit of plot which would not be completed until the next issue of the magazine appeared. Sometimes a succession of stories would appear over two or three years. The stories would not necessarily be connected in terms of plot but would consist of a new series of adventures in which the characters alone united the series, but this made them no less exciting opportunities for the reader.

As a somewhat more advanced reader, I remember the delightful shock of recognition when a librarian friend led me for the first time into the adult section of the town library and there pointed out to me two whole shelves of novels by John Buchan, who was later to become Lord Tweedsmuir, Governor General of Canada. That windfall of reading left me standing there before the laden shelves, almost breathless with excitement. *Greenmantle, Mr. Standfast, Thirty-nine Steps, Three Hostages, Huntingtower, Castle Gay, House of the Four Winds* . . . all were read in a headlong rush of pleasure, a kind of breathless delight. I think not one of those clever yarns was a disappointment for me. True, some had greater appeal than others, but each one was read in a great gulp of pleasure and then reread in greater leisure, but with no less delight. There have been few times when a single author has given so much satisfaction to a young reader, now grown older and perhaps more sophisticated in his reading tastes.

There have been some authors whose works have been reread as an entirely new experience. To read *Treasure Island* as a youngster results in one kind of experience. To reread that same happy work as an adult, with values somehow sharpened, with taste more recently attuned to different kinds of reading satisfaction, makes for an experience which is not only intriguing, but also enthralling. To meet Soames Forsyte for the first time, to dislike him heartily for his voracious sense of property, is one sort of experience. To read *The Forsyte Saga* for the second or even the third time reveals Soames in an entirely new light, which somehow graces him with a new dignity not recognized on first acquaintance. To examine from a more mature point of view the tangled involvements of the Forsyte family brings on a wonderment as to what readers of a hundred years from now (and Soames will certainly live for that long) will think of the paradox of Victorian rectitude and turn-of-the-century morals.

It is to all intents impossible for any individual actually to "reread" a book. In each reading there are at least two things which are inevitable. First and most certainly the reader must have become a different reader between any two readings of any book. Only the dullard does not change. The thoughtful reader is a different individual, a different person, at the time of his second reading. Therefore, the response to the stimulation of a good book cannot help but be slightly and, in some cases, importantly different with each new exposure. In the course of thirty-five years, I suppose I have reread John Drinkwater's *Robinson of England* no fewer than fifteen times, and each reading has brought some new enrichment of the meanings of English literature or of England's history. On more than one occasion, some passage carefully underlined on a previous reading has seemed to gain an enhanced or entirely new meaning. This endless system of change, within the reader or in the context of the approach to a literary work, presents new challenges and new joys with each rereading.

Perhaps the real significance of what I have tried to express here is made clear to me as I sit comfortably in my favorite reading chair and glance over the two or three shelves of favorite books, which show by their well-worn, slightly discolored spines that these are friends that patiently await each happy renewal of friendship for us both. These are good friends. In physical appearance they do not seem to change at all through the years. The words are just the same. The pages are ranged with ordered lines of type. Yet, between me and these friends of such long standing, there has occurred over the years a kind of mutual growth, of respect, and contentment; I would not change a word or line in these books, but I am sure that they have greatly changed me.

Letters from Anagnostes Solitarium,
October, 1972

The Power of Books

As a librarian I am quite aware that I have been blessed with many more privileges than I would have dared to hope for or expect had I remained a layman, content with only those few books which I could afford for myself. Among the privileges, and I truly consider them such, I suppose the greatest for me is the unlimited association with representatives of the world's fellowship of writers. This fellowship, this fraternity, if you will, is composed generally of great minds, and the pleasure as well as the terror of such association are something the everyday reader cannot escape. As for the pleasure, there is the warmth and richness books provide for any reader, whatever his or her mood may be. As for the terror, there is the sometimes shattering experience of having one's prejudices and silly beliefs stripped away, and finding oneself standing intellectually naked in the bright light of reason, in the burning light of a truth which cannot be denied. There are, however, other privileges to be gained in a library, where the shelves of books range across a hundred thousand regions explored by other men and described in their writings.

I find two delights, which are at the same time frustrations, as I spend my days among the treasures which men have mined in the caverns of their minds. Delight is to be found always in seeing these monuments to man's intellect ranged in orderly patterns on the shelves. Books are for me symbols of such real pleasure that even being aware of their presence in a room brings contentment. In a library in particular the patterns of the tapestry which the shelves provide is pleasant to observe. Sometimes the patterns are created by bright, new bindings, not yet worn or faded by use. Sometimes the patina of use creates shadowed designs, quite mellow and pleasing to the eye. The frustration lies in the true impossibility of ever being able to delve into more than a relative few of those thought-filled volumes. As I remember, when I was young it was my habit to read from left to right across a shelf, devouring every book that came to hand. But even a lifetime of reading hardly provides sufficient time or opportunity to continue such a scandalous habit, pleasing as it may be. Reading for me nowadays must consist of careful selection of a few, in order to exploit only those I can be nearly certain will pertain to my personal interests.

The simple experience of wandering up and down the regimented ranges of bookshelves provides a delightful experience and one which, I am quite sure, represents a nearly unexplored aspect of reading and research. Just recently I went to the shelves where books of exploration are to be found, intent on finding the first volume of Theodore Eliot Morison's *European Discovery of America, the Northern Voyages*. I found the volume quickly, but my eyes wandered along the shelves, finding interest in the tempting titles which were joined with Morison's splendid work. First one and then another I pulled down, tempted by each, gently excited by their variety. And then my eye was caught by an Italian name, Pigafetta, and saw that the tall two volumes were entitled *Magellan's Voyages*. Here by accident in the happy experience of browsing, I had rediscovered a book which thirty years ago had fascinated me. Pigafetta was a secretary under Magellan and had accompanied the explorer on his fabulous voyage around the world. Magellan's secretary was a delightful mixture of Pepys and Boswell, reporting in a personal way all of the shipboard difficulties, professional scandals, as well as every act and spoken thought of the great explorer during the long and for Magellan fatal voyage. The book is not one to be read through in great gulps; it is a book to be savored, and I have, since rediscovering it, picked it up over and over again to sample Pigafetta's narrative skills.

More than once I have come to a university library, when its doors were closed for a long weekend, to find myself surrounded by a multitude of whispering shades. This is no matter of idle imagination, for when the busyness of daily work in a library has been stilled, there remains, for any reader who enters alone, a strange and mysterious "aliveness" in the shelf-lined rooms. I am not a man of superstition, but I believe that books have a power of their own to draw readers toward them. Their "voices" are not heard by everyone, but to some they cry out to be noticed, to be taken from the shelf, to be read. Those who handle books, not as simple commodities or artifacts, but instead see in them the great catalysts between modern readers and their predecessors, cannot help but be aware of their mysterious power to communicate the thoughts which have been considered important enough to be preserved for newer times.

Letters from Anagnostes Solitarium,
January, 1975

Surprised by Joy

As I moved down a busy city street some days ago, I passed a store front where the door had been carelessly left partly open, and from it came a flood of that warm, sweet, yet gently sharp scent of bread baking. I did not pause, yet as I moved on my thoughts were filled with memories of other mornings, in a house where bread baking was an almost daily occurrence, and those familiar scents were a daily pleasure to a young boy's senses. Another day, in the middle of our coldest January in years, I went into my back garden, and there, in a little glade formed by an encirclement of azaleas, I discovered a tiny scene laid out before me, where tiny twigs, unevenly cast away by the winds and thrust into the good soil, had been decorated with frost and little snow curls, making a scene of faery, which quickly brought back another youthful memory, when in an open field near my home on the shore of Lake Erie, I once found a similar scene. Under an overhanging berry bush, I discovered a tiny pond, where, in the shallow, frozen water, twigs had been trapped in the quickly-freezing ice and turned into miniature sailboats with snowy, crystal sails, little boats which seemed to rush across the pond lake in a race for the far shore. Each of these childhood memories, brought into consciousness by an adult experience, "recalling in tranquillity" an earlier moment of observation, created an instant in which the viewer, in C. S. Lewis's words, was "surprised by Joy."

Lewis makes it clear in his biography of his early years, *Surprised by Joy*, that there is a marked and significant difference between joy and those other related elements of experience, happiness and pleasure. Happiness and pleasure, he says, are sensations, experiences which may be sought for they are as a matter of fact of an essence which one may expect to find again and again . . . momentary releases into a warm climate in which the mind and spirit revel, knowing full well that such sensations are passing things, but knowing too, that one may very well seek and find them over and over again. But it is joy, says Lewis, that comes upon one with an unexpected rush, sweeping around a corner to wrap itself about one's very being, to swell the heart, the spirit, the secret soul in such a way that one is left breathless, nerveless, happily shaken, fully aware that one has without warning come upon one of those secret springs provided by the Almighty in an ever-outward flowing of sheer delight. Joy makes it possible for the simplest as well as the most blessed of human beings to know that he or she is part of the great universal experience of being alive, part of that dreamed of but seldom recognized Master Plan.

I have said that there are marked and significant differences between happiness and pleasure and this greater joy. Yet it is not a simple matter to separate out and identify the differences. But the definition of experience might help somewhat in this matter. I think that as a young college student I mistook, in a reading of Lewis's own little masterpieces, *The Screwtape Letters*, an experience of joy. I came upon that wise and witty book in a bookstore in a little college town. I picked up the slender volume, read the first letter, and knew that I had touched upon one of those little jewels of Christian wisdom. I purchased the book, tucked it into my pocket, and then took it out to read it as I dangerously threaded my way through street and sidewalk traffic, lost in the wise incisiveness of Lewis's "Dutch uncle" advice to the junior devil, Screwtape, who was badly botching up his assignment to tempt the soul of a weakling human Christian. Screwtape's instructions as to the best and most obvious means to play upon the foibles of the human spirit made one squirm as one recognized one's own petty weaknesses and soft-minded attitudes towards matters which, when fully seen, can only be seen as crystal-hard in their reality. In that first reading of *The Screwtape Letters*, I was sure that I was finding joy. That I was not finding joy is obvious enough now . . . it was merely very great pleasure, which I have sought and found time and again in many rereadings of the letters.

Having suggested, therefore, that I knew something of both pleasure and joy in the reading experience, I began to wonder if I had ever experienced the higher element of joy. I hardly think so, at least in the specifics of the term as defined and described. I would, however, go on to make a more general abstraction of the total experience of reading. Yes, I am quite sure that there *is* to be found in the act of reading (an act we have never fully been able to comprehend in terms of what actually happens in the process of that act) an experience that falls within the limits that joy encompasses. Let me see if I can explain. It can occur in numerous ways, but in two ways in particular. There is always that moment when one is seeking something new to read, for pleasure or for some reason of discipline, when one's hand touches for the first time a new book, new to oneself, that is. For me, the first glimpse at the running lines of print, a passing look at whatever illustrations there may be, a quick examination of the table of contents or index . . . all provide, without a moment of actual reading, an anticipation, an awareness of starting out on a new adventure. There is a tension in the experience, a drawing together of one's senses and one's intellect, that in the mind does what in one's bloodstream a surge of adrenalin does. The mind trembles, as the lover's hand trembles in touching the loved one's fingers. It is a moment of anticipated pleasure that in its essence so nearly approaches joy as to beggar the difference.

The experience, too, of yielding one's mind to the impact of another's mind enters into this experience of near joy. A new author or a new book by a familiar author brings about that curiously abrasive relationship that brushes the two minds together, the reader's and the author's, and assures that if there is something to be changed, this abrasive relationship will bring about the change. The light of ideas results from the heat of mutual contact, and that light widens the reader's view and possibly even brings about a new capacity for wisdom. When this occurs, joy is clearly present.

Letters from Anagnostes Solitarium,
March, 1977

A Long Dinner

Reading for most people seems an occupation which is carried out in a mechanical and unthought-out way. A colleague, asked recently how he read a book, laughed a little in embarrassment, and then replied, "Oh, I just pick up the book, open it to a page, and begin to read the words." In an oversimplified way this is all true, but it leaves something to be desired in a description of everything that occurs during the act of reading. Pursuing this matter a little further, two quite different kinds of reading, recently experienced, proved rather interesting in their contrasts. The first reading experience was the result of a demand placed on this writer to produce a brief essay concerning the life and writings of an Ohio author, Charles Waddell Chesnutt. The second experience came as a single book, read for sheer pleasure, provoked and prodded the reader into a whole series of brief reading adventures, all oddly held together by the book which made them necessary. The two reading experiences were so different in their nature that viewing them in retrospect they seem to represent two separate functions entirely.

The essay concerning Charles Chesnutt began with a quick and entertaining reading of one of his short stories, a delightful bagatelle entitled "Baxter's Procrustes," which appeared in the *Atlantic Monthly* in 1904. It was an urbane and semi-sophisticated bit of raillery directed toward a club of bookmen who had both amused and irritated Chesnutt until he had lampooned them with dry satire. An essay concerning Chesnutt became a necessity, and so a brief adventure began. First a checklist of his works was created, and then they must be read in a rushing venture into a world which was surprisingly current, though its creation had occurred nearly sixty-five years earlier. Two works seemed quickly to set the pattern, first a volume of wise, earthy stories, entitled *The Conjure Woman*, and then a solemn piece of poignant social satire, *Wife of His Youth*, followed in quick reading by another three or four of the author's lesser works. There was too little leisure in this reading, but it had a purpose, to touch as much of the author's creative skill as possible in a brief time. Next a half dozen critical essays, concerned with Chesnutt's writings were devoured. A contemporary criticism, written in 1907 by William Dean Howells, was perhaps a high watermark in the critical writings reviewed, but there were four or five other essays, each examining a particular work by Chesnutt which were of interest. Then a long chapter in a work entitled *To Make a Poet Black*, by Jay Saunders Redding, produced solid criticism of Chesnutt in the 1930s, when the Black writer was first beginning to assert himself in critical reviews. These were then followed, first by a brief biographical article about Chesnutt, in *Ohio Authors*, and then by a full biography of Chesnutt by his daughter Helen. This was reading done in a headlong effort to gain as much information as possible in a limited amount of time. It was not without pleasure. The reading was inherently of interest, but it was done under some pressure and with the mind alert for only those essential facts and bits of related information which would contribute to a later summing up of the material. It was a reading experience of absorbed, concentrated concern. It held vital interest at a high level for the space of two or three days, and it brought together and into the hands of the reader a surprising amount of information to be used within a short space of time in producing a written summary review of Chesnutt's life and works.

A few weeks later, an experience in reading of an entirely different sort presented itself. An early copy of the latest volume of Edwin Way Teale's exciting series of volumes concerning the four seasons appeared on the reader's desk. *Wandering Through Winter* was the title, and it represented a piece of writing which had been awaited for three or four years by the reader as the final volume in the series. It was a volume which was quickly glanced through and then set aside for leisurely and relaxed reading later in the day. But once it was begun, it was an experience of such pleasure and such fascination that it provided one of those unique experiences that a reader may have. There was first the temptation to hasten through each of the succeeding chapters, to hurry along to reach another heart-warming description of Teale's long journey through the varying winter scenes across the country. But there was an equal delight to be found in the savoring of the author's fine prose style, of his philosophical observations, and of his perceptive comments about the men and places visited. There were, too, provocations to leave the delightful book to seek out the writings of others mentioned by Teale as having parallel interest. Not all of these byways of reading were in direct relation to the material with which the Teale book had to do. A chance quotation from a speech by the White Queen led the reader to a reading of that speech in its full context in *Alice's Adventures in Wonderland*, hardly a matter of concern for the naturalist but a matter of sheer pleasure in its rereading. Another passage made it seem imperative to reread a dozen pages in Thoreau's *Week on the Concord and Merrimack*. Still another suggested a pair of chapters in Burroughs' *Signs and Seasons*, and these in their turn led the straying reader to a half dozen pages of Hazard's *Johnny-Cake Papers*. A paragraph in *Wandering Through Winter* called up a chapter in *Snowshoe Country* by Florence and Lee Jacques, with Lee Jacques' stunningly bright illustrations. And before the Teale volume was half read, it became necessary to look into his earlier work, *The Lost Woods*, written twenty years earlier, and yet showing the same fine writing style and the same perceptiveness.

This last experience was one of sheer pleasure, and something more, for it was like a long dinner, with each succeeding course a new temptation, and each shift from one author to another bringing out the excellence and subtleties of the other. This was reading which kept the reader wide awake and alert, and at the same time drew him out of the commonplace of everyday happenings into a world of another sort, not unreal, but intensely real, not of escape, but of restfulness and adventure combined. It was reading which, as the fresh, cold air of a bright winter's day sweeps the lungs clear and brings fresh temper to the body, enlarges and enlivens the mind and spirit with new sensations and gives new meaning and consequence to old recollections.

These two experiences are so alike and yet at one and the same time so unlike that they seem comparable, and yet when they are tested, one against the other, are almost impossible to compare. The one is certainly not lacking in excitement, for the seeking out of new information is always an adventure worth pursuing. There is a tension in such an experience which is sharp and fascinating, sometimes exhausting, always challenging. But the other experience, so pleasurable, so leisurely, so seemingly without purpose, yet filled with the purpose of continuing satisfaction, must remain for any reader an opportunity which can never come too often. Nor will it present itself so often as to dull the pleasure it gives. It may come once, or twice, or even a dozen times within a lifetime of reading experiences, certainly no more. Gilbert White's gentle *Selbourne* provided one such opportunity for me, leading me on to a baker's dozen of byways of reading. Admiral Richard Byrd's *Little America* sent me headlong into a whole year of reading in the literature of the poles. Even a rereading, after many earlier readings of Christopher Morley's *Parnassus on Wheels*, never fails to yield me a harvest of parallel readings. And there have been at least another half dozen which have provided similar provocation.

I would not lose either of these two experiences nor do without them. The first is blessed with the excitement of the hunt, the casting about in a field where the quarry is suspected to reside. The quartering of the field, the first glimpse of the quarry, as perhaps a fleeting form, which is then slowly exposed and clothed in its full nature, this is a hunt which never ceases to bring delight. But the second opportunity is perhaps more like a springtime walk along a swiftly moving stream, when soft sounds call the attention to some new meadow or half-hidden and forgotten clearing in the woods and partly out of a new world through which the seeker walks. No reader can truly claim to be such with absolute privilege until he or she has found this kind of opportunity and taken full advantage of it, holding still and breathless with the wonder of the light that his or her reading sheds on commonplace things.

Letters from Anagnostes Solitarium,
August, 1980

Dialogue With the Author

It has been said that reading is a one-way communication from the author to the reader. This is, of course, manifestly untrue, for despite the fact that it is the author who has some concept which he wishes to transmit to others, it is just as true that in the reading experience the reader must contribute something to the situation as well, and in so doing establishes a kind of dialogue which develops eventually into a relationship adding considerable meaning to the entire process between reader and author.

There can be little question that the act of reading is one which involves many aspects of which we know very little. There is sparse information, for example, concerning the miracle which occurs when a reader opens a volume and applies himself to the printed lines. The physical act of reading has been examined with considerable care, but the astonishing event which comes about when the reader's eyes receive the signals from the printed letters, combines them into concepts called into being by the arrangement of the letters, and then accepts them in more and more complex combinations with the developing sentences and paragraphs is not well understood. The purpose and presumably the end product of this sequence of action and reaction is comprehension of the thesis or ideas the author has seen fit to put in writing.

It is not the purpose of this brief commentary to discuss what occurs in the process suggested. It is, however, perhaps worthwhile to look briefly at the two most easily recognized elements of the writer/reader dialogue. The writer at one end of the dialogue and the reader at the other have certain relationships and responsibilities which are interesting to look into. The author's part in this two-way communication has been much discussed and much analyzed. He or she is normally thought to be responsible for being well informed about the topic being dealt with; he or she must have a special awareness or perceptivity concerning the theme or thesis under review; he or she is expected to be disciplined in the subtle arts of rhetoric and syntax. The writer is given a certain license in the mysterious area of creative writing, especially when narrative fiction is being undertaken. This license permits the writer to hold up in the clear light of common day the entire spirit of his hero or heroine and to turn that spirit this way and that as thoughts about that character are communicated to the reader. Beyond this, the writer can proceed with double purpose, first to reveal his or her own thoughts and feelings about a character, and second, to call upon the reader to join in this appraisal, whether it be sympathetic or antipathetic.

In short, the author's responsibilities are those of initiating the dialogue, or communicating through a careful organization of words and sentences an idea or series of ideas, with logical development, with purpose, and with a modicum of grace.

At the other end of this line of communication, not quite the same responsibilities are to be found, although certain similarities appear. While the author has responsibility only for his or her own individual part in the dialogue, he or she is faced with a great variety of receivers or interpreters among his readers. Thus the line of communication between, shall we say, Plato and his modern reader may very well be blocked at the receiving end by the incapacity of the reader to comprehend the full reach of that author's intense logic. Indeed, there seems always to be some such risk, a risk at least of a difference of interpretation, since, for example, words must always have slightly different connotations in their transfer from one mind to another. These variations of interpretation become even more involved when they exist between ages of time than when they occur between two individuals writing and reading in the same time. And it is this, among other things, that makes for the most significant responsibility which must be accepted by the reader.

First, in joining in the dialogue with the author, the reader accepts at the start some significant obligations. He or she must assume from the beginning, for instance, an attitude of sympathetic responsiveness to what the author has to say. This is not to place any claim upon the reader for agreement, but it is at least the reader's responsibility to attend to the expression of the author's ideas for long enough to comprehend what the author is attempting to do. Second, in the case of the reader who takes up a book from another age than his or her own, there is an obligation to gain at least some concept of the context within which the author lived and wrote. To read William Morris, for example, or Walter Savage Landor, without some awareness of the time and culture in which they lived and wrote is to read half blindly. To read *The Education of Henry Adams*, without being at least dimly aware of his background and his keen awareness of family, is to miss the implication of the work entirely. One does not ask the reader to prepare for reading a particular book by taking a course of some sort, but this is to say that a volume read without at least some awareness of its frame of reference will all too often prove of little worth to the reader.

At least one other obligation laid upon the conscience of a thoughtful reader is that he or she shall not simply lie down before the flooding words of the enthusiastic author, permitting them to flow over himself or herself, with their "mental sound" dulling the ears and mind. Nor should swiftly flowing sentences be taken in great gasping gulps. Instead they should be savored and enjoyed, first in their simple context of sound and organized ideas, and second in their impact upon the reader's own sensibilities and opinions. The reader, caught by some sudden beauty of phrasing or soft cadence in a sentence, should sometimes at least reach back to the beginning of the passage to see just what it is that catches the mind's ear with so lovely a sound or that brings so swift a quickening of wonder in the world's marvels. And in so doing, astonishment and joy in watching another's mind at work are the result. This is not in the least a business lacking in purpose or personal gain, for often in retracing the author's regimented words, the reader will find both enlightenment and pure joy.

In the course of some forty years of more or less continuous reading, this writer has had the opportunity to read to all intents in their entirety the writings of some half dozen authors. The reason for this relatively complete exposure to the wholeness of these half dozen authors has been simply that the marvelous combination of their thoughts and their capacity for expressing these combinations have made a real and yet intangible appeal to this reader's mind and spirit. No other reason worth recording can be given. But in the somewhat intensive exploration of the thoughts of these six or seven writers one reader at least has found not only stimulation and a peculiar delight but, even more, the comfort and joy and endless surprise of friendship and companionship. Doubtless the authors themselves might be surprised, perhaps even chagrined, to find that they have become so much a part of another man's life, a life found in a century with which they might have little sympathy. And yet this has occurred, and has given warmth and great happiness and even strength to one reader who has cultivated their distant and yet very real acquaintance.

Letters from Anagnostes Solitarium,
April, 1981

SECTION II
LITERARY CREATION
AND TYPES OF LITERATURE

The reader will notice that many of the examples selected for discussion in these essays are taken from English and American literature. However, the same comprehensive reading, methods of analysis, and enthusiasm can, and should, be brought to whatever discipline the collection development librarian is responsible.

Exceptional Pleasures

There are numerous pleasures for the reader who persists in an exploration of the world of books, which is an unmapped world, an uncharted sea of wonders and delight. There are few of us who do not envy the excitement of the young reader, who still has the world of books to explore. But exciting as the vista is for the young reader, an even more exciting opportunity exists for the reader who has spent a lifetime in following the highways and byways of the book world. There is always, even for the most jaded reader, that miraculous experience of discovery which occurs when he finds a fine new book or one which he has somehow left unread. It is in this joy of surprise that perhaps the most satisfying of all reading experiences may be found.

There is a small and choice group of books which might be called springboard books. These have the capacity to lead one into such an experience. Christopher Morley's *Parnassus on Wheels* and *The Haunted Bookshop* are books of this sort. Another such book is certainly the simple, and disarmingly childlike little volume by John Drinkwater entitled *Robinson of England*. To this book the present writer owes a most important debt of gratitude, for John Drinkwater in his little work describes two other books in such enticing manner as to make their reading an imperative matter. Drinkwater causes his hero to talk with his niece and nephew about one of the most charming books in the English language, Gilbert White's *Natural History of Selbourne*. White belonged to that breed of men which England seemed to foster once, who were amateurs in every sense of the word. White lived in the village of Selbourne all of his lifetime exploring his village and his county, savoring every facet of the community and its people, exploring every niche, pondering over most of the natural wonders to be found there. His series of "letters," each describing some special feature of the community or county he loved, go to make up a truly delightful volume on natural history. His description of the Hangers, a wood which hung above the town and dominated it in a mysterious way, is one of the loveliest nature passages in all of English literature. His curious consideration of the swallows, which he felt surely slept underground in a neighboring cliff, while mistaken in its facts, is nonetheless a triumph of the amateur working with planed tools. Each of the little essays is a triumph of literary organization, each provides a cleanly drawn vignette of some natural aspect of the countryside which he loved more than England itself, it seems. It is a book created in such delicate balance that its reading becomes almost painful at times because of the perfection of its simplicity. The joy of surprise which it provides for the reader who comes upon it for the first time, and unsuspecting, is something to be treasured and remembered.

Another work which Drinkwater made seem important to read because of his comments in *Robinson of England* is the nineteenth century utopian novel, *News from Nowhere* by William Morris. Morris has a special quality of writing which makes his paragraphs seem strangely sunlit and warm, even while under their sunny passages there may be sensed the gentle knife of the satirist. Just as certain of the Scandinavian writers have the capacity to paint with words the transformation of the bleak landscapes of their homeland when these are flooded with clear northern sunlight, so William Morris has created a panorama of light-filled prose which sweeps the reader up into a world he or she never knew, one that is oddly comfortable while at the same time disturbing.

Another book that is full of joyful surprises for the reader is one of the minor masterpieces of American literature, that collection of unbelievably perfect short stories by Sarah Orne Jewett, *Country of the Pointed Firs*. Written at the close of the Civil War, Mrs. Jewett's clear sounding, clean sounding prose, portrays a world which perhaps can never exist again. Yet her book has that timeless quality which makes it as fresh today, and as readably modern, as though it had come from her pen in the mid-twentieth century. Few more poignant character sketches have been drawn than that of the little gray lady who ran away from the poor home to seek adventure. Nor can there be found, anywhere in American writings, such limpid and cleanly fashioned prose as is found in these brilliantly created tales of the Maine coast.

Still another joyous surprise for the complete reader may be found in two late gothic novels written by John Meade Falkner. *The Nebuly Coat* has a haunting quality of ominous doom which grips the reader almost from the first page and holds him or her until the final pages crumble in the dust of the dying abbey. Falkner wrote with a kind of eighteenth century grace and with the vigor of the gothic horror writers. *The Nebuly Coat* along with its companion piece, *The Lost Stradivarius*, represents a remarkable rebirth of the sense of the macabre which permeates the writings of Mrs. Shelley and of such gothic legends as the *Mysteries of Udolpho*, but with an added quality of swiftness of expression which makes them a joy to read and a delight to remember.

Edmund Gosse should not be forgotten in gathering up that little group of books which bring about the joy of surprise. Gosse's important little narrative which will stand for centuries as an important human document, *Father and Son*, represents the terrible struggle which ensued between the traditional fundamentalists of the first half of the nineteenth century and the men of science who followed the scientific explosion set off by the publication of Darwin's *Origin of Species*. Gosse, himself the son of a fundamentalist minister, was in truth a man of the age of science, and his account of the heartbreaking struggle of the older man to hold the son and of the son's final break with his parent and with the past is a remarkable and provocative story which will stand as a convincing record of the century in which the two Gosse men lived, gazing at each other across the Darwinian chasm that separated them.

Not one of the books named here stands as a gigantic literary creation. Yet each is secure in its own right as a book capable of offering joy and delighted surprise to the reader who opens its pages. There are few enough such works, but those there are invariably exhibit in their pages an incomparable fitness of expression, style and purpose, and each brings comfort, joy, satisfaction and surprise to the person who pauses long enough to read them.

The Printer's Mark,
July, 1961

Books to Live Without

A librarian is supposed by the general public to like books. A librarian is thought by most to be a sort of reading machine, into whose receptive heart all books may go, to find a warm reception and a careful response. If the truth must be known, however, there is at least one librarian who has a healthy and well developed set of negative reactions toward some books. In the course of more than forty years of reading I have compiled a list of books which are anathema to me, for one reason or another, and because these books bring the worst out in me, I think the time may have come to express my feelings on the subject, and exorcise my soul of their effect.

My list of books which I would not take to a desert island with me is of considerable length. The essence of the list, however, I wish here to present, not necessarily in the order of my disapproval, but as a group of books which are simply not for me:

Lloyd C. Douglas	*Magnificent Obsession*
Hemingway	*The Old Man and the Sea*
Grahame	*The Wind in the Willows*
Lewis	*Babbitt*
Dickens	*A Tale of Two Cities*
Clemens	*Tom Sawyer*
Dreiser	*An American Tragedy*
Thackeray	*Vanity Fair*
Scott	*Ivanhoe*
Steinbeck	*The Grapes of Wrath*

This is a list of ten, to which another fifty could be added, but certainly those here named stand among an unhonored group in my personal gallery of distaste. Why do I dislike these particular books? Well, there are a dozen reasons, I suppose, not the least of which in each case is the suspicion that their presence on lists of books which must be read by all and sundry is due to a kind of conspiracy among teachers to keep these books alive, not because of any essential merit in their pages but because someone else thought them of mountainous stature.

I do not think it truly necessary to justify such a list. It is not one which I would impose on any other individual. Far from it, for if truth were known the existence of this list of mine is as much due to the impressing of some of these titles upon my consciousness without regard for my own tastes and preferences. I mean that teachers and librarians I have known have been guilty of trying to force my reading and the reading of others like me into a mold too closely resembling their own reading pattern. This kind of forced reading is as dangerous in its way as is the censorship which some would impose on unsuspecting readers.

Now as to the list and the titles it contains, while I reserve the right to list these titles on my own personal catalog for limbo, I am willing to present at least some of my reasons for distaste. Let us admit from the start that some of my reasons are as unreasonable and as ill defined as the adolescent's "I don't know" reply to any question. But there are some reasons which bear validity, at least for me.

Magnificent Obsession stands near the head of my list merely as the symbol of the entire list of Douglas's writings. I hold two things against him, first that his philosophy is dangerously insincere, and despite his protestations to the contrary all but non-Christian. His preachment, which runs through every volume that he has placed upon our shelves, is the preaching of a false kind of sweetness and light. Be good, he says, not for the sake of being good, not for what being good will do in the way of helping others but rather as a means of storing up a kind of kind of insurance in heaven. Be good, because if you are good, you will reap benefits in heaven. The kind of goodness which he urges on his reader is to be repaid somehow in heaven, and this concept is as far from the truth of the Christian ethic, which Douglas professes, as it can be. Beyond this, Douglas's style I hold against him, partly out of jealousy, I am sure, for it is so smooth and so wonderfully applicable to his narrative that the falsity of his teaching is hidden deceptively beneath the sunniness of his words. His message is not for me.

Hemingway's *The Old Man and the Sea* is another highly polished piece of shining literary gloss. Papa Hemingway in the course of his increasing years had mastered his trade completely. Mastered it at least in terms of his capacity to turn out a richly illumined prose, regardless of the shallowness of the content it clothed. Set *The Old Man* beside the stark, sunlit agony of *Death in the Afternoon*, and its slim thesis becomes apparent to any reader. Yet I have heard in recent weeks a half dozen critics imposing upon *The Old*

Man a marvelous costume of meaning, turning it into a strange allegory of a contest between man and his fate, which from my point of view is utterly without reason or purpose. Let us take the little tale for what it is, and let it stand on its own true merits. And if those merits leave it something less than blessed with the stature of the mighty, let us not try to endow it with riches which it cannot carry. Far rather the morbid probing of *A Farewell to Arms* than the trumped up emotion and phony drama displayed by *The Old Man.*

My distaste for *The Wind in the Willows* finds its explanation in more than a single element, I suspect. The quaintness of the tale is first of all abhorrent to me. I do not like the foolishness of animals endowed with human characteristics, even for the sake of satire. An occasional short story I can stomach in this vein, but a whole volume couched in this quaint imagery is more than I can stand. If one is to be quaint in this manner and also successful, let us at least have the kind of tongue in cheek writing of that fine sentimentalist, A. A. Milne, for Pooh and Eeyore and Tigger have at least their splendid humor to help them survive the black days, a humor Rat and his companions sadly lack, so busy are they aping the ways of men. Another factor in my distaste, I must admit, are the drawings by Arthur Rackham which adorned the pages of my first copy of *The Wind.* His dainty, overbusy and scratchy plates suit the quaint mood of Grahame's writing to perfection, and so add only that much more to the deadly mood itself.

Sinclair Lewis, I am sure, and in fact I even heard him say so once, wishes that Babbitt could have gone to his grave fifty years ago, from where he might even now arise on All Hallow's Eve to haunt his creator, but to have had to live with *Babbitt* through a lifetime, without ever having intended to create a deathless figure, is more than any author—or reader—should have to bear. Now as a novel of quick, biting wit, aimed at holding up a mirror for a brief while so that Sinclair's dreadful middle class might see itself, *Babbitt* served a splendid momentary purpose. But it was, when all is said and done, a novel not written with any idea that it would stand as a model for other satirists to follow, or that its title would become a misused word in the native tongue of its author. All of this has occurred not because of the novel itself but rather because of the imposition by the critics, those wonderful extenders of meaning, of a whole set of special meanings and satiric thrust upon the original work. Let me explain. Some novels possess within themselves a peculiar catalyst which allows them to live on and on and preach their little sermons through the years, while other novels, as this one of Lewis's, must be supplemented by the critics, who go on adding chapters and meanings to the original prose for dozens of years until the original work stands in the arena, weighted down with armor it can hardly carry, a helpless symbol adorned with meaning it was never meant to have.

Years ago, on first reading *The Grapes of Wrath*, when the lowering days of the depression made such searching of the national soul fashionable, I was taken in by the splendid narrative skill which Steinbeck displayed. I remember very well thinking that here was a book for the ages, with the sweep of destiny in its paragraphs and across its pages. It certainly is not original to suggest that it is only a little more than a social tract that Steinbeck disguised in slick prose. Just the other day, riffling through its angry page, I felt a certainty that it lacks the timeless qualities of those earlier tracts by Robert Greene, which, hidden beneath his skillful rhetoric, have somehow managed to survive the times and terrors of history and have even gained stature as literature. But literature applied to sociology, though the conny-catching papers of Greene were written before the birth of the statistical frustrations of sociology, leaves more to be desired than I can say in terms of truly deathless prose. Let us leave the sterile social tract to the professional scholar with his carefully documented jargon and concentrate on writing of literary worth in the entrancing forms for which fictional narrative was devised.

Dickens, Thackeray and Scott have for these many years been introduced to young readers with examples of their writing which do not represent them at their best. *A Tale of Two Cities* is no more like Dickens than day resembles night. Indeed, I have often wondered if Dickens wrote that maudlin tale himself or ill advisedly lent his name to its publication. Not that Dickens is incapable of the sort of sentimentality here to be seen. The morbid pages of the long, slow death scenes in which Little Nell holds the center of the stage in *The Old Curiosity Shop* are ample proof of this. But compared with such sturdy representatives of Dickens's pen as *Great Expectations, Bleak House, David Copperfield,* or *Oliver Twist,* to say nothing of *Dombey and Son, Two Cities* pales into insignificance. In my opinion *Pendennis* far outreaches Thackeray's other works, though *Vanity Fair* and *The Newcomes* are the fashionable titles to recommend to high school reading lists, while Scott's *Ivanhoe,* a piece of hack writing unexcelled as representing the worst of Scott, is jammed down the throats of young readers still too disciplined to resist. And the result? A lifelong distaste for these three writers, brought on by surfeit of their least admirable works. And instigated by whom? Teachers who pass on from generation to generation of young readers only those titles which they themselves came early to despise and which they cannot exchange for better because they have not read the better ones themselves.

Tom Sawyer? It is an American classic, to be sure. But is it this only because America has produced about as poor a lot of juvenile writers as an English-speaking nation could and because adults have laughed over Clemens's highly colored recollections of his boyhood days, nodding their heads sagely and saying, "Ah yes, I remember days like that. My salad days were filled with escapades, with adventure, with drunken Indians named Joe, with smoking behind the barn, and with superstitious midnight ceremonies." One reason that the adult reader clings to this tale of a river boyhood is that more modern juveniles consist so entirely of everyday experience that romance is almost absent from them. Our rage to have our children know the facts of living, as revealed in *The Little Farm, The Little Fire Engine* and similar masterpieces of practical everyday things, has left our juvenile literature devoid of imagination and sturdy romance, and dropped our children's reading into the realm of stodgy how-to-do-it prose. And when one comes down to it, what is there about *Tom Sawyer* that is so truly amusing? The wonderful scene in church in which the stray hounddog breaks into the sermon with his yelps as he sits down upon an escaping pinchbug is countered by the almost cruel humor displayed as Tom watches his own funeral and his aunt's brokenhearted attendance at that funeral. The whitewashing of the fence has been for too many years overplayed, and other scenes have at least been matched by other writers, even such as Thomas Bailey Aldrich in *The Story of a Bad Boy*.

What do I decry? Chiefly that too few readers are willing to give enough of themselves to the experience of reading to find books which have some special place to hold in their own lives. We live too much in an atmosphere of canned reading. We subscribe to book clubs and settle back to be told what is good, instead of finding for ourselves books and poems which have value for us and which make us eager to share them with others. So too today, books are read by too many of us only because they are being read by others, because they are in fashion . . . not because any book recommended as a bestseller necessarily has value for a particular individual. "Have you read this book? EVERYONE is reading it." So what? I have almost never heard in recent years any one of my acquaintance say, "I've just read a book, and it had something to say to ME."

It is true perhaps that very few serious readers are willing to admit that this book or that book holds a special place in their hearts. To make such an admission is to give away something of one's self . . . a dangerous procedure in any day or any society. To speak with feeling of something that one loves or cares for deeply is to die a little. But is this any reason to accept, publicly or privately, only books and ideas that are foisted off on one by a changing fashion?

I have suggested in this brief diatribe that there are some books, even some writers, who for one reason or another are not for me. There are, for certain, at least as many others I hug close and hold as part of my very self, for comfort, for sheer joy, for provocation, and for something more which I would not confess for worlds. To know the joy of this special kind of possession, a book of one's own, I know no better thing to suggest than to read and read until one finds those writings which possess in some measure the magic touch which is truth. In savoring those books, those words, one comes upon the wealth of the universe, which when all is said and done is more often than not found only within the self.

The Printer's Mark,
October, 1962

Christmas Packages

To begin with, Christmas packages are things of such excitement that they carry with them a peculiar aura of breathlessness, something akin to that tense moment as the curtain rises at the opening of a play, when the audience holds its collective breath and waits for the first burst of light upon the opening stage set. The characters, already placed upon the stage, stand motionless, and like puppets seem to await the first twitch of the invisible threads to give them life. Just so, these Christmas packages wait for the moment of exciting introduction to the world. For me the heap of carefully piled packages, each with its ribbon and bow, each with its sparkling wrapping, turn the base of a Christmas tree into a thing of sheer excitement. And for me those packages, more often than not, contained those still more exciting packages of pleasure which are books. I know of children in recent days who are so loved that their parents do real damage to them on Christmas by giving them too many packages to open, with a resulting confusion and frustration which is pitiable, despite its laughing excitement. My own days of Christmas were of a somewhat different sort.

Long before Christmas came, usually early in November, there would begin for me moments of delightful anticipation. I very often spent hours before the fireplace in my home in company of a grandmother who was herself so delighted a reader that we had a particular affinity, and would stay quietly together reading for hours on end, with hardly a word between us. In one of those moments she would say, "What do you want for Christmas?" The answer was always the same for me. "A book." "What kind of book?" And then would begin that delightful anticipation.

I used to be subscriber to and ardent reader of the old *St. Nicholas Magazine*, and from September on its pages were more and more crowded with advertisements for the new books coming into the bookstores. I used to pore over those advertisements and memorize the "blurbs" of those books which gave most promise of delight for me. And so we would talk about books, discussing the new titles, choosing some, and setting others aside, agreeing that this author had been usually worth reading in his last work, wondering if this new author would live up to the promises in the advertisements. I remember very well that I became aware of a secret little game that my grandmother used to play with me. We would discuss a particular book and come to an apparent agreement that it should be placed on the Christmas list, and then subtly the discussion would change, and she would convince me that perhaps it was not such a good book after all, and so should not be listed as a special Christmas wish. There were times when I was somewhat disappointed with these little shifts of opinion, but she was so always right, that grandmother of mine, that I was willing to go along with her. It was only after we had played this little game for several years, five perhaps, that I became aware that some of the very books which had been discarded in our discussions of what should be on the Christmas list were in fact under the tree on Christmas morning. I came to realize then that this was her way of saving a few special titles to give to me herself. The Christmas list, you see, was shared by the whole family—mother, father and a few aunts and uncles—but titles which she and I discussed so avidly, only to decide ultimately that they were less desirable than some others, were saved for her own purchases. It was a quiet little deceit of hers, but a loving one. I do know, too, that after I came to a realization of what was happening I loved it quite as much as she did, and I think each of us was aware that the other knew the rules of the game, but we continued to play it, she and I, until she was in her seventies, and I was in graduate school. And there was a happy zest in the game that brought a special joy to our Christmas Day.

Christmas Day itself was of course a day of great joy. My Christmas used to consist of few games or toys and, most acceptable of all, a double armful of books. Those books, each wrapped in its own package, sometimes disguised as a kind of joke to look as though they held larger objects, were opened carefully to reveal the colorful dustjackets. The books were piled carefully, close beside the chair which was always mine, and as the pile mounted up, with five, then ten, then twelve or fifteen, my own impatience to begin to do more than glance at the dustwrapper and the title became almost unbearable. There were times, I remember very clearly, when I would have been content to leave the other non-book packages under the tree so as to be at the absorbing business of choosing the first book which would be read.

It took a half dozen Christmas mornings to complete my set of the comfortable leather bound Nelson edition of Dickens, all bound in dark maroon, with gilded edges, the leather soft and smooth and inviting to the touch and the white pages crowded with close-set print. That set stands still upon my shelves, the backs somewhat worn, and the gold spine titles rubbed and now hard to read. But each volume of that set contributed to a Christmas holiday of reading that has not yet lost its glow of satisfaction. A set of Scott, in the same edition, these bound in royal blue, were likewise joined in the regiments of Christmas books, and every one bears the marks of time and comforting use, for these were books to read and then reread.

I can remember the arrival one Christmas morning of Howard Pyle's *Book of the American Spirit*, a conglomeration of historical tales, each illustrated in Pyle's flamboyant and swashbuckling color. I remember the first copy that I came to own myself of Kipling's *Captains Courageous*, a book that I had read a half dozen times in copies from the public library before I knew that I must have it for my own; I remember, too, the game played with my grandmother, a game which I won to our mutual amusement by returning to discuss half a dozen times my wish for this particular book. I remember my first introduction to Will James's horse story, *Smoky*, remembering it chiefly because one year there were three copies of that same title among the packages which came from relatives. There was a surfeit of *Smoky*, and perhaps because of that it is a book for which I never have had much feeling.

There was a Christmas of especial laughter when *Skippy Bedelle* and *The Varmint* by Owen Johnston made their appearance under the Christmas tree. There were three years or so when each Christmas meant a change in ideas as to what I would be, with the arrival of one of Henry Hold-Wheeler's books of the year, *The Boy with the Secret Service*, or *The Boy with the U.S. Weather Service*. I never understood why he could not write about a boy who would be a librarian, but such an occupation evidently did not lend itself to boyish books. There were years when Christmas was made most complete by a new book by William Beebe . . . *Nonsuch, Land of Water, Jungle Days, Galapagos, Worlds End*, these were titles fraught with romance. There were those outrageous tales of romantic travel by Richard Halliburton, *Royal Road to Romance* and its less successful sequels. Christmas was a time for dreaming, and for reading of the empty places on the map of the world and of those others whose names were miracles in themselves.

There was a year, too, when four autographed first editions arrived of Robert Frost's classic New England poetry, so gracefully simple that its ulterior qualities only barely glowed through the swiftly moving lines. There was a year of wonder when Sara Teasdale, and Edna St. Vincent Millay were wrapped together in a package that made a lovely sound upon its opening.

Christmas was and is a time for any reader, but more particularly it stands as a time of excitement for a young reader who has only begun to sense that there are more books in the world to read than can possibly be encompassed in a single lifetime; it is a time of impatience, when a dozen books unopened make the choosing of an evening's reading a thing of vast importance and utmost anticipation; it is a time for rereading, too, for there are books which must be dipped into every year as part of the ceremony of Christmas; and best of all, it is a time for glancing along one's private shelves to see titles that recall that merry game of deciding which books were to be among the gifts from that small, special grandmother, who loved to buy books at Christmas, who gave them with obvious pleasure, who often read them aloud and who discussed their special value as easily as if speaking of the weather. Christmas is for everyone, but especially Christmas is for the reader, for whom every book represents the merriest of Christmases.

The Printer's Mark,
December, 1962

Counting Cats in Zanzibar

A pungent phrase attributed to Thoreau has been teasing my mind for several days. The philosopher of Walden, speaking in his superior fashion of travel, once said, "It is not worth while going round the world to count the cats in Zanzibar." It is a remark that strikes sharply home, for there are all too many travel books which are little more than an account of the number of things seen, or the number of miles travelled, with a result achieved which could only be expected. Such travel books are all too often devoid of understanding, their authors having failed utterly in the effort to catch the essential spirit of the countries visited.

It is of course exceedingly difficult for a traveller to sense in a hurried visit the spirit of a people or the warm nature of a community. An occasional fortunate traveller will experience a peculiar revelation as he pauses in a fishing town or mountain village. I remember, some time ago, standing on the deck of a coastal steamer as it slowly crept to the dock of a northern community in the eastern reaches of the St. Lawrence. A first glance at the little town, resting uneasily along the curving, scaly beaches of an uninviting harbor, revealed only a group of unpainted houses, somehow garish, somehow naked in the half-warming sunlight that slanted briefly toward the pole. The dock itself was almost bare, with a few tangles of tarred rope and rusty and decrepit-looking fork-lift on it. But there was a tension in the air, too, for beside me stood two priests, one a young man, who was quietly watching the narrowing strip of water that separated us from the pilings of the pier, and the other an ancient and sorely tried, sad-eyed priest, his hands folded firmly before him as gazed down at the deserted pier which let up to a deeply shadowed street. The young priest stirred and glanced triumphantly at me, for he had warned me of what would come. "Monsignor comes home to die, so the doctors say," he had informed me as we left our last port in the morning before reaching Havre St. Pierre. "But his people will make him forget, they will make him glad. I have told them of the illness which the doctors have spoken of. But his people will make him glad to come home, you will see." And as he stirred, the ugly shed was suddenly brightly lighted. The great doors swung open, and crowds of people who had been waiting inside streamed out upon the dock, with a makeshift orchestra blaring and whinnying from the shed entrance. The people crowded to the wharf's edge, cheering and waving and letting their monsignor know that he had come home. It was a spontaneous gesture of kindness and of love and affection for a man who had been a leader of that community. I had watched his face throughout the days of the voyage down the river, patient, yielding only occasionally a brief shadow of pain or perhaps something deeper than pain. Now I glanced at him again, a little shy myself, to see the effect that this wonderful welcome would have on him. And there was on that wise and patient face a serenity, a pleasure, a pride and quiet joy that made all the sorrow of his terrible illness slip away. He raised his hand in the traditional movement of blessing, and I turned away, for his joy was meant to be a secret thing.

Now what has this to do with the kinds of things that usually are taken up in these brief papers? Very little, I suppose, and yet a great deal, too. The point to these introductory remarks is that the casual passerby seldom has an opportunity to savor the true value and spirit of whatever is seen in so fleeting a way. And, in the nature of things, the words a writer uses to describe an experience or his or her reaction to it or to any thing which has given him either pleasure or displeasure, are so tenuous as to make them of little use, even in the most intimate of communication. Let me try to explain the sense of futility most writers feel as they hear others' responses to their thoughts and words.

There is in *The Barren Ground of Northern Canada* by Warburton Pike, a most unusual and interesting book published in 1892, a lovely passage in which Pike reports a conversation between a missionary and an Indian of those northern wastelands. The missionary has, in the course of a lengthy preamble, spoken to the Indian concerning Christian faith, and in so doing has spoken of the wonders and beauties of heaven itself. His words have impressed the Indian to a point, but the concluding remarks by the Indian are worth noting. "Is it as fine as when the caribou move in the spring? Is it as fine as when the great trees color in the fall?" Here, in a moment are the swift sense of beauty and the quality of longing which enters the spirit of a person who has found contentment in the past and is not eager to change his concept of what the future may hold. And no amount of travel, to Zanzibar or the ends of the earth, will make a difference worth the price of losing that sense of value in the past.

A good friend recently came into my office to tell of a particular moment of excitement which had turned his day from a gray, December emptiness into a day of joyous optimism. He said that he had been watching a television program in which the sordidness and ugliness of modern times had left him enervated and depressed. He had picked up his copy of Thoreau's *Week on the Concord and Merrimack Rivers* and found, among the entries for Monday of that splendid week a passage which somehow made the world seem right again in spite of its unhappiness:

> Far in the night, as we were falling asleep on the bank of the Merrimack, we heard some tyro beating a drum incessantly, in preparation for a country muster, as we learned, and we thought of the line,—
> "When the drum beat at dead of night."
> We could have assured him that his beat would be answered, and the forces be mustered. Fear not, thou drummer of the night; we too will be there. And still he drummed on in the silence and the dark. This stray sound from a far-off sphere came to our ears from time to time, far, sweet, and significant, and we listened with such an unprejudiced sense as if for the first time we heard at all. No doubt he was an insignificant drummer enough, but his music afforded us a prime and leisure hour, and we felt that we were in season wholly. These simple sounds related us to the stars. Ay, there was a logic in them so convincing that the combined sense of mankind could never make me doubt their conclusions. I stop my habitual thinking, as if the plow had suddenly run deeper in its furrow through the crust of the world. How can I go on, who have just stepped over such a bottomless skylight in the bog of my life? Suddenly old Time winked at,—Ah, you know me, you rogue,—and news had come that IT was well. That ancient universe is in such capital health, I think undoubtedly it will never die. Heal yourselves, doctors; by God I live.

What a magnificent passage. What a healing insight leaps out of those lines. What a sense of timeliness and hope is here revealed. And what a vision of those starlit deeps where one finds hope of one's eternity and is able to set fears aside as the darkness vanishes.

Counting cats in Zanzibar. I have recently read and reread because I could not believe what I was reading, a series of travel books in which the author counted out the days he'd spent abroad and cast like dice before my eyes the numbers of castles he had seen, the landmarks he had noted, and the museums he had hurried through, catching now and again a glimpse of some masterpeice which lit up but faintly his jaded memory. This kind of travel book is hardly worth the ink that has gone into it. But there are others, worth the reader's patient reading. A rare sort of experience may be had, for example, in T. H. White's *England Have My Bones*, a book which details a number of "fishing week ends" and vacations taken across the countryside, with nostalgic accounts of the fishing inns where White spent his evenings and of the curling English streams which he and his rod explored. Here is travel writing at its best, with cheerful accounts of fireside meals in the company of fellow anglers and with a keen sense of the beauties which were his to savor as he cast his line.

A tale of adventure of an entirely different sort is to be found in what at first seems to be a most unlikely source. Dard Hunter produced a combined tale of adventure and work of scholarship in his stunning and beautifully produced *Paper Making in Indo-China*. In this he tells of his lengthy visit to the paper villages of Indo-China. Describing a world which is now all but lost, Hunter's book is a marvel of the genre. Place names ring like bells out of his graceful paragraphs, such names as Annam, Phi-dinh, Vu-yen, Van-phy, Thach-de and Yen-luong, where the ancient papermakers discovered how to create the lovely rough-surfaced sheets of paper which were perhaps the first writing material ever. His narrative is filled with word pictures of the hidden valley towns, where the paper mills were huddled about pure springs of water and where the silent artisans stooped above the vats to stir the mash which would soon be turned into paper and children played beneath the drying lines of paper. Leisurely, comfortable reading, it is a book both for the scholar and general reader, whose interest never lags in the narrative, despite the technical details provided along the way for the scholarly researcher. To write a travel book, it seems to me, there must be more than simply a desire to tell of where one has spent his vacation. Baedekers and such travel manuals are to be had for the asking, and a thousand times a thousand men and women have been sure that they have seen for the first time some sight of London or Cologne. To write a truly worthy travel book the author must be a person who has some special rapport with what is seen. As this is so, the number of great travel books is relatively small. One traveller may well sense the power of London by standing in Trafalgar Square. Another is awed by the Lake Country, not by the lakes themselves, with their pleasant shores and rainy afternoons, but instead is able in some miraculous way to glimpse what Wordsworth saw, and in that fleeing vision find himself or herself in touch with particular realities. One person remembers shivering in a cold wind facing out to sea at Plymouth, knowing very well that that rock is almost certainly not the place where the Pilgrims first stepped ashore, and yet sensing truly what those Englishmen felt as they left their ship and stepped ashore in the new world. Most of us have few enough of these moments of swift insight in our own experience. In books, however, the reader may find such moments over and over again, and in these flashes of comprehension are excitement and inspiration, the stuff that makes the world go on.

The Printer's Mark,
October, November, 1963

Books and Winter

Of the four seasons of the year there are two which lend themselves best to the comfortable occupation of reading. While spring and fall seem to place heavy demands on one to spend much time preparing for the growing season and clearing up after the harvest, the other two seasons offer time for the enjoyment of that gentle art which both rests and invigorates the mind. Within the winter season there are special times when reading offers different kinds of enjoyment. The first blustery weekends of December bring about a sense of security when those stormy days are viewed from the vantage point of a comfortable chair beside a warming fire. And in that security the joy of a good book is peculiarly heightened and transformed into miraculous wonderment. Later in that season when long days of storm make even contemplation of outdoor activity unattractive, then the good companions on our bookshelves provide us with great satisfaction.

It is to this season which Chaucer called "the colde, frosty sesoun of Decembre" that certain books somehow belong especially. I know of very few published works which deal entirely with the cold of winter, although there are of course a few. But there are many old favorites which within their covers present passages devoted to a depiction of the wonders of snow and all that goes with it. Therefore, in this last month of the year it is appropriate that we glance at least briefly at some of these wintry works.

One volume which has for all the years that this reader has been reading held a place of honor on the shelves close beside a comfortable easychair is that account of a New England boyhood, *The Story of a Bad Boy*, by Thomas Bailey Aldrich. Two chapters of that delightful work are given over to a description of two unforgettable episodes of youthful memory. One describes the first snow of the year, and is so filled with boyish surprise and excitement that despite its icy subject is a heartwarming testimony of what winter can mean to the young at heart. Tom's delight with the great gateposts at the front entrance of his grandfather's house, which were overnight "turned into white-turbanned Turks" guarding the door, is as infectious as it is imaginative. The account in that same chapter of how, after the heavy snowfall the town's "oldest inhabitant" broke out his record of memories and pronounced the storm the greatest in history, is both amusing and wise. Still another aspect of winter in Portsmouth recounts the great "Battle of Slatter's Hill," a snow fight between two boyish gangs which begins with ordered plans and regulations, only to end in wild battery and assault. These are wintry tales, both historical and nostalgic, which make for fascinating December reading.

New England winters, it seems, hold a charm, particularly in memory, which is pieced together of many things. To some a Maine winter means long, windy days along the coast with the great American fjords streaming in raw easterly winds. To others it means memories of sleet and hail crashing against the windows shuttered against a January storm. But to John Gould, Maine editor and author, a Maine winter is filled in recollection with the pungent scent of apples stored in the cold basement beneath the kitchen and of apple pies brought fresh out of the oven and placed to cool a half hour before dinner. In one of the most delightful wintry books, Gould spends a too short chapter drawing comparisons between various kinds of apples in the production of those apple pies. His amusing *Farmer Takes a Wife* is a mouth-watering narrative of the events which transpire in his farm kitchen as his wife prepares man-filling, lusty soups, bakes bubbling apple pies, stirs meaty stews, all intended to ward off the winter's chill. This reader always tries to reread John Gould's little book at Thanksgiving time, when our house is filled with seasonal preparations, for Gould's enthusiasms only add to the spicy climate of the day.

Winter is hardly a time when one would choose to spend the days in any kind of solitary environment, and yet one narrative comes to mind which details an entire winter season spent by a woman alone, save for the mischievous companionship of a dozen ponies, on a farm in western Massachusetts amid the Berkshires. *The Lone Winter*, by Anne Boxworth Greene, is a simple, sometimes mildly sentimental story which evokes quiet pictures of that graciously rolling countryside, with clouds of snow sweeping across the valleys to hide the hilltops and shut out the light of neighbors' friendly barnyard lanterns. It has passages of noisy racing in pursuit of thundering pony hoofs as the swift little beasts break through their pasture fences and escape down snowy, rutted roads. It tells of loneliness during stormy evenings and the joy of clearing weather when the sun picks out nearby snowcapped hilltops that contrast with the brown stains of winter woods along the shoulders of the hills. Here is a book for a quiet afternoon or evening with just enough action in it to stir up the reader's interest, but not so much as to demand that the volume be put down unfinished. It is a book to be dipped into over and over again, to seek out passages which one cannot forget, for the enjoyment in them.

There are times, of course, when most of us would welcome an opportunity to remove ourselves from the wearying daily intercourse with others in order to determine for ourselves, if we can, what matters in the world and what does not. Two books, each quite different from the other, give accounts of such retirement into the silence and solitude of self examination. The first of these is an introspective study of lonely danger, *Alone*, by Richard E. Byrd, the arctic and antarctic explorer. Drawn from his diary and notes of a terrifying winter spent entirely alone in a miserable hut dug into the antarctic icefield a hundred miles from his well-staffed base camp, *Alone* is tragic in its revelation of the need of man for man. It is at the same time a measure of one man's bravery, facing death yet refusing to call upon his colleagues to endanger their lives in a rescue effort. The volume leaves the reader with a stunning sense of unbearable cold and hardly less bearable loneliness. It holds no violence, other than the toll which nature takes when one dares challenge her. Yet there is a kind of agonizing evil portrayed in Byrd's story which makes the book into strong reading fare.

An equally contemplative work may be seen in Henry Beston's striking *Outermost House*, in which he tells of a whole year spent alone in a cottage built facing the Atlantic on the high beach of Cape Cod, some twenty miles below Provincetown. Built with windows which face both the sandy dunes of the Cape's backbone and gray mystery of the sea, Beston's tiny shelter afforded him an opportunity to observe all the natural events and seasons which sweep inexorably across the Cape, and a chance also to turn inward to examine his own thoughts and attitudes. Here is one of the most delightful of modern American classics, and one which draws for the reader a full portrait of man's inconsequence in the face of what nature produces.

The loneliness of windy autumn nights; the comfort of occasional calls from coastguardmen marching lonely beats along the winter beach; a sharpening interest in the sudden appearance of migrating geese; the discovery of tiny juncos, resting in the shallow valleys of the dunes after their perilous flight not along the coast, but directly across the wind-driven seas from Nova Scotia to the mainland and the Cape . . . all these go into Beston's book, and they hold the reader spellbound.

Letters from Anagnostes Solitarium,
December, 1968

Books About Books

Books about adventures with books and books about people who deal in books have a peculiar fascination about them. This is so in all probability because the reader must often wonder what the magic is to be found in books, and what the impact of that magic, whether it be white or black, is upon those who spend their lives in close company with the mysterious world of print.

That the magic is not all white is evident enough in some of those fantastic tales which have been written concerning the evil which books seem to have wrought. There is an eerie short story, written by Octave Uzanne, and published in translation in the first volume of that delightful journal of printing, *The Dolphin*. It carries in its narrative enough evil and bibliographic hatred to make content even the most violent bibliophobe. The story has to do with the obsession of M. Raoul Guillemard for the book collection of his deceased rival, Jules Sigismond. Entitled "The Sigismond Inheritance," it tells of Guillemard's total lack of sorrow over the death of his friend and his gleeful anticipation of the day when his rival's library will come to the auction block. But Sigismond, in anticipation that his demise would result in the dissemination of his book collection among his bitterest rivals, has willed the rich array of editions to his cousin Eleanore, a sharp-nosed, cantankerous spinster, whose hatred for her cousin is only exceeded by her hatred for the books which had been his preoccupation for so long. The legend is concerned with Guillemard's decision finally to seek the hand of the harridan if he can by that means alone achieve possession of the library. In announcing Sigismond's will, the lawyer in the tale deals the final insult by allowing that Sigismond's rivals will be permitted once each year to view the collection on the anniversary of Sigismond's birth. On these occasions they are to have twelve hours in the library moving the books, turning their leaves and enjoying their beauty.

On the first anniversary of Sigismond's birth following his demise, his bibliomanic friends discover to their horror that the new owner of the library has permitted the roof to develop leaks and has exposed the rich volumes to the rains of fall and winter and spring.

Another season passes, and they find, to their horror, that the wretched cousin has ordered the placement of whole families of mice into the library building to be free to nibble and digest the rich bindings and the priceless works. The roof the bibliophiles will have repaired, but the mice present another problem entirely. Guillemard counters this destructive purpose by dropping cats into the building through its broken roof. Eleanore counters this by installing wolf traps, and the cats are destroyed, while the library slowly crumbles into dust. The macabre tale, for the bibliophile a thing of horror, has its moments of high humor as well as of scholarly chicanery. It is, in fact, a splendid spoof on book collectors and bookmen in general.

Another tale with a curious kind of sadness is Roswell Field's half-sad story *The Bondage of Ballenger*. Poor Ballenger, blessed with little wisdom, is all the same capable of enjoying the pleasures of learning through devoted perusal of books. But the little learning he gains leads poor Ballenger into sinful ways, for he becomes so completely a slave to his reading that he loses all sense of proportion, spending not only his leisure hours buried in his books, but the hours of work as well, until his life and the life of his family are slowly lost in his ineptitudes and incapacities. It is a sweet, sad tale, not lacking in interest, but also a tale of the slow erosion of a man's spirit, and in effect a condemnation of books and reading. That such a work should become a part of an essay as this may seem strange, yet despite the fact that Field's little volume shows the tragic effect of overindulgence in the pleasure of reading, it is a little masterpiece of character drawing and of gentle satire. It has at least the merit of being a study of the development of a fatal flaw in a scholar, and, when all is said and done, the fatal flaw is the essence of great tragedy.

One of the most delightful and readable works having to do with books, bookshops and book dealers, is a quiet masterpiece now almost forgotten save by a few who have had it called to their attention by Roger Mifflin in Christopher Morley's *The Haunted Bookshop*. E. V. Lucas takes his hero in *Over Bemerton's* to an apartment above a London bookshop. This person immediately recognizes the advantages of living above a bookstore, as he suffers from insomnia. He anticipates being able, in the darkness of a sleepless night, to slip down to the crowded shelves of the bookshop to find either a novel of adventure to while away the waking hours or some serious, soporific volume which will induce sleep. But the hero's purpose is thwarted by a steady succession of people of books which move before him. His delightful, half-serious series of quotations from a Chinese dictionary of biography are as amusing and as fascinating as they are without doubt nonsensical. The ridiculous chapter in which the hero takes over as shopkeeper for a day is so filled with whimsical nonsense as to make it a true gem of turn-of-the-century humor and fantasy. And the stream of characters who move in and out of the shop provide Lucas with ample opportunity to display his capacity for lampooning all mankind. The book has moments of seriousness, too, which are both pleasant and worthwhile. His comments on the quality of the English stage, his brief diatribe against the irreligious in English stage comedy, his reactions to Victorian poetry at its worst, all merit the reader's attention.

Perhaps a little less appealing because of its somewhat stilted style, a kind of typographic detective story, is to be found in Lawrence Blochman's *The Aldine Folio Murders*. A kind of tour de force, this little bibliographic fiction depends upon its detective hero's knowledge of typefaces to unmask a bookish thief who is not quite bookish enough to carry off his thievery. The story proceeds at a happy pace, and contains an unusual element of suspense which makes it readable and worth remembering.

But of course the book about books to ascend above all others must remain Christopher Morley's altogether satisfying *Parnassus on Wheels*. Roger Mifflin, the owner of the original Parnassus, so completely dominates the story, despite the homely charm of its heroine, that he has become a kind of bibliophilic figurehead for the whole profession of booksellers if not, indeed, for the whole world of book lovers. The double handful of little homilies on reading, on the reading of particular books and authors, and on the ills of the world, which Roger Mifflin is convinced may be solved by the panacea of reading, makes for amusing and provocative reading. The red-headed bookseller's enthusiasms are so patent and infectious that the deep wisdom which lies beneath his diatribes on reading is easy to accept. More than this, his speeches concerning individual books draw the reader to those books and make them seem not only attractive but imperative to read. Roger Mifflin is a most amusing combination of playful scholar, mild philosopher, ardent reader, and aggressive promoter both of books themselves and of the art of reading. He must stand squarely at the head of the long line of bookish characters who are not in the least retiring or shy about singing out the praises of the world of books.

I, Anagnostes, blessed with considerable experience in the world of reading, would add my soft enjoinder to Roger Mifflin's constant cry that reading is for the person who would be free. Roger would say, without doubt, that to be a captive in the world of books is to be free in any other world. What can books do for such a person? They set the mind in action and lead the way to the farthest horizons of research. They ease the heart in moments of sadness by transporting the reader into the wonderful and healing world of imagination. They bring the reader the thoughts and words of people he or she would not dare approach in person, and still leave the reader free to agree or disagree, accept or reject, whatever is spoken by the other. A liberal education, as the gods well know, is never freely given, but is gained at great cost by those who would have it. A liberal education is one which sets the mind free, liberates it through contact, often abrasive, with other minds. This is a contact best made face to face, across the lines of printed words and thought which books and reading make available to any who choose them. Books are for free men. Free men find in books the strength to keep themselves free.

Letters From Anagnostes Solitarium,
March, 1969

Family Sagas

The day of the literary family chronicle seems long past, and occasionally when one sees on the library shelves the long sets of Galsworthy and de la Roche, one feels a pang of regret that the richness of those leisurely studies of generations of Forsytes and people of Jalna seem to modern readers tedious. Yet, a recently begun television series from the BBC brings into vibrant life the splendid group of property owners who went by the name of Forsyte, and makes their family history once more a thing of wonder, even for the young viewer. One of those responsible for the rejuvenation of the Forsytes has spoken with some astonishment of the interest this series has stirred up. He admitted that, when the television version of *The Forsyte Saga* was begun, he had suspected it would appeal only to those viewers over forty-five. To his astonishment he is now fully aware that it has found appeal among young men and women who hardly remember World War II! With this in mind, I turned over the pages of the long series of novels which make up *The Forsyte Saga* to see what there could be in those gentle chapters to appeal to those whose reading tastes, according to publishers, center more on violence and shock effects than on such genteel introspection as found in Galsworthy.

The one thing which seems most obvious as an explanation for the timelessness and continuing interest of the Forsyte story is that the central figures of the long narrative are completely real, well rounded in their characterization and entirely human in the ways they develop and change in face of the circumstances in which they find themselves. Soames Forsyte, so self contained, so conscious of the value of property, whether it be real estate or stocks or bonds or, for that matter, his marriage, moves through the narrative as an altogether convincing character. His uncle, Old Jolyon, a moving personality, perhaps in a real sense the true Victorian, bends only slightly before the winds of change and fortune which beset him, but bend he does. Young Jolyon, a sensitive artist and overwise for his years, becomes the individual he is in the face of his rejection by family and relatives for his refusal to subject himself to an unhappy, though fashionable, marriage. And Dartie Montague, half wastrel, fool, impetuous gambler, is clearly drawn in all his brazen and loathsome conceit.

In short, there is hardly a figure in the nine novels and half dozen interludes who is not alive and recognizably human. Even Soames, determined as he is to dominate his own personal and materialistic world, moves about in that world bustlingly and disturbingly human. He is not the hero of the saga, for in fact there is no distinct hero at all. But as the narrative extends into the lives of Soames's daughter by his second marriage and his granddaughter, he does assume the tragic role of a man defeated by the very things that mean most to him. Soames's tragic and indeed uncharacteristically impetuous pursuit of Irene Herron brings about his first personal defeat. He is puzzled and troubled by the fact that Irene cannot and will not live the coolly ordered existence which Soames has disciplined himself to lead. He is equally puzzled in later life by the utterly realistic, cynical acceptance of himself by his second wife, a practical, dismissive Frenchwoman who matches his own coolness and shrugs away as too romantic his desire for a household dedicated both to his comfort and his need for affection.

If there is a truly tragic figure in the saga, it is probably Irene, a sort of patient Griselda figure, moving through life in beauty and grace, drawing to her unwillingly men of all ages and all kinds. Old Jolyon is drawn to her beauty and her kindness. Young Jolyon is caught up in the web of her resistance to Soames, her sorrow over the death of her lover, and her ineffable quality of gentleness and goodness which appeals to his own deep need for affection. If Irene is a little less clearly drawn than she might have been, it must be laid to the fact that she is a picture of the author's own lover, and so perhaps Galsworthy found himself unable to bring out her being in bright, sure colors and had to leave her instead partly in shadow. That Irene appealed sharply to James Forsyte, a bumbling sportsman, to Dartie Montague, a gambler and rake, to Soames Forsyte, a man of property, and most of all to the sensitive Young Jolyon is understandable, as she is shown moving about her world in search of peace, yet she somehow is a little less real than her companions. And she is to younger readers of today the least understandable of all the Forsyte characters because she echoes somehow a portion of the unreality of Victorianism.

Galsworthy was in effect painting a picture of England and London from the turn of the century through the 1920s, and this picture is more realistic than that found in any other fictional study of those years. There is a neat balance in the saga between the utter respectability claimed by the upper middle class and the oddly decadent society which they created. I cannot help but wonder what moral judgment will be leveled against the Forsytes and their kind, when a hundred years from now a new society looks into their lives through Galsworthy's observant eyes. What a mixup of human lives is to be seen in the *Forsyte Change*!! Irene marrying Soames Forsyte for security, finding him unbearable, falling in love with the buccaneer architect Bossiney, and then, after his death in a foggy London street, turning to Soames Forsyte's cousin for comfort and a different kind of security . . . Winifred, a respectable Forsyte woman, caught by a gambling fool and paying with her own happiness for the rest of her life . . . Old Jolyon, protecting his children and their children when he can, condoning even the confusion of the little lives of his family . . . it is all a little soap opera-ish when laid out in this fashion. Yet the whole saga is convincing, strangely powerful, especially remarkable in its characters . . . they are not mere stereotypes, but are truly types—recognizable, lovable, detestable, puzzling, human, real.

If one were asked what is the best thing about *The Forsyte Saga*, it would be difficult to pinpoint this. But if there is a kind of universal best, it must be said that two of the beautiful and thoroughly readable vignettes or interludes inserted usually between the longer novels must stand high indeed. The more delightful and moving of these two is certainly *Indian Summer of a Forsyte*. In it Old Jolyon finds comfort and quiet joy in visiting Irene and her small son during the final weeks of his life. It is a gentle and altogether beautiful little vignette, one worth reading more than once. The other interlude is entitled *Awakening*. In this young Jon, son of Irene and Young Jolyon, awaits his mother's return from the Spanish holiday, and alone with her that evening, discovers that his mother is the most beautiful thing he has ever known in his life. It is a small boy's awakening and a jewel of characterization, a thing of laughter, quiet tears, amusement, and child-like rapture.

These are among the elements which make *The Forsyte Saga* timelessly universally appealing. Galsworthy has occasionally been reviled as an author whose works will be forgotten because they were so strongly concerned with their own narrow span of time, but now the Forsytes are beginning once more to be seen as individuals whose personalities will live on. So real was Soames to those who read the long saga that when in the final novel, *Swan Song*, Soames meets his death, the London *Times*, staid and stolid as it is, printed an obituary, under the name of Forsyte, Soames, to mark the death of an Englishman who stood for more than just the value of property as someone in fact who represented English ideals and standards as well.

Letters from Anagnostes Solitarium,
November, 1969

John Drinkwater and T. H. White on England and America

Over the past weekend I had as companions two men, speaking to me from the pages of two quite different books; yet, as they spoke, they were so alike in some ways that they could have been close friends. Each of them was in love with England. Each of them was in love with America. Each of them wrote with passion of his loves. And each of them brings to his readers echoes of the kind of world which seems in these days of strife to be slipping away from us.

The first of my companions was Robinson Dare, the scholarly uncle of John Drinkwater's *Robinson of England*. Robinson Dare was the kind of man who attempted to gather about him antiquarian objects which reflected by their very existence the nature of life in the world they served. He liked to bring out, before the delighted eyes of his nephew and nieces, such commonplace things as a wimble, mentioned so often in the descriptions of farm life in Hardy's masterly tales. He showed them a muller, a cone-shaped copper pot with a brass handle, in which ale was heated over the coals of a kitchen fire and brought to heady bitterness. He brought out for his guests two short ash poles, joined together by a leather hinge, that was used to flail the grain in harvest time. This was Robinson Dare's way of keeping alive in his own mind and bringing alive in the minds of his nephew and nieces the simplicity, grace and homeliness of the England which he feared was passing away.

Robinson Dare calls up for his young relatives the words of one of England's truly astonishing geniuses, William Morris, and these words echo a philosophy which now strikes home with deadly accuracy as a criticism of our own time:

> The world with its machinery has gone another way, but it will have to come back sooner or later to Morris's way. All he asked was that people should have less work and greater pleasure in it, and more spare time with better means of spending it. It's just as simple as that, and yet it seems too difficult for civilization to understand. But until it does understand it

> there will be no peace, no real coming of what Wordsworth called "joy in widest commonalty spread."

Morris, according to Robinson Dare,

> had the faith of the old prophets that against all odds a few just men might yet redeem the mistakes of a multitude . . . but we have always to remember that there is an immense drag of indifference, which is really the root of all evil. It is against this drag that the few seers and poets have set their powers, and there is no calculating how effectively.

This is John Drinkwater's expression of the English spirit, perhaps a spirit somewhat daunted in this day, yet still one met up with occasionally.

John Drinkwater was an admirer of America throughout his life, but, in his affectionate observation of his western friends, he focussed most of his attention on Robert E. Lee, the great Confederate general. Drinkwater wrote a thoughtful, sympathetic drama which depicts Lee as the great general and fine gentleman that he was. This is one of the rare literary treatments accorded the life of this great man. If Drinkwater was somehow less able to comment freely upon America itself, he was at least sincere in his avowal of concern for its unity.

A second Englishman who loved both England and America was Terence H. White, whose involved and freewheeling treatment of the Arthurian legend has delighted American readers so greatly. White, whose *Once and Future King* so quickly caught the imagination of American readers and whose *Mistress Masham's Repose* brought him his second Book-of-the-Month-Club award, refused for twenty years to make an effort to come to the United States because of his own withdrawal from public appearances and a mistaken feeling that Americans would be less than enthusiastic about him. At long last, in 1963, only a short while before his unexpected death, he made an extended speaking tour from coast to coast across America. Like so many of his modern confreres, he fell in love with the sprawling, self-conscious breadth of America and reported his excitement, his joyous acceptance of the America he did not expect to discover, in the last work published by him, *America at Last*.

White had a genuine passion for learning, not only for reading history or translating medieval Latin, but for learning to fly airplanes or catch salmon or train falcons or plough with horses or fence with foils or paint pictures or do anything else which required the lovely effort of learning. He applied this eclectic enthusiasm to the business of learning about America and Americans during a six months' speaking tour in the United States. He found, to his intense delight, that the big, burly country to which he came prepared to be condescending, was made up of people who were as eager as he was himself to learn, and his journey became a prolonged and passionate love affair. White had the temerity to speak with Virginians and South Carolinians questions of Americans about their regionalism, their provincialism. He delighted in their ready and frank responses. He found within himself the warm pleasure of speaking with small groups and with large ones; he found that presenting prepared lectures was rather more like acting than he imagined, and he enjoyed "playing to the gallery" in order to observe their reactions. The only time he quailed was when asked in Salt Lake City to speak to an audience of 12,000 concerning "the pleasures of learning." And even in that situation he discovered the power he had to sway his audiences.

America at Last is a kind of travelog concerning America, not unlike, in many ways, the pleasurable *Travels with Charley* by John Steinbeck. Both men observed the country through which they were passing with clear eyes and some prejudice, but with understanding. White adds to his observation of America a kind of lyric celebration which makes his chapters rich and colorful. A startling portion of his book provides the reader with an Englishman's quite intimate reaction to the swiftly moving events which surrounded the Kennedy assassination. The sensitive response of a creative writer to the tragedy which he was somehow able to observe as a neutral is both provocative and interesting and leads the reader to self examination in a way which very few American historians or critics are able to do. White's caustic and only half serious proposal that America and the world return to slavery as a means of caring not only for non-whites but also for inept whites who are incapable of rising from their own variety of ghetto, is an expression of a critical idea which is both annoying and subtly provoking. Like Steinbeck, White rises to anger at the injustices which lie beneath American complacency. Yet, as any thoughtful man will admit, he concludes that a great many of America's ills are the result of its oversize, its unwieldy mightiness; while its little people, its individuals are, for the most part, warm, unselfish, and unselfconscious, rather desperately eager to be loved. Far from being a great book, *America at Last* is nonetheless a book which any reader will find well worth the hour and a half that will see it read.

Letters From Anagnostes Solitarium,
July, 1970

Literary Creation

Robert Louis Stevenson once said, "Every book is, in an intimate sense, a circular letter to the friends of him who writes it." What a happy concept this is! For it provides a sunny bridge between the author and those who meet him in his writings. And if one accepts this idea of books representing the art of communication between two minds, then the author is the richest of individuals, with countless friends the world over.

It must be said that the art of creative writing is one of the most miraculous of man's gifts, providing as it does for this opportunity to share with others thoughts one feels are worth preserving and worth passing along. Thoughts locked away in the dark prison of a miserly mind are not living thoughts at all but are only the dim specters of ideas. An idea shared with others becomes a living thing, a bright and vibrant presence, capable of expansion and quick to call forth other new ideas from the minds of those it touches. This is not necessarily to say that creative thoughts are easy to share, or the strange process of literary creation is often fraught with an agony of labor. But when there is a will to put such thoughts into written form, the result is an oddly cleansing process for the creative writer, a cleansing process which leaves the creating mind with both a kind of ecstasy and an exhaustion. But once having been put into written form, an idea becomes a perpetually living thing, which will never completely die but will forever have the power to bring light to the mind of any individual it touches.

There is a mystery which cloaks the entire business of literary creation. What is it that occurs before and during the act of producing a work of art, whether this is a painting, a piece of music or a literary work? Just what is the spark which ignites the creative process? Or what is it that rides the shoulders of the creative artist, urging this person, often against natural will, to express whatever it may be that has filled his mind? It is impossible to say, yet a few clues exist. In the nineteenth century it was suggested there are ideas floating about in all of the universe like little electric impulses and that these ideas, these quickening thoughts, touch men's minds and souls in such a way as to give expression to the intelligence they contain. This is a fascinating idea itself—the universe floating in a sea of electric ideas. Moreover, there is something convincing about the theory. It might well explain why some inventors seem to develop identical inventions at about the same time, while living half a world apart. It might provide an explanation of the suddenness with which ideas flash without warning across the human mind. It might even explain how solutions to puzzling problems sometimes seem to come out of nowhere. It is a haunting theory.

Another part of the mystery may be seen in what one probably can best call the association of ideas. A familiar landscape, for instance, may bring to mind a sequence of memories, ideas, hopes and fears, and these in turn develop into a picture which must be put to canvas or the framework of a melody. Walking along a sunlit street in summer, when the store doors stand open to the air, one's subconscious sets in motion whole floods of mental pictures, memories and new ideas. A half heard but clear melody will often prompt its own swift moving sequence of recollections. Are not all of these reflections, at the least, aspects of the creative process? And do they not intensify Stevenson's idea that an author is eager to share with others what has been written?

Letters From Anagnostes Solitarium,
August, 1970

The Familiar Essay

It is sad to think that in this day and age when the presses turn out thousands of pages of print every hour of the day, the art of the essay, and particularly the familiar essay, should lie so nearly dead. This, one supposes, can be laid to the mad pace at which we live today. There is too little time in our rushed age for the reader to sit down for a moment to contemplate some gentle aspcet of our lives. We must be caught up in activity that is so frantic that sitting at our ease becomes a lost art. The day is long past when Charles Lamb could contemplate the joys of dining upon roast pig in a delightful essay. The days are longer gone since readers stood on the street corners and read aloud the quiet comments of Sir Roger de Coverley. *The Tatler*'s politics were expressed in terms which today would hardly be heard in our noisy marketplace. It repeat: It is a thing of pity that the friendly essay and the good conversatioj it betokens have all but disappeared in this day and age.

About the only examples of the familiar essay one can find today are those that deal with the amiable field of natural history. It is quite interesting, as a matter of fact, that it has been in this special area that the essay has persisted for more than a hundred years, while in most other areas it has been ignored. Thoreau would doubtless find it an insult if his extended essays like *A Week on the Concord and Merrimack Rivers*, or *Maine Woods*, or *Cape Cod* were called familiar essays. Yet they are that. The delightful *Clerks of the Woods*, by Bradford Torrey, is still another example of this friendly sort of essay. Edwin Way Teale has carried the familiar essay in natural history to its highest peak, especially in his splendid series of seasonal works beginning with *North With the Spring* and ending with *Wandering through Winter*. Joseph Wood Krutch turned from literary criticism to writing familiar essays that included his musings on the wonders of the desert. In recent times the author of *Stalking the Wild Asparagus* and *Stalking the Blue-eyed Scallop*, has charmed his readers with his preoccupation with the natural foods people so often ignore. Now what is there about this form of writing that makes it a natural for the contemplation of the wonders of nature and no longer a vehicle for the contemplation of people's foibles?

The familiar essay is actually a form of conversation. It does not present the sort of communication found in the formal essay. The latter represents a tightly woven argument that dissects its subject under the cold light of logic, exploring pros and cons, weighing and balancing them, and ultimately organizing them into a tight structure of pros. The familiar essay, on the other hand, is a report of an experience; more than this, a recalling in tranquillity of a moment that brought its author into touch with his universe. In *A Week on the Concord and Merrimack Rivers* the author watches the river banks slip by, contemplates the effect of the warm sun on rippling water, lies under the stars at night and, at the sound of a drummer in a nearby village, senses, as he recollects all these things, a deep meaning, a sense of wonder, pervading his whole existence. Charles Lamb, in an earlier time, under the guise of a little fable, recollects the pleasure of eating, extols the virtues of roast pig, and in so doing carries on a pleasant conversation with his reader. It is as though author and reader were sitting together before a warm fire and remembering old times.

Just as the familiar essay has slipped into the wings of the stage of modern communication, so has good conversation been pushed aside in our time. I remember that, when I first knew for certain that my life would be spent in the academic world, I looked forward with eager anticipation to what I was sure would be found there. There would be pleasant evening hours in our living room, our feet reaching out toward the pleasant fire of logs, while our minds, my colleagues' and mine, would play the happy game of putting thoughts into words. There would be the clash of mind on mind to spark ideas, and on and on into the night we would converse, agreeing and disagreeing congenially. Alas, that halcyon dream never came to pass. On some few occasions, by spontaneous accident, a friend would arrive, a conversation would develop, two minds would reach accord. It was, however, no regular thing. Good talk seemed a thing of shreds and patches. Friendly converse was for the most part lost in a welter of academic committee meetings and the press of research. The need to publish the scholarly papers was so urgent that producing or perishing in the academic battle had become a general and all-consuming preoccupation.

Conversation of the sort we speak of here is never forced. It cannot be dragged into being. One does not say to one's friend, "Let us sit down tonight and talk about . . . " True conversation simply happens. It is the result of an instant of warmth, a momentary meeting of two congenial minds, a miraculous discovery of common ideas, of a coalescing of thoughts. It is like the remarkable moment of recognition when two individuals meet in a strange street and suddenly become aware that they have known each other all along, without being aware of it. Just so, the familiar essay is the result of a coming together of a set of circumstances, which, falling into place under the intellectual eye of the essayist, take on sudden meaning, a new kind of significance. The essayist observes an interesting fact or situation. In it he or she recognizes some deeper truth, relates what is seen to his or her own experience or the experience of people in general, and then draws conclusions, usually philosophical in tone, concerning the meaning of the discourse. Conversation and the communication of refined ideas in an essay are matters that to our loss have fallen on evil days.

Letters From Anagnostes Solitarium,
April, 1972

Books and Journeys

I have always found that on long and tedious journeys my best companions have been books. I cannot say how many long and boring hours have been brightened by the company of the books I have carried with me. When I have gone on vacation journeys, I have made it a habit to pack, along with other necessary things, at least two or three books, among them an old favorite for quiet rereading at the end of a day of driving; another, a new book which has caught my attention; and usually one which might be classified as serious reading. Each will find its own and proper time for perusal, and each carries its own purpose for entertainment, relaxation, exploration and release. The old favorite makes for a pleasant hour or so of reunion with old friends; the newly published title offers the pleasing opportunity to meet new friends, to explore new places; the serious reading provides the material to sharpen one's mind when it has perhaps become dulled by the clicking of railway wheels or the hum and roar of the airplane's jets.

A great many men before me have found books their good companions on long journeys, and many have expressed their delight in gathering for themselves those companions best suited to their tastes. Some have gone so far as to construct travelling libraries for themselves. One of these was one Julius Caesar, Master of the Rolls in the time of King James I. His library went with him wherever he went. It was arranged in a box shaped like a folio volume which was covered with olive green morrocco, finely tooled in an elaborate pattern. On the inside of the lid there was a catalog of the forty-four books which comprised the library, together with Sir Julius's arms and other decorations. His books were bound in vellum, tooled in gold, and furnished with various colored ribbons, the colors indicating whether the book was theological, philosophical, historical, or poetical in nature. The ingenious device is now preserved in the British Museum. The use of the colored ribbons seems to me to be a particularly clever device, although I must confess that, if Sir Julius had in fact been a reader of extensive experience, he would surely not have needed any such form of identification.

Other men of substance have shown their taste of reading and their concern that books should accompany them wherever they went. Napoleon had a shelf of books fitted into his coach. There is a passage in Cicero's *Pro Arachia* which acclaims, "Books delight us at home, and are no impediment abroad; they go abroad as they go into the country." Do you remember the character Dr. Okeborne in the novel *Camilla*? He would stuff the coach or post chaise in which he travelled with books and read them as he proceeded on his journey across the city or country. Sir Charles Lubbock suggested in a letter to a friend that there should be two or, better, three books for a long rail journey, at least one of them to be of an amusing character so that possible tedium could be avoided by "ringing the changes," the traveller thus coming back again and again to each book with renewed zest, as hour after hour went by. Aldous Huxley, writing in an essay in *Along the Road*, has some sound advice and one rather startling suggestion for the traveller-reader. He advises this person to carry any good anthology of verse, perhaps a volume of aphorisms (for himself he says that he always carries a miniature volume of La Rochefoucault in the pocket of his waistcoat), a copy of Boswell's *Johnson* and, finally, something he nearly always carried himself, a volume of the *Encyclopedia Britannica* in the so-called pocket edition. He says, "I never pass a day without taking a volume [of the *Britannica*] with me. It is the book of books." While as a librarian I grant the wonder and power of especially the eleventh edition of that encyclopedia, I have hardly considered it for casual reading on a journey.

Boswell reported in his account of Johnson's tour of the Hebrides that the great man carried with him on that journey a copy of Cocker's *Arithmetick*, saying, "If you have but one book with you on a journey, let it be a book of science, for when you have read through a book of entertainment, you know it, and it can do no more for you, but a book of science is inexhaustible." That Johnson practiced what he suggested is evidenced in more than one instance in Boswell's record of his friend's comings and going. Another inveterate reader, Sir Edward Cook, advises that if a book is to make a good travelling companion, it must not only be readable and portable, it must also within its range be a full book. And Cook hints that the selection of a travelling book is not easy. "No test of real liking for a book is so searching as the choice of a travelling companion."

There is one truly astonishing record of a man reading on a long and necessarily boring journey by sea. Trevelyan quotes from a letter Macaulay wrote after his journey by sailing vessel to India in 1834, that Macaulay achieved one of his most Herculean feats as a man of books. Wrote Macaulay, "I read insatiably, the *Iliad*, and *Odyssey*, Virgil, Horace, Caesar's *Commenatires*, Bacon's *De Augmentis*, Dante, Petrarch, Ariosto, Tasso, *Don Quixote*, Gibbons's *Rome*, Mill's *India*, all the seventy volumes of Voltaire, Sismondi's *History of France* and the seven thick folio volumes of *Biographica Britannica*." And as he devoured, he brooded, comparing authors and previous readings, liking the *Iliad* a little less on a second reading and the *Odyssey* considerably more; he was more than ever charmed with Horace, not quite so much with Virgil. A glance back over this list makes the modern reader quail before Macaulay's accomplishment. Even with our serious efforts at "quick reading," the sheer quantity of what Macaulay read makes one stand aghast. That he actually read so widely is well attested to, moreover, in the astounding complexity of his own writings, which provide ample evidence of the wide and insatiable quality of his reading.

To travel is to learn. To read while travelling brings both knowledge and pleasure, as well as relief from the endless hours of moving across the world. The brief glimpses we have seen here of men who cured the loneliness of travel through reading surely make it clear that books make the best and most pleasant companions in the world.

Letters From Anagnostes Solitarium,
January, 1974

What Makes A Good Book?

What makes a good book? It is a question that has been asked by writers and readers of all kinds and of all levels. Too often the answer given must be recognized as personal opinion. Too seldom have those who have tried to answer the question been able to distill from personal opinion, or even from reading experience, those abstract elements that characterize what can be called a good book. Seldom enough have even critics, blessed with real authority, stretched their minds beyond personal reactions and prejudices to evaluate a book and place it in its proper relationship with others on the long ranges of a library's shelves. There must be, however, some abstract elements which are recognizable and useful in determining just what makes a book a good book.

More than one approach is available in making the sort of clinical observations that book appraisal requires. Let us look at some of these approaches to see if any are truly useful. And for purposes of this discussion let us define the term "book." A book is made up of fiction, drama or verse. Now, what is meant by a *good* book? To be brief, a good book is one which has in some way managed to communicate its themes, its ideas, its mood, its *self* to a reader. That is to say that the author has managed, by the miracle of creative thought, to communicate his or her ideas by means of the printed word to a reader or readers. Obviously then the degree of goodness or success attributed to a book involves the ease of flow of ideas between author and reader. And the dual nature of this goodness or success is dependent upon some tenuous elements. What are these?

They are elements of such delicacy that they make it a double miracle when a book—the author's product—achieves acceptability by any reader or group of readers. To begin with, the state of mind of the author at the time of writing determines in large part the enthusiasm and fervor brought to the task and whether or not inhibitions of any sort are allowed to interfere with it. The next major element in the establishing of communication between author and reader has to do with the receptiveness of the reader. This receptiveness is greatly complicated in several ways. First, the reader's capacity to identify with the author's point of view affects receptivity. Second, the reader's vocabulary level and verbal skills enter into the picture. Third, the momentary mood of the reader may limit the ability to enter into the spirit of the exchange.

And there are other elements, too, that complicate the process. These include such things as the work's esthetic worth, the style of the author, the power of presentation and the author's enthusiasm for the subject being dealt with. The list includes likewise the reader's initial interest and intellectual curiosity and whatever catalyst presents itself to light the spark between author and reader. It will be seen in considering all of these complexities that the *goodness* of a book is not something imposed upon the writing or creating of the book alone. Both active and passive conditions are concerned. And even the active ones, those provided by the author, may be thwarted by the resistance of a reader. Conversely, as the old axiom of the horse led to water suggests, the reader can be offered even the most carefully and enthusiastically prepared piece of writing, but without at least a modicum of enthusiasm on the part of the reader the author's offering may fall before closed eyes.

Having established this series of barriers to a book's acceptance, we have still to examine after the fact some elements that tend to insure the acceptability of books of high quality. It is not easy to discover these. As a matter of fact, if such elements existed and were literally visible, the world of publishing would enter into an age so golden as to boggle the imagination. E. B. White's curt title, *One Man's Meat*, carries the suggestion that describes the problem here. A book which appeals to my friend may well be anathema to me. A book which is good in my estimation is quite possibly bad in my friend's. There are books which have been most belligerently rejected by the critics but which have met with wide appeal among everyday readers. And books which have achieved wide acclaim in one period of history have been known to slip into oblivion in the next. Some books, regarded over hundreds of years as great, are in modern times agreeably acknowledged as classics (whatever that may mean), but left unread.

It is nevertheless true that some conditions do seem to determine a book's goodness. Such things as immediacy, artistic quality, perceptive depth, fervor, compassion, conviction are the building blocks of goodness in a book, but the degree to which any of these tenuous elements enters into the equation varies with the day and hour.

This very difficulty of determining a book's goodness is the factor which makes reading one of the last freedoms we all can enjoy. Choosing for oneself what is good or not is the important thing.

Letters from Anagnostes Solitarium,
May, 1975

Bibliographic Ghosts

One of the banes of the bibliographer's life is the presence in some bibliographical lists of ghosts. There are some classic examples of such ghostly publications. Perhaps the most famous is that standard bibliography of scholarly works in German, published by Julius Petzholdt in the mid-nineteenth century. Petzholdt was for the most part a reputable bibliographer, but for some reason he could not resist the temptation to insert in his otherwise useful listing of serious works of scholarship, titles and names of authors which were false. The danger in such a practice of course is that the existence of even one false entry in a work alleged to be the result of sound scholarship destroys the worth of the entire bibliography. False bibliographic entries are much more difficult to uncover and display than are faked footnote entries or plagiarized passages in the body of a text. Even the most casual reader can easily detect that John Gerard was having a bit of fun when he describes in his *Historie of Plants*, published in 1633, a plant he calls the Goose tree, which he says he had observed in the marshes of western Scotland, a plant whose seed pods, once dropped into the wetness of the marsh, would produce young geese. But since "of the making of many books there is no end," it is easy to believe that a book title, no matter how improbable it appears to be, might well exist.

There is a lighter side to this matter, however; for writers of one sort or another have often amused themselves by listing the titles of books possessed by their heroes, or have created imaginary libraries of titles appropriate to some particular person, or produced booklists which would seem to support the theme of a novel or that of even a more serious work. A marvelous example of such bibliographic skullduggery occurs in Austin Tappan Wright's splendid utopian novel *Islandia*. Wright very convincingly lists a group of books written by a Frenchman, an Englishman, an American and members of a few other countries, all of which he suggests represent the results of careful observation by adequate authorities of the utopia of Islandia. Wright himself actually prepared a delightful set of books about Islandia, including an atlas, an almanac, a military history of the country, a philosophical history and a detailed account of the succession of prominent families in Islandia.

Wright's fine novel stands every chance of living on in the history of utopian literature, but it could well be that some bibliographer of the future may so completely believe Wright's work that those ghostly titles will be accepted as actually existing. What a wild goose chase could result!

A delightful aspect of this bibliographic disease occurs in a list of book titles produced by one of the Thomas Hoods, supposedly at the request of the Duke of Devonshire, who needed the titles for a group of dummy books to cover an unsightly door at Chatsworth castle. This hesitant writer suggests that you brace yourself in order to bear up under a discreet sampling of some of Hood's suggested titles:

— On the Lung Arno in Consumption, by D. Cline
— Dante's Inferno, or Description of Van Demon's Land
— Pygmalion, by Lord Bacon
— Boyle on Stream
— Chronological Account of the Date Tree
— Kosciusko on the Right of Poles to Stick up for Themselves
— On Sore Throat and the Migration of the Swallow
— Peel on Bell's System
— Cursory Remarks on Swearing
— Shelley's Conchologist
— Johnson's Contradictionary
— Grose's Slang Dictionary, or Vocabulary of Grose Language
— The Scottish Boccaccio, by D. Cameron
— In-I-go on Secret Entrances

Hood's list goes on ad nauseum, but it cannot be denied that its nature has elements of wit and humor, even though puns sadly predominate.

Anyone who has become acquainted with Roger Mifflin in Christopher Morley's *Parnassus on Wheels* and *The Haunted Bookshop* remembers Morley's list of books, painted on the walls of the box wherein Mifflin's dog, Bock, slept. Bock's "library" consisted of titles appropriate in one way or another to a dog's life. There was *The Rubaiyat of Omar Canine*, a copy of *Bonar Law* and a set of Bohn's *Classics*. And best of all, Bock's book collection contained *Catechisms on Dogma*. To make the collection even more appropriate, Roger had built Bock's home within a home in the form of a little Carnegie Library.

A fascinating variation on this business of creating an imaginary library is to be found in Cervante's *Don Quixote*, where the creation of a book collection possessed by the Knight of the Sorrowful Countenance is used as an integral part of the narrative. Cervantes provided the Don with a collection of real books which, as he read them, caused the variety of madnesses which brought him up to his adventures. It is not the title of any of these volumes that was significant but the content of the book which he had read most recently. To a careless reader this might well suggest the danger which many who resist reading seem to fear, that any reader can be changed by the act of reading.

Of course the ultimate infamy in the creation of imaginary books is the invention by an author, editor or scholar of a book which purposely bears misinformation. While this is in the eyes of the scholar or librarian or bibliographer the sin of sins, such evil books have been created. A most famous one is the late nineteenth century biographical dictionary, Appleton's *American Cyclopedia of Biography*, a work of several volumes in which it was discovered that literally hundreds of the biographees never existed. The editors of this reference set, it seems, were paid by the inch for type which was set, and so proceeded to invent biographies of nonexistent persons, mostly with Central and South American connection, to pad the set of biographical volumes as a way of adding to their income. Such practices, while they can have entertainment value, are in general regrettable.

Letters From Anagnostes Solitarium,
October, 1975

Too Many Books?

One of the strangest illnesses which besets the human race is a persistent fever which creates in the average human a burning desire to put his or her thoughts on paper. In an advanced stage, this illness leads to putting even the meagerest of thoughts down in print. The result is a rash of published works of little use to anyone. A modern cynic suggests that this disease of breaking into print is most acute among elected officials. For every passing thought in the halls of government it seems a dozen documents will appear. One of our leaders will express an opinion of some other leader's opinion on some subject on which neither can claim to be an authority. And this biased expression of opinion will give impetus to as many as a dozen or more rebuttals and counterattacks. Each will become engraved upon public awareness through the appearance of a dully-printed product from the GPO or other such body. As if the mere production of these inconsequential documents were not enough, the feverish disease next appears in a more contagious form, as each author and counter-author distributes his or her published expressions of opinion with the intention of securing among his or her constituents an audience of some size and presumably attentiveness.

And so the disease spreads, bringing along with it side effects described variously as boredom, complacency, or confusion.

Now this extended metaphor has a purpose. It is to point out that one of the major problems of our bureaucratized and overgoverned world is a surfeit of unnecessary printed works, printed forms, published statements and printed directives which lead into the labyrinth where only the vines of red tape prosper. I know of a state which requires of its innumerable agencies, that each prepare, when ordering some supposedly necessary item, not one or two copies of a purchase order but NINE. One copy of the order the agency is permitted, indeed required, to keep. Another copy must be sent to the supervising agency immediately above the ordering agency. No individual has succeeded as yet in discovering where the other seven copies of the purchase order go. It is most evident, however, that those seven copies are filed somewhere, somehow, for they never have been know to reappear or become once more visible. At some location in that confused and profligate state there must be the vastest and most dangerous fire hazard known to man. A flinty spark, an unbroken match still burning, a flash of fire from some fuse box, and that huge mound of duplicate order forms could burst into flame, and seven-tenths of the records of that state would be lost in smoke and fire.

I would offer a suggestion which could well solve all of our human problems, a considerable portion of which I am certain rest comfortably in the hands of government. Take from Government its sources of paper. Cut the production of newsprint as well as the glossy stock of governmental publications by two-thirds. I am willing to guarantee that society's problems would at once be reduced by at least the same amount. Such a reduction in the availability of this important material would lead to more than one benefit. It would increase the need for personal communication and would reveal at first hand the author of needless documents. It would stifle the temptation to produce printed proposals in sufficient quantity to make possible endless committee discussions and thus force expeditious decisions from persons in positions of authority. It would undoubtedly bring down the cost of government. It might even reduce or eliminate senseless Senate and House debates, since it would remove the temptation to oratory.

This recommendation, made only mildly in jest, is not of my own direct invention. It is the result of a seed placed gently in the soil of American literature in another century. Not long ago I found it flowering happily in a little verse by none other than Oliver Wendell Holmes, and for your pleasure I repeat it here:

Cacoethes Scribendi

If all the trees in the all the woods were men;
And each and every blade of grass a pen;
If every leaf on every shrub and tree
Turned to a sheet of foolscap, every sea
Were changed to ink, and all earth's living tribes
Had nothing else to do but act as scribes,
And for ten thousand ages, day and night
The human race should write, and write & write,

Till all the pens and paper were used up,
And the huge inkstand was an empty cup,
Still would the scribblers clustered round its brink
Call for more pens, more paper, and more ink.

Letters From Anagnostes Solitarium,
March, 1976

Literary Criticism

Two things seem to have fairly well disappeared from the literary world in modern times. The familiar essay has not been of real significance for at the very least fifty years. And the fine art of literary criticism has not been seen in the world of letters for at least as long. That both have nearly disappeared is certainly a loss to modern readers. It is true of course that in the 1930s there were excellent critical essays written in such journals as *The New Yorker* by Clifton Fadiman. And he was followed very successfully by Edmund Wilson. It is likewise true that both the familiar essay and the critical review were celebrated in the writing of Christopher Morley. And if pressed, perhaps another handful of names could be dredged up, whose works can be said to have honored these two literary forms. But by and large these two aspects of literature are not part of the current scene. Now this writer could be said, I suppose, to have a vested interest in the familiar essay, and so little comment will be made here concerning it. But there are a few things which should be said concerning the place of the literary critic in the world of letters, a place which has to a great extent been abandoned in these latter days.

In the classic days of French literature, the critics took it upon themselves to establish standards to serve as guides to writers employing every literary form, from poetry to drama and all that comes between. Those standards maintained for two centuries and more, well up into the nineteenth century, did a great deal to provide guidelines concerning style, rhetoric, grammatical construction, and purity of content. Unfortunately the standards established by the French masters became idols which took the place of all other literary virtues. Form and style became the sole criteria for acceptability, and French literature became stultified and lifeless. Such a situation could only result in rebellion, and the opening years of the romantic period produced revolt and dissent that all but destroyed the standards which had been maintained so rigidly.

To a somewhat lesser degree, literary standards in England in the seventeenth, eighteenth and early nineteenth centuries were set up, and these standards served to keep many aspiring writers from breaking into the literary scene. Early in the nineteenth century, however, criticism began to take the form of attacks against personalities instead of providing definitions of perfection, or of quality. Critics writing in such journals as *Blackwood's Magazine* and *The Edinburgh Review* assumed the posture of "godly criticism," and went out of their way to rain down blows upon the heads of upstarts like John Keats, and all of the youngsters who were battling for literary freedom against the hard-headed and heavy-handed critical conservatives.

Now despite the fact that the ultra-conservatives of literary criticism became insolently arrogant in their demands for purity in literature, there is still something to be said for those detractors of literary freedom. While they may have been blind to new kinds of creative greatness, they at least assumed a responsibility for leading or directing younger writers in the elements of literary value. They were well aware that failure to observe standards could result in literary chaos, and they did their best, if mistakenly, to stem the tide of careless, inept literary production which they saw rising. If they had had their way, the flood of romantic poetry and prose soon to overtake the literary world in a strange admixture of greatness and ineptitude could not have taken place. If giants like Scott, Thackeray, Dickens and Trollope stand out like the Alps above the lowlands, it is because those very literary critics, who destroyed lesser literary figures failed in some part to the standards they propounded.

In our own times, there has been a serious retreat from responsibility by those who call themselves literary critics. Criticism, in terms of the critical review of newly appearing books, poetry, drama (though drama has been better served than most other literary forms) has generally been content to restrict itself to reporting on the publication of some new work of literature. *The New York Times Book Review* section is little more than a news sheet announcing a weekly list of new publications. The reviews of *The New Yorker* magazine are so far beneath the quality of its reviews of earlier times, say of the 1940s as to be hardly recognizable as criticism. As strong as the latter day *Saturday Review* is, it also suffers sharply by comparison with the *Saturday Review of Literature*, especially of the period 1929 to 1935. In that period the quality of the reviews that appeared was at its very best, for among the reviewers were such luminaries as Henry Seidel Canby, Amy Loveman, William Rose Benet and Christopher Morley. A golden age of criticism, hardly to be seen again.

The real point, however, is that there were critics and editors in those halcyon days who took it upon themselves to lead young writers into quality production. Thomas Wolfe would have seemed sophomoric and dull had it not been for his editor, who cut away the nonsense from Wolfe's lush prose and held up to view only the brilliant literary jewels that remained. A handful of critics and editors in the period between World War I and the beginning of World War II made certain that out of the flood of writings which appeared, the best were polished and honed to the point that their real worth became apparent. This is not to say that some less worthy publications did slip through the sifting machine of criticism and editorial leadership. *Gone With the Wind*, for all its astonishing acceptance and sale, could have been a far better novel had it been given into the hands of a responsible editor. But be that as it may, the critics and the editors placed before the world a shimmering, golden supply of highly skilled writing, and for this we should be grateful. Nowadays, alas, the voice of the critic is heard only faintly in the land.

Letters From Anagnostes Solitarium,
February, 1977

Across Canada

Some years ago I planned what was thought by many of my friends a ridiculous trip across Canada by train in mid-January. I had heard of the quality of rail service offered by the two great railroads of our northern neighbor and felt that a winter trip not only would offer interest but also several days of uninterrupted opportunites to rest and read, with the world going by outside the window. The trip far more than came up to expectation. It began with a drive from northeastern Ohio to Niagara Falls, and thence to Toronto. From Toronto we boarded the Toronto section of the Canadian National Railway's crack transcontinental train. We had spent much of a day exploring Toronto in pouring rain, and a taxi delivered us to the vaulted National Railway station a little before six in the evening. Once we had settled our things in our comfortable bedroom on board, we walked through five or six cars to the dining car, where tables shone in clean whiteness and the burnished silver glistened. There is something always pleasing and exciting about such dining places. Our dinner ordered, and the sturdy soup placed before us, we were suddenly aware of a gentle movement of the train, and with no jerk of starting, we were in a few moments watching the bright lights of the city streaking by our window.

Dinner completed, we returned to our bedroom where two comfortable chairs faced the countryside with twinkling lights marking now and again a lonely farm house or a quick inundation of light revealing a village or small town as we raced northward through the darkness of the January night. We had packed a book bag with things that we were sure we would read on our westward journey, and that evening I remember reading the last half of Thoreau's *A Week on the Concord and Merrimack Rivers*. The cadences of Thoreau's prose seemed especially fitting as our train rushed along the rails. As we passed through villages and towns we could see that the storm was continuing in a heavy downpour, and our warm, and softly lighted room seemed secure and somehow snug. At eleven the porter came to turn our room from a living room into a bedroom, and well before midnight, with the muted clicking of the wheels making a rhythmic melody that was soothing and sleep-producing, we were nodding and ready for bed. Before retiring I had pulled up the heavy shade and left the window uncovered, with the driving rain beating against the double glass. So it was that I wakened in the night, and lifted myself to peer into the dark outside, and in those two hours of sleep a miracle had occurred, as the train was now driving northward through a world blanketed two or three feet deep in sparkling snow. We had entered the colder air that was pouring down across the Canadian shield; the sky was clear and bright with stars that seemed larger than I had ever seen them before, and the moon, riding above, was like a finger pointing down at the earth. And as I leaned on my elbow, staring out at the whiteness, shadowed here and there with the blue of trees and the deeper tones of an occasional building, a sudden streak of light marked the path of a falling star.

The next morning the world was revealed in brilliant sunlight, carpeted with snow that reflected the sun in millions of diamonds, and the scattered towns that we rushed through seemed somehow snugly buried in that blanket of white, while chimneys sent crayon blue fingers of smoke straight above the houses we passed, into the cloudless blue of the sky. The great train was now swinging slightly northwest, toward Nakima, where it would join with the section which had begun its journey in Montreal the afternoon before. The train slowed now, for Hornepayne, for a change of crews and to take on water and fuel. We seized the opportunity to get off, and walked for a few minutes in the icy cold of the northern winter morning. The air slashed at our lungs, and every breath resulted in a cloud of crystal breath, so that we were glad to return to the warmth and comfort of our room and see the town slip by and disappear. We climbed down the latitudes, moving farther and farther north and then at last swung directly west, north of Lake Nipigon, the train now twice as long, and with an extra monster engine ahead to share the pull.

Along this northern railroad line, the towns were now fewer than before, and their huddled buildings seemed somehow stark and on the defensive against winter storms. At lunchtime we watched Sioux Lookout slide by, its very name telling of troubled past history, and as the afternoon waned, the shadows of the forest grew long, there was an austere mystery about the scenes which we watched, and the snow turned rosy pink as the sun fell to the horizon. Northwest of

Lake Nipigon, we were now heading for the central prairies and Winnipeg. From the high seats of the domed observation car we watched night overtake the flattening countryside, and then, with a suddenness that was startling, a line of star-like lights showed across the entire curve of the western horizon, as the Queen City of the Prairie came into view. Winnipeg in that moment was a shimmering necklace in the night.

The next day, still racing across the great plains of Canada, was spent reading *Runes of the North*, an introspective seeking after peace in the northern lake and river country, which reminded one of that splendid account of a journey in *The Barren Grounds*, a book that served as a prototype for most of the diaries and accounts of life in the sub-arctic world of the northern territories of Canada. Then suddenly in the late afternoon, a glance above the page of print revealed the looming of the great escarpment of the northern Canadian Rockies, their gray granite shoulders nudging the sky, and cradling the sinking sun. Just two hours later we stepped from our coach at Jasper into a chilling darkness where the temperature as we stood in the station platform was already $-32°$!

Two days spent in Jasper, followed by a night climbing through snow-choked passes, then a rush down the western slopes and along the valley of the Fraser River, finally to reach Vancouver, where there were roses and pansies blooming in the station yard in a 65° temperature.

This long preamble to a short tale led to the discovery, in a side street near the great Hotel Vancouver of one of the finest bookshops in the Americas. It is Duthie's Books, a cavernous, five story building, each floor laden with an enormous supply of English, American and Canadian editions. The five floors overflow, down wide stairways into a vast basement room, where what looks like the largest collection of soft bound and paperback publications ever gathered together is made available. That visit, one of three made to that book-filled building, gave an opportunity, for one thing, to gather a double armful of the English editions of C. S. Lewis, Charles Williams, J. R. R. Tolkein, Owen Barfield and one or two others of "The Inklings." The result of that orgy of book buying was, after a few days spent in exploring Vancouver and its singular beauties, a long train journey back to Toronto. This time we travelled on the Canadian Pacific line, and the long days spent either in the spacious bedroom aboard the train or in the comfortable observation car made for more than seventy hours of reading time. What more pleasant a vacation could one ask—the security and peace of the long train ride, with only interruptions one wished for and a pile of books, unread, but to be seen to at one's leisure.

Letters from Anagnostes Solitarium,
February, 1978

Alone

"No man is an island," but almost in the same breath one can add that every man would like to live on some kind of island. It is quite likely that the human dream of finding a peaceful island, sufficiently remote and insulated against the world's intrusions, a place that provides peace and an opportunity to contemplate one's self and one's ideas, is, in fact, an ideal that is similar to the understandable desire to retreat into the security of one's youth and childhood. The seeking out of a place in the wilderness, a search followed almost universally by great prophets, philosophers and leaders, is in fact a kind of secret obsession of thoughtful people. Virginia Woolf expressed the idea's obsessiveness in the title of one of her greatest works, *A Room of One's Own*. The peace, the quiet, the privacy of the scholar's cubicle is but another expression of the need to retire into a kind of secret world of one's own. Those pleasant retreats which many religious orders offer for the use of people of the world provide happy opportunities for refreshment and rejuvenation after the weariness and turmoil of everyday life. The thoughtful reader can be grateful that a good many individuals who have sought the curative force of solitude have seen fit to describe their experiences in print. The idea of retirement to an island, whether it be in the Canadian wilderness or in the much travelled Puget Sound, say, returned to me recently when I picked up at random at a library book sale a copy of David Conover's *Once Upon an Island*. His work is not intended to be the final repository of philosophical insights into the human needs for peace and quiet opportunities for thought and contemplation. It is instead a happy narrative of two young people, deeply in love, who dream of living out their lives on a mile-long, two-hundred-yards-wide island, off the coast of British Columbia. Their dream comes true as a result of a series of minor miracles, and then begin some years of extremely hard work, as they homestead on their island. Their life they lead is characterized by a strong sense of partnership, by mutual understanding in difficult circumstances and by physical hardihood. The book makes for pleasant reading as Conover describes their labor to build their homestead and the heady pleasure they felt in living off the land and from what the sea produced for them. Their mutual affection might have become cloying had not the couple been possessed of salty good humor and amusement at inevitable shortcomings. This is no starry-eyed tale of an always successful homesteading effort, but instead a healthy report on how their "ways and means committee" sought and for the most part found answers to all kinds of problems. Their self-dependence, their insatiable desire for freedom, makes the reader shake his or her head in astonishment, but in admiration as well.

A story of another attempt to live free of the world's limiting demands is found in Leland Stowe's epic, *Crusoe of Lonesome Lake*. The narrative is of a man completely obsessed with the idea that he must be his own man entirely, totally free of the usual demands of society. The early chapters tell of his lonely venture into the Canadian northwest wilderness and his discovery of Lonesome Lake in a remote valley of the Northwest Territories. His self-discipline, his endless drive for minimal comforts through the long summers and the even longer winters, makes it clear that this man, a true example of the "loner," had the will and self-assurance to build his own utopia, despite the troubles created by blizzard and drought. But a flaw is evident when this Canadian Crusoe determines to have his wife and family join him in the wilderness. He is so sure of his own ability to survive that he dominates the others in a dangerous display of almost dictator-like control. Nevertheless, the story has appeal.

Still another wilderness narrative worth reading is much gentler, yet one endowed with enough excitement and fascinating experience to make it readable even thirty years after its publication. It is Kathrene Pinkerton's *Wilderness Wife*, one of the classic tales of seeking health, spiritual renewal and a satisfying life in the far reaches of the Ontario north. Opening with the depositing of a young couple from a newspaper family in Boston, at a railway stop where there was to be seen only a battered wilderness store, the narrative loses little time in taking them into the wildest north country. Their struggles to build a wilderness cabin are both amusing and pleasantly exciting; and their determination to make use of northern huskies to speed up their necessary trips back to what passes for civilization provides amusing, and sometimes frightening, vignettes of northern life. The birth of their daughter and the story of her growing up in the wild north country, is convincing, even though most readers could not contemplate such a rearing for their own children.

There are a certain number of common threads which weave through all of these wilderness narratives. Among them are a need to withdraw from the confusions of urban life; a need for self expression; a need to prove that they can be successful homesteaders and tamers of the wilderness; and a need to examine their own personal thoughts, ideas, goals and ways of life. These are admirable concerns, representing as they do an almost metaphysical attention to the details and priorities of one's life, but they are not for everybody. Most of us are non-wilderness participants; happily for us, the five or six shelves of such narratives that most public libraries offer make for unusually good reading—stimulating, provocative and entertaining.

Letters From Anagnostes Solitarium,
March, 1978

Classics and Bestsellers

It was Mark Twain who defined a classic as a book no one reads but everyone thinks should be read. It is curious certainly that in any list of great books there are titles which, by reputation at least, may be said to have had an important impact on the minds of men and women, but which, when given the test of continuing use, seem not to matter at all. This is so common that a list of classic or world changing books could well be described as an indication of "the power of the unread." Harriet Beecher Stowe's classic, *Uncle Tom's Cabin*, is perhaps an unfair example, but the fact remains that while it doubtless was a true "best seller" in its own day and time, today it is not even read as an historical or literary curiosity. Bellamy's *Looking Backward*, by many considered a classic utopian novel, to a modern reader, even to a reader interested in the theses of social order, is a source of boredom. The complete range of Sir Walter Scott's Waverly novels, looked upon by any and all teachers of literature as having been cast in the classic mold, today sit proudly on every library's shelves, untouched by most readers, unless imposed on them by some assignment in a course of high school literature. Even the giant Dickens, save for perhaps his *Christmas Carol*, is probably better known nowadays by the formula dramas made of his works for the moving picture screen or the television tube than by the works themselves.

Now what can be the reasons for the general acceptance of such classics, and at the same time their general rejections? What are the reasons, in the first place for the original recognition of a "great" book, and its final slide into honored but real oblivion? There are few who would disagree with the suggestion that there is a marked and more than significant difference in the literary value of any one of the classic titles and most modern-day popularly-acclaimed bestsellers. But why, then, does a modern bestseller explode into prominence, if its values are in fact beneath the notice of recognized critics?

It is suggested that some of this lack of quality in the bestseller can be attributed to modern day methods of production that are geared to making possible speedy presentation of a work to a large-scale reading public. Moreover, despite the legendary speed with which such nineteenth century authors produced enormous quantities of manuscript, they could hardly match the speed with which modern authors rattle material off the tops of their minds and through their agile typewriter-trained fingertips. And perhaps it is this very element of desperate speed which produces the ebbing of literary quality which prevails so widely today. Another factor no doubt is the almost complete disappearance of what, even forty years ago, was known as critical editorship. Thomas Wolfe, for example, would almost certainly have been lost in his literary heyday had he not been taken in charge by a good editor, who criticized, bullied, and persuaded Wolfe into careful reworking of his writing until he produced in final copy acceptable prose. Not only is the critical editor lacking in today's world of writing, but the critical review simply does not exist, especially in the world of the bestseller.

An answer to the first question asked earlier can only be gained with some difficulty. What is the difference between a work of high literary worth, accepted as a classic, and the nova-like explosion of prose which becomes a modern best seller? The answer would have to take into account a peculiar set of factors. The classic literary work generally is put together according to a well-defined pattern, very much like a sonata, with a beginning, a statement of theme, a development of theme, and a summation or return to the original theme. Such stylized but effective patterns probably began to disappear with the appearance in the 1920s of stream of consciousness novels, which tended to downplay the importance of beginnings, middles and endings. Much of today's fiction in fact continues in this same careless, unbalanced, and irresponsible vein. It requires a true literary giant to impose his or her own character and ideas upon so formless a structure. A Faulkner succeeds, but there are few Faulkners. The speed of production, coupled with the current penchant for a flat and wandering style, compounds the difficulty of literary production of high quality. Add to this the huge number of prospective readers reached by the popular advertising media, and the fact that journals tend to list rather than review new books, and the sale of a new title is quickly assured, regardless of its literary merit.

It might be interesting for a publisher to reissue in a series the works of classical authors, applying in the case of each of these works the same advertising techniques they use in promoting current bestsellers. Might it not be possible that the so-called standard authors would experience a renaissance? Something of the sort has occurred in the case of Galsworthy's *Forsyte Saga*, whose interest was reborn through the agency of the Public Broadcasting Service. Even as this is being written a new television production of Dickens's *Our Mutual Friend* is stirring interest among new and younger readers. A contraction of several of Trollope's novels, one *The Eustace Diamonds*, introduced a modern audience to that writer's brilliant comedies of manners. Could not, should not, this technique create a whole new market of readers for some of the little read classics? Thackeray, William Morris, Frank Stockton and a dozen others are waiting in the wings to make a new and lively appearance before a whole new world of readers. And think what such a rejuvenation of these "old boys" of the nineteenth century could do for the quality of the literary taste in our own time.

Letters From Anagnostes Solitarium,
April, 1978

Secret Worlds

In *Moby Dick*, Ishmael says of his friend Queequeg's home island in the South Pacific, "It is not to be found on any map; true places never are." Now this is a fascinating concept, because it represents a subtle idea that the true places of man's awareness are those secret but intensely real places that live within his mind. In a recent essay I spoke of the secret place commented upon by Virginia Woolf in *A Room of One's Own* to which she felt every soul should be able to retire, even though it might be only within his own mind, to rest and rejuvenate in that peaceful island that can be found on no map anywhere. It is almost platitudinous to suggest that such places should exist for every sensitive individual. However this may be, a galaxy of such unmapped but intensely real places have been created by writers. That these places of the mind are in all probability mere shadows of the real islands and private dwellings of those who create them need not concern us. It is enough that we have been allowed a glimpse of the places where these inventive writers lived a happier and more real existence than was theirs to all intents and purposes in actuality.

In R. J. Reilly's *Romantic Religion* is discussed the secret worlds of, among others, Owen Barfield, C. S. Lewis, Charles Williams, and J. R. R. Tolkein. One can hardly expect to find a more closely-knit group of men than these four, since in their association with each other there was a great deal of cross-fertilization of ideas, especially among the latter three. Yet even a fleeting look at this group of fascinating scholars reveals that each had a secret, unmapped place into which he could retire and from which he would emerge often enough willing to share some part of his secret place with the others, but not of course to give away all of it.

Barfield's unmapped island was his personal interest in and concern for the occult and a self-admitted dependence upon the thoughts and writings of the remarkable occultist Rudolph Steiner. Lewis found his rest and rejuvenation in a tri-corner secret land consisting of his juvenile kingdom of Narnia, a personal faith that shines out of so many of his serious works and his "frontier which divides the kingdom of the powers of evil, and the kingdom where men of good will stretch a thin line of defense against the evils of that outer kingdom." Charles Williams moved back and forth between a secret place where he entered into combat with the dark powers and the real world where he spoke with scholarly clarity of the basic elements of faith. Tolkein lived in a scholarly, secret world where his interest in linguistics and mythology and the mythical "middle earth," while evidencing scholarship of high quality, were interwoven with his faith.

Now this long preamble to what should be a short tale makes it necessary to point out that each of these four writers lived in at least two worlds. They had the unique ability of sharing those worlds in part with their colleagues, and even with lesser men and women who were touched by their writings. But, for good or ill, they would be the first to admit, it is certain, that never were they able, let alone willing, to open wide the doorways that lead into the secret worlds of imagination. This is somehow reminiscent of Truth in Plato's fantastic cave, whose burning brilliance the viewer feared to look at, preferring Truth's dim shadow on the wall to the real thing. Or like Shakespeare's world in which only the dim outlines of the world and reality are visible to the viewer.

Those who have been given the opportunity to glimpse such secret worlds through the partly opened doorways are fortunate indeed. These worlds, to be forever unmapped, are apprehended with wide-eyed wonder, perhaps even some envy, for they represent in outline the thoughts and creative instincts of persons touched with genius, able to instill hope at a time when little room exists for it.

Stop for a moment to examine the marvels which these unmapped places of the mind have brought us. There is Gulliver's Lilliput; there is the Utopia of More; there is the rabbit hole which led to Lewis Carroll's Wonderland; there is the strangely unreligious secret world of *Islandia*. There are whole galaxies of secret worlds and places, described by men who never saw those worlds. And there are our own "fine and private places" into which we retire, or would, if we could. And like a wonderful memory of real places to which we have gone, and which we cannot forget, these private, unknown and yet well-known places can never be taken from us, for they exist solely in our own minds and hearts. Moreover, they will continue to exist for as long as we exist, or for as long as we decide to go on visiting them.

Letters From Anagnostes Solitarium,
May, 1978

The Debonaire

It is curious and at the same time thought-provoking that in most translations of the Bible, whether in English or any other language, the nobility of the Sermon on the Mount is for modern readers lessened by the inclusion of the one word "meek" in the Beatitudes . . . "The meek shall inherit the earth." This curious lessening of stature is probably accounted for by the fact that the word "meek" has in some ways lost its significance, its true meaning. In modern day parlance, the word "meek" carries with it the connotation of a trembling, fearful, self-effacing individual, yet an individual not all that innocent. As we make use of the word, it carries with it an image somehow related to the hand-twisting, bowing and scraping figure of Uriah Heep. Being "meek" is, in the modern awareness, the equivalent of being helpless or weak. There is one translation of the Bible, however, a French translation, which makes use of an entirely different image for the ultimate inheritor of the earth. The French say, in their usual precise and effective way, that, "The debonaire shall inherit the earth." What a lovely idea lies beneath their use of that particular word. To be debonaire is to care-less! Just so, the inheritor of the earth in the French mind is one who simply could care less about himself, yielding up his body and spirit with absolute freedom, knowing full well that his mind, his body, his spirit, his soul, are safe in the hands of his Creator, thus making it a simple, obvious matter to offer his entire faith in his Creator, with no other thought than confidently giving himself in that faith.

Now it is without doubt a far cry from the utter simplicity of that debonaire self-yielding to suggest that one of the true measures of the great book, the truly great literary creation, is to be found in the degree to which a novelist or poet, a dramatist or biographer, is successful in being debonaire, if you will, regarding his or her own literary creation. What is important is the author's capacity for giving himself or herself wholly to the task at hand. Regardless of the fact that Boswell was labelled a fool by his contemporaries, his producing what is thought to be the single most successful biography ever written can be attributed to the fact that he buried himself beneath the domination of his biographee, and so permitted Johnson to parade his wit, his opinions, his philosophy in the light of common day. Boswell was properly content to remain a constant admirer, in Johnson's shadows. Only on rare occasions does Boswell move out into the sunshine which pours down on Johnson; and when he does, he does so to comment admiringly on his subject's splendid qualities and then slips back into the shadows to keep watch on Johnson's doings.

A frequent characteristic of great writers is a skill in standing back and allowing the character being described to move about freely and become fully-rounded. Thus, we can only suppose that Shakespeare, perhaps with tongue-in-cheek, wanted Mercutio to be laughed at, to be scorned. Instead, Mercutio prances and minces in full view, while his creator laughingly puts him through his paces, guiding him with invisible threads toward his destiny. Hamlet's hesitations, his inability to make decisions, his failure to meet successive challenges, are the weaknesses of the character on the stage, and only very rarely do we become aware of Shakespeare standing in the wings, using his own will to force his character toward his end. To understand just how this self-effacement comes about and marks the genius of a writer is to come to an appreciation of the difference between great books and the masses of mediocrity which all too often pass for literature.

Let us look once more at what this self-effacement by the author really means. It suggests that the author is content to stand apart from his or her creation, knowing, though perhaps subconsciously, that the characters being created will in this way attain full stature and credibility—they speak as themselves, not as robots or caricatures without a will of their own.

Charles Dickens in creating the formidable figure of Scrooge, did an unlikely thing for a man as self-interested as he was by giving himself up so completely to his character that Scrooge is real. The result is that the reader is able to laugh and weep and finally enjoy the company of the villain-cum-hero as he moves through the streets of Christmas-time London.

In Thomas Hardy's gloomy, fog-ridden scenes, we are aware of Hardy himself only in that we know that Hardy's own view of life was as pessimistic as that of his star-crossed leading characters, whose end was predestined and who had no power to change the events or course of their lives. Yet Hardy held himself aloof, and his characters, destined for tragedy, are somehow more real than their creator seems to most readers. Tess of the D'Urbervilles shines as brilliantly in her brief lifetime as does any heroine in literature, and brings fame to her creator, though he considers himself less important than his creations.

So there is at least a suspicion that the most successful literary creators are those whose care-less attitudes about themselves permit them to give all of themselves to their literary creations and to be content with whatever honor their heroes and heroines bring them.

Letters From Anagnostes Solitarium,
October, 1978

Springboard Books

Over the course of a good many years, during which an insatiable taste for reading books and talking about books has led some of my friends to suggest that I do little else but read, I have come to know a little group of books, not all that impressive as a group, but still worthy of consideration for what they can do for new readers and even non-readers. These books, a few of which I wish to call to your attention, are what I like to call "springboard books." A springboard book is a book that, more or less against its reader's will, or at the very least without any real awareness on the part of the reader that something has happened, tosses its reader into another book, and even into a set of books, and beyond that into a whole world of bookish interest.

Any librarian will agree that Christopher Morley's two delightful bibliographical confections, as well as many of his essays and short works, can easily be considered springboard books. Roger Mifflin, as the leading character in *Parnassus on Wheels*, and in its sequel, *The Haunted Bookshop*, is the propelling force in those two books which sends the reader into parabolic flight, to find himself or herself standing knee-deep in a wonderful world of literature that might well have never been known had Roger not provided some impetus in the matter. I remember very distinctly listening myself to Roger Mifflin whose voice sounded nearly identical to that of Christopher Morley, speaking with happy enthusiasm about the "sleeper book" of all time, *Dreamthorp, a Book of Essays Written in the Country*. This is no dreamy book of bucolic recollections engaged in before the fire after a country adventure. It is in fact a mixture of diary and philosophical examination of the life of a man, the ideas of a man who has chosen to seek in the solitude of a small country community, where the press and bustle of the city do not serve as interruptions, some of the underlying meanings of life. Is it a group of philosophical essays? Yes. Is it a kind of religious reflection on a person's place in the world? Yes. Is it a mirror reflecting the night thoughts of a man grown weary of the world revealed only by the light of common day? Indeed, yes. It is not a book to be rushed through at express train speed. It constitutes for its reader a view of a quiet world, as one sees that world riding through the countryside on horseback or in a horsedrawn cart. Every farm, every field, every hill and valley reveals itself slowly, offering itself for thoughtful examination. Certainly, I would have missed this book entirely, had not Roger Mifflin made the springboard send me in its direction. And had he not tossed me into its sphere, I would have missed some of the best and most provocative reading ever to come my way.

Long before I became acquainted with Roger Mifflin, I had read with childish enthusiasm Kipling's delightful *Puck of Pook's Hill*, but it was Roger Mifflin, again, who nudged me toward a more mature reading of this little masterpiece. And a fortuitous discovery of the fact that Kipling had spoken of his experience in writing of the Roman legions at Hadrian's Wall led me to still another book, Kipling's *Something of Myself*. It is an unfinished biography, but it tells of Kipling's almost psychic experience in "remembering" the names of the legions guarding a special point in Hadrian's Wall and naming the officers of the legions specifically. So, in two leaps I was led into two separate worlds by books which suggested other books, and so offered a wider horizon of reading experience.

Another "springboard book," but of a somewhat different nature, is the utterly delightful juvenile work by Morris Dolbier, *The Magic Shop*. It is a tale of a pair of youngsters who find themselves in a magic shop operated by Puck of Shakespeare's *Midsummer Night's Dream*. Their adventures under his pert and mischievous leadership are amusing in themselves, but the significance of the book is that no young reader with any imagination whatsoever can resist, in reading it, the temptation to know more about Puck himself, and his dramatic colleagues among the fairies.

Books such as those already mentioned provide of course an excellent means of inspiring young people to go on reading. But, to be truthful, there is hardly a book in existence which does not lead its readers toward still more reading. To the intellectually curious, the reading of a book is an act which cannot help but suggest further reading adventures. The reading experience is, for the serious reader, similar to that which occurs when one walks along the shelves of a library in search of a specific book, or of a book on a specific subject. The books, ranged side by side, provide an adventure of unparalleled excitement. To know that there is one book of a certain sort or on a certain subject, and then to find that it sits side by side with dozens, yes, hundreds of other books like it, is and should be a breathtaking moment of wonder.

I shall never forget the first such experience that I had. As a ten-year-old I had become the despair of the librarians in the children's division of the public library near where I lived, having read literally "across the shelves," book after book and then begun to reread them. The librarian finally brought me a copy of John Buchan's *Greenmantle*, an elegant spy story of World War I. I remember taking the book home, with special permission, since it was from the adult reader's section, and devouring it, racing through its exciting pages, before bedtime. The next morning, a Saturday morning, I was impatiently waiting at the library's front door, when my librarian friend appeared. I handed her the book and asked if there were any more like it. She sighed and leading me into the adult section of the library pointed out a double row of shelves where I saw the considerable armful of books John Buchan had produced. I was given an adult borrower's card and sent off on a reading adventure the like of which I had never dreamed possible. It was a new world of lively adventure, and I never recommend John Buchan to some young friend in these later days without envying the experience upon which he or she is embarking. To read for the second or third time a book of adventure or exploration is always a matter of pleasure, but to read such a book for the first time in one's life is one of those wonderful, heartwarming, mind-expanding experiences that can hardly be described, only experienced, and is never forgotten.

Letters From Anagnostes Solitarium,
January, 1979

Fairy Tales

Just about once a year I fall into conversation with a woman who is imbued—I started to say endowed—with the virtue of practicality. Knowing me as a reader of all kinds of books, but as one who has a penchant for those books which have a capability of carrying me off into some realm beyond the horizon of everyday existence, she likes to take it upon herself to chide me about what she calls my helplessness in the face of reality and with preferring a dream world to the world of everyday living. One of her chief lines of attack against such natures as mine is to rally her arguments against books which are built around pure imagination, and she holds that these dream-filled writings are fairy tales that are destructive of the true purposes of life and rife with the dangerous unrealities that lead men and women to lead less than practical lives. Now I have known this woman for long enough to recognize, at the first sound of her argument, that she will never have done with baiting me along these lines, and that I am drawn almost against my will into argument (she starts by calling it "discussion") which she has been carefully preparing agianst the moment when she entraps me with some new comment about my impractical reading interests.

The point at which our discussion always reaches its climactic moment of battle is when she asserts, looking superciliously down her nose at me, that, "Of course you always say that fairy stories are an important part of literature and that we should feed them to our poor children in spite of all else." This cleverly cast fly I watch alight in the very center of my consciousness, and in days gone by I used to go rushing out to swallow such barbed hooks and then find myself thrashing about at the end of her ever-tightening line of argument. But nowadays having gained a mite of wisdom, I no longer rush to my own destruction. Instead I let her tempt me a little, with little jerky follow-up statement, which often give away the newest line of her attacking argument, and so, sometimes at least, gain an advantage before entering the fray. The sad part of her willingness to enter into this annual contest is that she is, in fact, a person of considerable imagination, but at the same time, because of her long denial of the values of fairy tale realities, starved for the very things she continues to deny as having value.

Why should not a child be given a rich, ripe fairy tale, can you tell me? Does it really matter that things happen in a fairy tale which perhaps never can really happen in real life? Is there anything about that special kind of unreal reality that, when it is discovered as unreal by the child, is any more destructive to his growing spirit than the discovery, in everyday life, that all things are not quite what they seem? Even in this discovery, has not the child experienced a kind of growing, in that his mind has been stretched a little and then permitted to lie back and contemplate with wonder what it would have been like, had his discovery been a true reality? More than this, in common, day-in and day-out events, there are endless chances for the child to discover that matters are often considerably less than exciting, less than provocative, in their dull procession. But there are lovely, enticing opportunities in this exposure to the unreal that offer richness, happiness, color and warmth, if for only a moment; and these blessed experiences are never found, unless the world of make-believe is opened up and examined, through the sunny windows of imagination. If, as suggested, "It is better to have loved and lost than never to have loved at all," then it is surely better to have dreamed, to have looked through a window into the bright world of the imagination than never to have opened that window at all.

It was one of the romantic poets who sang of "sensing heaven through its partly opened door." That poet had not of course known in a practical sense what heaven was like, nor even if there really was one, yet he had sensed it, somehow, as its wonder flooded through that briefly opened door. Just so, there are lesser heavens, lesser kingdoms, if you will, which may be apprehended through the "sixth sense" of the imagination, a sense offering the power to explore places beyond ourselves, beyond our everyday lives, to catch glimpses of those things that might be, that we ourselves might bring to pass, having felt their tempting beauty and wonder, through the freedom of the imagination.

In books to read and plays to act in, it is well enough to insist that each fact shall be a thing of hardness, of cold reality . . . something which may be handled, and is known to exist. It is well enough to face reality and find bravery in that moment of facing. But it is a matter just as worthwhile, just as useful, to live for a brief moment in the brightly lit world of imaginary existence, for it is there that assuredly are found wonder and happiness and beauty such as seldom appear in everyday life.

So, my friend, you may have your practical, hard and fast reality;

you may trudge your way along that harshly lit road toward you know not what real city with its cold paved streets, its noisy din of commerce, its daily routine that gathers up and smothers most of us, despite our best efforts to resist this. But let the rest of us have the singular and blessed opportunity to know what may well be beyond knowing, to live for a while in the world of the imagination, for this is something that enhances our life forever.

Letters From Anagnostes Solitarium,
March, 1980

SECTION III
ELEVEN AUTHORS

These essays on eleven authors offer perceptions on writers and books which have a very personal meaning for the author of the essays. The essays are the result of close and comprehensive reading, and they exhibit a willingness to state opinion and enthusiasm, characteristics which are distinguishing marks of effective collection development.

A Succeeding Pleasure: Constance Holme

There is no pleasure so keen as discovering a book to one's taste, except perhaps that of passing it along to a friend when one is done with it. A book which has suddenly been discovered and read with delight cannot be said to have been read until it has been shared with another. And when the book is not a lone volume, but a double handful of delightful volumes by an author who is consistently excellent as though having written ten volumes at a single sitting, the pleasure of passing them along is a delight almost beyond description.

It hardly seems a year ago, and yet it is more than twenty-five, that I was forced by lack of funds to spend a between-terms holiday alone in my living quarters at college instead of making the trip home to Ohio. At loose ends I turned to the shelves of the university library and pulled from their places in the ordered rows a half dozen things which appealed to me at the moment. One of the slender little volumes that I carried home that early February evening bore the title *The Old Road from Spain*, a title that sang gently of adventure and of ships and the sea. I no sooner opened this book, by Constance Holme, than I was caught in the web of delight which she wove through its two hundred pages. I finished it by midnight, and wakened the next morning impatient to reach the library to seek other titles by Holme which I had seen on the shelves. I spent a good many hours during the remainder of that week in company with the Westmoreland people who live in her books, and in the strange, half realistic, half mysterious country through which her characters move. In the last twenty-five years I have travelled the roads of Westmoreland more than once in the lively company of Luis Huddleston, Ann Clapham and Simon Thornthwaites.

A haunting persistence has kept these remarkable stories alive and in the minds of bibliophiles and readers for the last fifty years, despite an almost total lack of advertising, of reviews, and of recognition of their literary value. Word of mouth recommendation and friendly sharing of Holme's charming tales have managed to keep them alive, when many volumes, more importantly supported by their publishers and the press, have disappeared into the limbo of forgotten works. There is a kind of cult of Westmoreland people, or at least of people who have come to love Westmoreland through Holme's writings, which persists in keeping her works in the hands of that goodly company of readers best able to spread the news of her writing.

Constance Holme was born in Milnthorpe, Westmoreland, and lived at Owlet Ash, the youngest of fourteen children. It was a legend of her family that her mother, who from her appearance was decidedly of Spanish stock, was the descendant perhaps of Spanish waifs who were cast up on the shore of Morecambe Bay when ships of the Armada foundered and were driven by storm into the narrow estuaries. Her family lived in an eighteenth century house, blessed with a rather unexciting and completely unproven ghost, whose exploits were legion but whose actions and appearances were dubious. Brought up by parents who had been "of the land" for centuries, given ample opportunity through an imaginative grandmother and equally imaginative servants to hear almost daily narrations of county legends and regional history, Holme said of herself that she "had lived, married, and would probably be buried" in Westmoreland, with little more than an occasional journey into Lancashire or Yorkshire to break her absorption with the local scene. She represents that rarity, the provincial writer, like Jane Austen, capable of careful character development and meticulously detailed backgrounds, but without allowing the intrusions of an extraneous world to trouble her heroes' existence.

In *The Old Road from Spain*, Holme tells an absorbing tale of the house of Huddleston, a brooding mansion situated on the last swell of the downs so that its dark paned windows could look down over the curving meadows to where the sea embraced the land. Dark fate hung over the house of the Huddlestons, brought by a ship of the Spanish Armada. From a Spanish ship was washed ashore a young Spaniard, who married the daughter of the house, and in so doing established a fated line. In the same storm from a Spanish ship came a flock of sheep that was to form the major source of income for the Huddlestons. The family legends make up the background of the plot: first, that in every succeeding generation a male descendant would be called to the sea, and invariably to his death; second, that his death would be foretold by a movement of the sheep, as these would break out of the meadows and move silently toward the mansion house, there to crowd about its porches on the eve of the doomed sailor's death. Holme uses these supernatural legends in establishing brilliant contrasts between them and the rural homeliness and earthy warmth of the countryside and its people. Descriptive passages of unmatched beauty, scenes of darkening terror that move relentlessly to their climax with black-faced sheep stumbling in a dreadful storm through breaks in the fences to surround the house with their foreboding message, patiently built up portraits of the characters, make for a perfection that is reminiscent of Hardy or Trollope, and yet is wholly her own.

An even more interesting narrative is to be found in *The Lonely Plough*, a second story of Westmoreland and the agents who manage the great estates there. It is a story of the integrity of one man, who makes promises in good faith that cannot be kept when he is betrayed by outsiders, but who holds himself responsible for the failure of a great dike erected against the encroaching sea. Somber in tone, yet touched with the warm colors of rolling fields, and the sunny hills of the coastal slopes of western England, here is a small miracle of the English language much in the style of such works as Winifred Holtby's *South Riding*, T. H. White's *England Have My Bones*, and half a handful of others that have caught, as John Drinkwater's *Robinson of England* did, the very feel of the English countryside.

Holme's peculiar and special gift to the modern novel is that of an intellect which has been kept almost entirely immune from the fretful haste of the ailing societies of the twentieth century cities. It is a gift enriched by messages of hill and sea, and filled with the sounds of plain and honest folkways. Her novels treat of Westmoreland types with the authority that personal knowledge allows. Perhaps her greatest skill is apparent in the manner in which she handles her characters against natural backgrounds. Without seeming stilted or unnatural in any way, she employs devices which correlate natural phenomena with mental or spiritual states in her characters. It is on lowering days that Rowley in *The Old Road from Spain* delves into his inner spirit to comprehend his problems; it is in the flood which is to destroy the dike that the hero of *The Lonely Plough* senses the cracking of his own solid integrity; it is on a winsome day of spring that the prince arrives to rule an unreal kingdom in *He-Who-Came*. All of this seems proper, it is not overdrawn, and is plausible and real enough to suit the most down to earth reader. And above all, the books contain prose values, lyrical beauty and a seldom matched rhetoric. These simple works are in short an embodiment of perfection.

In recent years, partly to evaluate my own deep sense of pleasure, partly to justify it, I have sought out critical comment by others concerning Holme's Westmoreland. Beyond an occasional paragraph such as the brief statement at the very end of a discussion of early twentieth century authors by F. A. Swinnerton in his *The Georgian Scene* and some brief comments by Bennett Cerf's predecessor in the *Saturday Review of Literature*, the literary ghost P. E. G. Quercus, there is almost nothing in print concerning Holme and her writings. It seems to me that this remarkable woman and her unusually fine country tales stand in danger of being forgotten, not for lack of value, but rather for lack of critical evaluation. Holme was unfortunate to have written most of her work at the time when the schools of naturalism and realism were coming into vast prominence. She is herself influenced by both, and yet she stands apart, writing with the skill and clarity of the eighteenth century, with the romanticism of the nineteenth, while living and competing in the twentieth. Coming just too late for the era of the romantics, just too soon for the revulsion against the naturalists which was to follow her peak writing years, she stands in the interim, wonderfully adept in her use of language, remarkably sensitive in her development of character, only a little less capable in her handling of plot, but deeply satisfying to the reader whose tastes are cloyed with the heady diet of modern prose and is hungry for the solid fare of simple people living close to the soil, where they live and love and are constantly themselves.

The Printer's Mark,
April, 1962

Last of the Procounsuls: John Buchan

It was as a twelve year old that I was first introduced to John Buchan. The librarian of the town library, who had watched me rifling through her shelves of juvenile literature and then begin the happy process of rereading all of my favorites three times over and more, led me on a rainy summer afternoon into the adult section of the library where she showed me a whole shelf of volumes bound in red and green and black and brown, each bearing witness to the authorship of John Buchan. Here was a wealth of new found riches! *Greenmantle* was the volume I took home that afternoon. *Greenmantle* it was that swept me into the world of spies and heroes and taught me something of duplicity and how this is combatted. *Greenmantle* it was that opened for me a world of pleasure and even today it holds joy for me, despite an awareness of its romantic limitations.

Buchan belonged to a breed of persons which has today all but disappeared. He was the scholarly man of affairs. He made his mark as a scholar, lawyer, classicist, publisher, editor, romancer, historian, essayist, poet, novelist and biographer. He also served as a war correspondent, propagandist, diplomat, parliamentarian, intelligence officer, administrator, churchman, sportsman, ethnologist, moralist and philosopher. All of this encompassed in a life of sixty-five years between 1875 and 1940. It is astonishing to contemplate both the variety of his interests and activities, and the degree of competence he demonstrated in each of his endeavors. One is tempted to speak more about the man himself, for he was a man of protean nature and vast accomplishment. Because of his general eminence, Buchan did not escape criticism. He was called a "professional Scotsman" and a "self made patrician," but those who used such terms only demonstrated their failure to comprehend the fullness and variety of his achievement and the delight his works brought to myriads of readers.

As a novelist, John Buchan concerned himself with a single theme, but it was a theme of many separate threads. Buchan believed, as did others of his kind, in the presence in the world of terrible forces of evil. In *Three Hostages*, for example, one of his characters states Buchan's own theory concerning this lurking force that is set upon the task of capturing and destroying people of goodwill. In urging Richard Hannay to accept a challenge of considerable danger, he makes clear the claim that the only reason these evil forces have not succeeded in conquering the world lies in the fact that men of goodwill have joined together to defeat them. He makes it clear, moreover, that only so long as pressure is brought to bear to hold these malign forces in check will the world survive intact. This is not a new idea, certainly, but it is clearly expressed by Buchan, and its problems are his concern in most of his fictional works.

Three separate narrative themes intertwine themselves about this central preoccupation. In the series of novels devoted to the adventures of Richard Hannay (*The Thirty-nine Steps, Greenmantle, Mr. Standfast, Three Hostages,* and *Man from Norlands*), Buchan uses a brave man who continually protests his cowardice as the dominant figure in the battle against evil. Hannay's greatest single virtue, aside from his actual courage, is his happy capacity for successfully bumbling through in the most difficult of circumstances. His serendipitous pursuit of the villain provides him with a highly satisfying series of adventures, and always there is assurance of a happy solution to his problems.

In another series, devoted to the activities of Sir Edward Leithen (*Sing a Song of Sixpence, Power House, Dancing Floor, John Macnab, Gap in the Curtain,* and *Mountain Meadow*), Buchan permits his readers to watch the reactions of a man far more sensitive than Hannay to these same threatening powers, although in this case the dark face of the enemy is less omnipresent and world affairs are less affected. And in a pleasant group of romances, a third hero, Dickson McCunn, a Glasgow merchant, has a merry series of adventures as a sheer romanticist (*Huntingtower, Castle Gay,* and *House of the Four Winds*). In this series, the powers of darkness appear in full force, to the astonishment of the gentle hero who had dreamed of adventure but was unprepared for the starkness of its reality.

The pleasure the reader finds in these tales of adventure in all probability is based upon two unobtrusive facets of Buchan's writing. His prose combines simplicity of style with swiftly moving narrative. Few writers of English fiction have ever had Buchan's ability to create, for example, the actuality and breathless pace of a chase. Richard Hannay's escapes and hurried journeys in *The Thirty-nine Steps* proved so enthralling that not even Hollywood could find a happier means of holding the moviegoer's attention than by providing in the movie almost literal translations of the Hannay chase scenes. Buchan loved to put his hero in a spot from which escape was possible only through use of his own legs and lungpower. In *John Macnab*, not content with a single chase, Buchan provides his readers with three separate chases, while in *Dancing Floor*, the entire novel develops as his hero prepares himself for a final race against both time and death in the form of a sort of olympic marathon. In all of these, the swift flowing passages carry bright excitement and tumbling sentences which carry the eye from page to page without stopping.

Perhaps John Buchan's experience as an intelligence officer and as a student of politics both before and after World War I, gave him some special information, but a peculiar aspect of his novels of adventure is a strangely prophetic foreknowledge of what has since transpired. In *Greenmantle* and *Mr. Standfast*, both of which are stories of cloak and dagger action during the First World War, Buchan spoke of the certainty that Germany would become an eventual buffer between the east and west and suggested that the real enemy was one whose ideology would challenge the vital strength of democracy.

More, in half a dozen of his novels he indicates that Africa is to be the focal point of a new area of contention. It would be interesting to know if he had ever had conversation with Arnold Toynbee, for many of his warnings against the complacency of the West and its failure to meet challenges, echo Toynbee's philosophy of history. Still more, in *Three Hostages*, that first appeared in 1924, Buchan presaged the rise of a madman who would dominate all of Europe, and even threaten England behind her channel moat. It seems no coincidence, although it must have been, that he envisioned a dictator who would seek to control the minds of those he conquered and attempt the destruction of whole nations of people to further his own ends.

Of Buchan, who later became Lord Tweedsmuir of Elsfield, it might be said that he was never a novelist of the first rank. And yet his qualities are those of the greatest of Englishmen. His love of country, his awareness of her power for good in the world, his certainty that it was not both an obligation and a privilege to serve first England and then the world, make him somehow the prototype of his own heroes. Hannay, Leithen, and Sandy Clanroyden, yes, and Dickson McCunn, Benjie, Dougal and his Gorbal Diehards, every one of them in his own way embodies a code of honor and action which may be smiled at by today's sophisticated reader as being of the essence of "old school tie" provincialism, and yet this code cannot be laughed at openly, for in every reader's heart there is a certain longing for the old verities and certitudes of which Buchan and his characters are foremost propounders.

I have collected first editions of Buchan's writings for twenty years or more, and it is true that some of the volumes in my now sizable collection have been read once and then put aside, kept only because of the collection itself, rather than their content. Among the volumes on my shelves, however, are some that tell such fine tales of the deeds of men of goodwill, that contain such good writing, that offer so much good entertainment that I cannot help but feel that Buchan will come into his own one day to stand as a proud representative of the time when others were producing mere sensationalism or were losing themselves in the byways of literary fashion.

That Buchan could write other than romantic tales is evidenced by a remarkable handful of unusually fine biographies, and a volume of autobiographical memoirs worth more than a second reading. His splendid *Montrose* is a classic of biographical writing and is listed regularly among the better English works in that field. Buchan's life of *Sir Walter Scott*, a man he admired greatly, sets that romantic British writer down in a spectacular recreation of the time in which he lived. Buchan's book both enhances Scott's reputation as a romanticist and his own capacity for detailed study and reporting. In his own memoirs, which appeared in England under the title *Memory-Hold-the-Door* and in America as *Pilgrim's Way*, Buchan's memories of his younger days are given full coverage. This portrait of his youth, which describes the factors that shaped his thinking and gives attention to his beloved Scottish countryside make for good reading and at the same time provide as revealing an analysis of self as may be found in any modern autobiographical work. This work, incidentally, serves as a fascinating introduction to his final and best book, *Mountain Meadow* (published in England as *Sick Heart River*).

I have wondered at times if *Mountain Meadow* were written in its almost allegorical form as a way of explaining Buchan's acceptance of the last great assignment of his life. It is a tale of Sir Edward Leithen's last days, in which Leithen travels into western Canada seeking a man estranged from the world by mental illness. Leithen's life, endangered by his lingering illness, finally achieves equilibrium by his discovery of himself and the settling of his personal accounts. It is a remarkable piece of prose, beautiful in its almost biblical simplicity, exhaustive in its searching after truth. I have said more than once to friends who know of my interest in and fondness for Buchan's writings, that I was glad he did not live to see the crumbling of the great empire he loved so well. He might well have gloried in the successes that followed Dunkirk, but he would have writhed as he watched the dispersal of English power. Yet, as I re-read *Mountain Meadow* not long ago, the thought arrived that perhaps his acceptance of the position of Governor-General of Canada might well have indicated his hope to bind that northern giant more closely to her parent Britain, and that his narrative of Leithen's death in the clear, cold purity of the northern tundra is in truth a recognition that this was not likely to take place.

A hint of his final mood may sound in a passage quoted from *The Power House*:

> Civilization is a conspiracy. . . . Modern life is the silent compact of comfortable folk to keep up pretences. And it will succeed till the day comes when there is another compact to strip them bare. . . . A little mechanical device will wreck your navies. A new chemical combination will upset every rule of war. . . . One or two minute changes might sink Britain to the level of Ecuador. And yet we never think these things possible. We think our castles of sand are the ramparts of the universe. . . .

The Printer's Mark,
July, 1962

A Murderous Love Affair

The detective story, like the sonnet, all too often falls into a set and procrustean pattern which leaves the author of such works at the mercy of the form and with little opportunity for development of any original theme or character. Agatha Christie has said more than once in public statements, that she grew weary very early in his career of the "little grey cells" of M. Poirot, her sterling and indefatigable detective hero. Margery Allingham, too, despite the fact that she embellished the character of her detective hero with an assortment of both philosophical and psychological trimmings, lost much of her enthusiasm for Albert Campion and allowed him to become little more than a robot figure through whose hollow voice she permitted traditional mechanics of detective work to be enunciated. There is one lady Pygmalion, however, who so fell in love with the product of her imagination that she was able to continue the development of his character to a point of perfection unheard of in the annals of mystery writing.

Just after the close of World War I, when it was fashionable in literature to portray young English lords as fops and relatives of lesser children of the *Scarlet Pimpernel*, Dorothy L. Sayers erected the character of Lord Peter Wimsey, as the hero of a detective story in the chessman formula, *Whose Body?* Lord Peter, in this first story was a hopelessly effete young gentleman whose carefully shined monocle served as a kind of disguise for a nimble wit, and whose chattering drove his companions and the murderer himself into making errors of judgment which were eventually to unravel the mystery. The story, thoroughly readable despite its uneven characterization, established a fascinating puzzle which left the reader in the dark until the final pages.

There must have been something about the young Wimsey (the second son of a noble but somewhat jaded house, whose coat of arms consisted of "three mice, rampant upon a shield of blue and silver") which appealed mightily to Miss Sayers, however. Her second detective work, *Clouds of Witness*, saw Lord Peter begin to develop into a person of more stature. In this novel he is placed in the curious position of having to save his dolt of a brother who is being tried on a murder charge before the House of Lords. Lord Peter is up to the challenge, displaying from the start his remarkable detective ability. Even more interestingly, however, it soon is apparent that he possesses a huge variety of skills and an incomparable body of knowledge. He is revealed as an amateur book collector, as something of an authority on Donne and as a musician of some capacity, with a strong leaning toward the works of Bach, whose intricacies seem to release Wimsey's own creative genius. And from this point on, through nine succeeding mysteries, Lord Peter grows and reveals himself as a man of singular stature, noteworthy acumen, charm and grace, a lover of unquestioned reputation, a traveller of the world, a man of business and a man of letters. If he appears now and then as a "chattering icicle," he does so as a means of misleading the villain of the piece. His most notable characteristic is flashing brilliance in the deductions he makes. Somehow, unlike other writers of detective fiction, Sayers manages to bring her leading character off as a live, zestful and thoroughly engaging individual.

She does this, I suspect, by allowing Wimsey a freedom to grow and become a super detective, while at the same time remaining a man of natural impulses. She surrounds him with a cast of supporting actors who are so natural and delightful themselves that they serve as admirable foils to the great detective himself. Who can forget the pick-lock turned fundamentalist revival leader who appears and reappears at needed moments to help Wimsey unravel some puzzling crime? Or Wimsey's Dresden-doll-like mother with her charming and *non-sequitur* remarks? Who can forget his assistant, Miss Climpson, who provides him with information about various murderers and who offers refuge for poor souls caught up in the web of murder? And who can forget Bunter, the butler of such vast virtue that he makes Jeeves and every other English butler seem nonentities?

Sayers creates in Wimsey a figure who is believable in even the most extended of situations because there are moments also when he is without question merely human. For instance, his temper flares when his sister-in-law persists annoyingly in expressing her lower middle class Victorianism. And Wimsey, a man of independent thought, relaxes occasionally in the face of custom and tradition, now reading the lessons in the chapel of his noble estate, now accepting the responsibility of caring for his dependents. Moreover, it amuses the reader to learn that when he takes his bride to the country for their honeymoon he is looked upon as being none too good by Mrs. Ruggles.

Now what does this all have to do with Sayers and her "murderly love affair"? It suggests fairly convincingly that Sayers was actually in love with her leading character, and it is not improbable that Wimsey stands as a model of the sort of man Sayers could indeed have loved. She found this young lord so filled with grace that she could hardly help but endow him with additional graces. Oddly enough, Sayers never describes Wimsey fully. No full, life-sized portrait of him exists. Yet the series of tales, from the first of 1923, *Whose Body*, through *Busman's Honeymoon*, published in the late 1930s, do present a reasonable, if fragmented portrait of Wimsey. We know him, of course, to be a man of quick and brilliant wit, one whose mind so quickly probes the evidence of a case that Sayers in one novel even leaves one page blank, agreeing with the reader that to follow her hero's swift analysis, as he first views the case, would make the telling of the story unnecessary. This occurs, in case you have forgotten it, in *Suspicious Characters*, as tightly knit a bit of detection fiction as one would care to find. We know him, too, as an athlete, a cricketer who had won his "blue." He is, moreover, a master of the academic debate; we watch the quiet dons in *Gaudy Night* pay homage to his scholarship, and hear the sweet, pedantic vicar of the *Nine Tailors* praise the quality of his published work on bell-changing. Librarians love Wimsey for his penchant for book collecting, envying him his first editions of John Donne and the manuscript letter of Donne given to our hero by his bride-to-be in *Busmans's Honeymoon*. Any book collector would give much to be able to check the shelves of her personal library, where the warm firelight from his comforting hearth flickers on the glowing spines of calf bound volumes. And to hear Wimsey tracing out at the keyboard the intricacies of Bach, what a sublime treat! Which of us has not smiled at the picture of his singing of fundamentalist hymns for the delight of some of his London-backwater acquaintances? Who has not watched impatiently as Wimsey sought information in his collection of texts on historical crimes on some obscure poison? His knowledge of medicine, art, architecture, business, history, the subtle black arts, the ways of youth and the quiet scholar's life as well as the noisy ways of the extrovert, all gave him a special wisdom and charm which made him a delightful companion to those about him, and, one can conjecture, to Sayers herself. Her own endowments as a medieval scholar, as a translator of Thomas the Norman's exquisite version of Tristan and Dante, all are to be found among Wimsey's own skills. He is endowed with still further graces, and, it must be admitted, a few weaknesses. His knowledge of languages, his skill in the diplomatic dance, are often employed by his country when, as a troubleshooter, he is sent to Rome to soothe the ruffled feathers, "repair the plumbing," as he says to Harriet Vane, his true love, disturbed or broken by some inept diplomat. His weaknesses are not by way of genuine failings but are rather physical and moral trepidations. He is after all only human. For one thing, he has a tendency to respiratory ailments, and a capacity for hideous dreams that are rooted in past experience as a World War I army officer whose life was nearly lost under artillery fire and a later gas attack. That he has a conscience is apparent, and this causes him agony as he dreads the consequence of punishment that awaits the villain he apprehends.

Those who have not had the pleasure—and it is something more than mere pleasure—of acquaintance with Lord Peter Wimsey have missed one of the great joys that come to readers of detective fiction. The development of Sayer's capacity as a weaver of taut mystery and her remarkable ability to create living characters provide a memorable reading experience for those who read her books. Leisurely in pace, her detective novels nonetheless are filled with the tension of danger and surprise. Beyond this, she invariably develops a fine and fitting background against which her characters move. All in all, one finds in Sayers a group of murder tales just about unmatched in English writing. In so many other instances, the stiff patterns of the detection novel tend to stifle the author's inventiveness and make for an outcome that is all too predictable. Sayers, on the other hand, manages to make the form with its narrowing demands her own. Her characters may be stereotypes in name, for in her novels are to be found the brilliant sleuth, the plodding perfectionist in the person of a Scotland Yard chief and the dull-witted sergeant, but one hardly recognizes them as stereotypes because of the freshness of Sayers's prose, the deft drawings of character and the novelty of the situations she presents. Murder in an advertising agency, a mysterious death in an English church at Christmastime, murder committed on a honeymoon, the murder trial of an English lord in the House of Lords, and on they go, all fresh, all tightly wrought, and all presented in a form that challenges perfection.

The Printer's Mark,
March, 1963

An Enemy of the Devil

During the Second World War I was commuting each day from the far western edge of Cleveland to the heart of that city. It meant that there was nearly an hour of travel each morning and evening that could be devoted to reading. As a result I fell into the habit of looking over the shelves of new books which came into the library where I worked with the idea of finding some comfortable reading for the boresome daily journey. In this mood I was struck one afternoon by a title which seemed almost to leer out at me from the top shelf . . . *The Screwtape Letters*. I took the book with me that afternoon, and during the long bus ride home and dinner I read it through entirely. I was caught up at once in its quick and incisive brilliance. Its sly, biting, insidious wit soon had my mind in a whirl, as the author stripped away the nonsense in which we garb so many of our thoughts, and left me laughing at my own idiocies, something more than half ashamed of my own weaknesses, and wanting to turn away a little from his sharp, probing scrutiny.

Since that day Clive Staples Lewis has had a steady influence on my thoughts. Practically every one of his works has found its way to my own shelves, and I have found him a remarkable companion on many journeys, both of the body and of the mind and spirit. I would hardly say that he is a comfortable companion, but the fact that he persists in his efforts to clear away the dustiness and the worrisome darkness of one's mind simply cannot be denied. No reader probably can accept all that Lewis has to say without sometimes finding himself or herself in difficulty. And it would be unfair to say that Lewis's writings all have equal appeal, as they reach across a broad range of ideas and intellectual attitudes. But it would be equally improper to suggest that he is anything but a stimulating and provocative thinker and writer. And more than this, he is a writer who speaks from a strong and deep religious conviction, unwavering in its certainty and startling in its power and clarity.

One of his most interesting efforts is to be found in a trilogy, loosely hung together in form but well organized in theme, in which he makes a series of studies of the never-ending combat between men of goodwill and faith and the forces of evil. The first of this trilogy is a piece of science-fiction, entitled *Out of the Silent Planet*. A fascinating tour de force, the tale makes no bows to pulp magazine fiction, but instead stands quite firmly on its own foundation of fantasy. It consists of an adventure in which Dr. Ransom, its hero, is kidnapped and taken on a swift voyage through space to Mars, where he is introduced to a utopian civilization of supermen and minor gods. These people, greatly superior to the race of earthling to which Ransom belongs, have developed a cultural and ethical existence far beyond the dreams of ordinary persons, and their civilization has reached such perfection that its inhabitants have succeeded in sealing off the earth, which has thus become "the silent planet," riddled by wars and evil, in the possession, in fact, of the powers of evil.

One of the most pointed passages of this fantastic tale occurs when Ransom, the hero, having accustomed himself to the appearance and actions of his hosts, finally meets again the earthling villain of the piece. Ransom watches his earthmate come across an open square toward him. He begins to describe this person to himself, and so completely has he been immersed in the sentiments and attitudes of the people of Mars that the shock of suddenly recognizing the unflattering description as that of earth people in general is remarkable and crushing. The sum and substance of the story, of course, is the shrewd commentary Lewis provides on the failings of our own modern society. His comments are sharp and bitter, to the taste, but brilliant.

Out of the Silent Planet was quickly followed by a second member of the trilogy, this time a work called *Perelandra*, which is the story of a voyage to the planet Venus. Once more Lewis succeeds in creating an imaginary world of goodness. Perelandra, a planet still in the formative stages of development, is peopled by a society untouched by evil and ruled by two totally innocent (though sophisticated) persons, one called "the King" and the other "the Lady." These two pure creatures come under the attack of an evil being, a human professor of physics, who has voyaged to Perelandra for the express purpose of tempting the King and the Lady and so destroying their natures. This evil human is a representation of course of the devil, and only through the efforts of Ransom, a human and so less blessed with either goodness or innocence than those he would protect, are these lovely creatures of Perelandra saved. The tale of course is a subtle retelling of the Adam and Eve legend. As such, one might expect to find the narrative thin but Lewis has managed to inject new vitality and wonder into his telling of the story, and the complete work is most rewarding reading.

The third member of the trilogy, *That Hideous Strength*, is perhaps the most terrifying bit of fantasy in modern literature. It is an account of a massive attack upon the community of goodwill, in this case a small community of business people. The first hundred pages of the work consist of some of the most chilling events imaginable— the infiltration of the community by the powers of evil, who slowly and inexorably are able to dominate and who almost through the most insidious means destroy it. Without the violence of J. R. R. Tolkien in the final volume of his massive trilogy of fantasy, *The Fellowship of the Ring*, this great battle between the forces of darkness and the legions of good faith depicts a blood-curdling, last ditch stand by an honored few, and reading the final pages in the light of recent wars, there is an interesting echo of Winston Churchill's throaty phrases about how so much is owed to so few. An astonishing thing about the work is that it may be read as a simple tale of conflict in which various jealous interests do battle. But regarded, as it should be, as an allegory, the reader is left breathless by its naked suspense, and the terror of some of the scenes is of the sort from which nightmares are born.

Still another Lewis venture into fantasy is found in a book which represents, for me at least a high point in this literary genre. *The Great Divorce* is as subtle and at the same time powerful a piece of religious fantasy as can be imagined. It is the account of a group of people who meet on a dimly lighted street corner in the center of hell, there to await a fantastic bus which will transport them to a meeting in the outer reaches of heaven with some heavenly representatives. The purpose of their journey is to be cleansed of their sins and offered an opportunity to enter heaven. Lewis's picture of hell is a fabulous description of a vast, eerie and smoke-filled city whose inhabitants have become so bored with the day after day frightfulness of their fate that they continually leave their homes for new but still empty-hearted dwellings in the suburbs. The resultant evacuation of suburb after suburb has left the heart of the hellish city abandoned and desolate. It is as frightening a picture of hell as can be found, despite its lack of fire and boiling cauldrons.

However, it is upon the company of people who enter the bus and take the trip to the edges of heaven that the reader's attention is primarily focussed. These are the common everyday people—none guilty of a monstrous sin, but each encumbered instead with the petty sins we all know: greed, lust, overbearing possessiveness, selfishness and the rest. One of the bus riders has been a petty thief. Another is a woman whose domination of her son has turned him into a wastrel and ruined his life. Each of the riders demonstrates some species of shoddiness, and the victim of his or her own flawed character.

On the clean windless plains of heaven these smudgy little characters are met by the shining creatures of the heavenly state, and in the dialogues that follow each is given a choice to make—accepting an opportunity to cleanse himself or herself and enter at least the outer halls of heaven or refusing this invitation and so returning to the endless boredom of the lower world. The tragedy of the little story is that only one of the bus riders refuses to return to the lower world. The one who refuses is the man guilty of lust. This person succeeds, in a vivid scene, in tearing his sin from his being. The rest slowly re-enter the bus and start back along the road they had followed early in the day with such hope.

Lewis belongs to a select and brilliant company of men, including such striking figures as J. R. R. Tolkien and Charles Williams who, it is said, all wrote under the influence of a mysterious literary figure of the latter part of the nineteenth century, George Macdonald. Readers may remember from their childhood reading Macdonald's *At the Back of the North Wind.* Macdonald's influence was seminal in the work of Lewis and the others, although each followed his own unique path.

Lewis employed his skills in the world of fantasy as a means of retelling the Christian story, and in so doing has held out words of inspiration and hope to countless readers who without him might never have felt the impact of Christian moral teaching.

Lewis's works are so filled with inspiration and what he calls the "surprise of joy" that one cannot help but revel in the wonderful spirit of the worlds he describes.

The Printer's Mark,
September, 1963

The Jewel Naulakha

North along Putney Road, across West River where the three bridges stood, then west along Black Mountain Road, passing the old farm once known as the Waite Farm, and crossing Waite Brook on the way we went. The names somehow struck familiar notes . . . Putney, Waite . . . for these are names that appear in a charming short story written by Rudyard Kipling which he titled "An Habitation Enforced." We sought out the fork to the right which announced itself as Kipling Road, and at once began ascending a steeply curving blacktopped road, now swinging boldly across a sunny meadow, now darting beneath overhanging trees which left the road surface dappled and leaf-patterned. We proceeded up the mountain side, glimpsing vistas below of steep meadows where the Connecticut River glistened in the sun, and then we came to the narrow gate, guarded by eight foot stone pillars that bore no name but somehow suggested clearly that the land they guarded was a piece of England.

Swiftly the road, now narrower, swept upward to emerge at last from a sweep of second growth maples, bright with color in the October sun, and we found ourselves in a courtyard with curved stone walls that leaned back against the hillside, shouldering it away from the tiny court where horse-drawn carriages seventy years before had paused for their passengers. And there, gray and brooding on its mountain ledge, stood Naulakha, the American dwelling place of Rudyard Kipling. It was a place such as only an Englishman would have built. It is so withdrawn, not in an unfriendly manner, but with quiet dignity and finality. In the 1890s, few visitors entered its frowning gates. Good friends, established friends, were welcome, to be sure, but this jewel called "Naulakha" was not meant for all to see but for only the few who were Kipling's intimates.

The entrance to Naulakha is quietly forbidding, for the house has turned its back upon the visitor, choosing to face out across the sloping Vermont meadows. The people at Naulakha chose to look out at the world, and not to have it look in at them. Built upon a shallow ledge, the house is one room in width, with only narrow windows that face the western mountainside, while the great expanses of glass admit a sweeping view of the Connecticut River and far off, twenty-four miles as the crow flies, the misty peak of Mount Monadnock. "God's finger nail" Kipling called Mount Monadnock, and the glimpse of that distant mountain in New Hampshire became for Kipling an object of comfort and contemplation.

Its shingles weathered to the pearly gray only New England cedar shingles acquire and gravely matching in tone the granite ribs thrusting out of every pasture, Naulakha seems to have become a very part of the mountain upon which it rests, and there is a kind of sullen indifference about the house as it looks out across the fields, and awaits the return of its long departed owners, who found happiness in their early years of living in its splendid rooms, but who found tragedy, too, which made them feel Naulakha a place too haunted with sorrow and pain ever to become a home for them.

Rudyard Kipling lived at Naulakha for four years, from 1893 until 1896, and while there wrote a sequence of novels that are peculiarly "American" despite the fact that he himself resisted angrily almost everything that was American. Coming to Vermont with his young American bride, Kipling first saw his temporarily adopted state in the middle of winter, and he wrote with amusement and some tartness of the bitter cold of its snowy countryside. Yet he greeted that first cold winter with delight and spent that winter with his wife Caroline in a little house half way up the mountain toward the spot where he and Caroline (they called themselves "The Ways and Means Committee") decided to build their American home. There in the Bliss Cottage, Kipling began work on *The Jungle Book*, which was completed later in the study at Naulakha. It was through a doctor friend, James Conland, that Kipling became acquainted with the rigorous life demanded of the Gloucester fishermen, and from this acquaintance came his well known *Captains Courageous*. And while at Naulakha he gathered the poems which were to be published under the title *The Seven Seas*. Other Naulakha writings included the short stories of *A Day's Work*. Among these is one, already mentioned, that has a peculiarly American character. This is *An Habitation Enforced*, a delightful tale of a New England couple who went to Britain, there to discover that their ancestors had come from the English community in which they had settled. Another of Kipling's short stories, *A Walking Delegate*, is a picture from a somewhat bizarre point of view of the life that Kipling saw about him in Vermont.

Kipling's study at Naulakha is a place haunted by the man

himself. Standing before the desk where he liked to write, one catches, if vaguely, a glimpse of what life must have been like for Kipling when he was there. The cane-seated chair behind the table-like desk shows on its low arms the signs of his hands rubbing the darkened wood as he sat staring out across the pasture and the river to Monadnock. The fireplace, darkened by a hundred winter fires, must have given comfort to him, when the snow was drifting along the porch upon which the study opens. Over the fireplace was a favorite Biblical quotation his father, John Lockwood Kipling had carved in the bricks: "The night cometh, when no man can work." Kipling was apparently fond of such sentiments, as over another desk in another room where he sometimes worked is carved: "Oft was I weary when I toiled at thee." The walls of the study carry framed sketches by his father for the illustrations of *The Jungle Book*. Mowgli seems to leap out of one, while others of the jungle characters appear everywhere.

Kipling was a man whose shyness and desire for privacy led him to speak harshly of Americans, whom he thought in general brash, and of American news reporters in particular with their persistent chasing after lions. It is not surprising that he gained a reputation among his Vermont neighbors for caustic comment and unfriendliness, though perhaps odd that Vermonters, of all people, with their own austere opinions about their neighbors and with their own passion for restraint, should have blamed Kipling for what they themselves were doing. Yet Kipling was not unfriendly, and a story, told of a spring visit by the Kiplings to a hillside farm across the Connecticut River valley in New Hampshire, typifies both the warmth of heart of the Kiplings and the interest they took in his neighbors. Kipling and his wife introduced themselves to the farmer's wife, whose house they could just see at the apex of a cleared pasture, and when they pointed out Naulakha across the valley, the woman shook their hands and said, "So you're the people whose light I've seen across the valley! It's been a comfort in the winter nights, often enough." And from that day on the lights at Naulakha were never darkened but kept on as a sign to the woman across the river that all was well. A small enough gesture, but a warm one.

The Printer's Mark,
November, 1964

Charles Dickens

For most of my life I have found the greatest pleasure and delight in the works of Charles Dickens. Whether he was exploiting all of the sentiment of Christmas in *A Christmas Carol* or ranting against the evils of the English courts, the English school system or England's prisons, Dickens always spoke out loud and clear, bringing squarely into view the shortcomings of his society. Now, with at least a fair share of those evils eliminated or at least ameliorated, the true wonder of his writing is becoming visible. No longer need his works be read as social tracts. Instead they may be seen for what they are—marvelously intricate narratives, in which innumerable threads and themes intertwine, back and forth through the warp of each novel and create a wholly satisfying and elegant pattern.

It must be pointed out, however, that Charles Dickens fell into the trap unintentionally set for him by the publishers who brought his works to the English reading public. Early in his literary career it was common practice for a writer to publish his writings in serial form. Thus, each of Dickens's long novels was published in nineteen or twenty parts. Each part appeared as a biweekly or monthly "magazine," complete with advertisements and, with illustrations tipped into the first pages, each illustration numbered so that it would face the proper page when the book was complete and bound as a total volume. The speed with which these little parts were completed accounts for some of the points by which first issues of certain works are determined. For example, in the *Pickwick Papers*, in the first part to be published, there appeared an engraving, familiar now, of Mr. Pickwick delivering an address before the Pickwick Club. He stands with one hand tucked into his waistcoat, the other beneath the tails of his dress coat. The original engraving showed his waistcoat buttoned up tightly about his rotund figure by *nine* buttons. Shortly after the printing run was started, however, this plate of Pickwick snapped under the weight of the press. Hurriedly the publisher rushed to the engraver and requested that a new plate be drawn. The engraver produced the plate in record time, but later, when the run of this first issue had been distributed, it was discovered that in the second engraving the waistcoat showed only *seven*

171

buttons. The loss of those two buttons creates a difference of hundreds of dollars between the collector's value of the first issue and the first printing of the second issue.

I have gone astray. The fact that Dickens's works were, for the most part, published in serial form, is no doubt responsible for the fact that they tend to ramble on and on. Take, for example, *The Old Curiosity Shop*. Very early in the book Dickens let it be known that Little Nell would die a lingering, sorrowful death. Little Nell was of course saccharine sweet, and she appealed greatly to the sentimental Victorians. As soon as it was known that Nell would die, the letters began to pour in. "Please, Mr. Dickens, do not let Little Nell die!" "Please, Mr. Dickens, Little Nell is too good to die!" "Oh, Mr. Dickens, if you let Little Nell die, I shall never forgive you. I'll never read another of your books again!" So many of these letters of protest arrived that Dickens realized he had in Little Nell something of a good thing. And so chapter after chapter she lingers on, always close to death and with the reading public hanging on every faint breath until it might be supposed that Little Nell would not die after all. Then, in one of the middle chapters, it happens and Little Nell is gone at last. The market for this tale had in the meantime grown greatly. The ploy was a success.

It was Charles Dickens's habit, too, of working on several novels at the same time. He would write a part for one novel, then a part for a second, and sometimes even go to a third novel. No writer, not even Dickens himself, could possibly work on two or three novels at once without coming to grief. And come to grief he did. This production line of literary activity led, I am sure, to the confusion that exists in some of his work. That he carried the complicated pattern on as successfully as he did, however, is a tribute to his remarkable creative power, versatility and stamina.

To suggest that Dickens was a careless craftsperson would of course be wrong. Dickens had a genius for using the right word in the right place. A recent publication of *A Christmas Carol*, in facsimile, with each page of manuscript facing a page of printing, provides an opportunity to study just how meticulous Charles Dickens was as he worked away, even at the feverish pace which he maintained in producing this Christmas classic. In October of 1843, as a filler between numbers of *Martin Chuzzlewit*, Dickens started on a Christmas story. In debt, he had need of an immediate success, and he had to write the story quickly enough to have it ready for December publication. Seven years earlier he had included the basic idea of *A Christmas Carol*, including even a mention of Tiny Tim, in Mr. Wardle's tale in *Pickwick*. Dickens rewrote this tale at white heat and as he wrote he fell in love with what he was doing. The effort, undertaken as a means of making money, had turned into a labor of love. Before the end of November the story was complete. Critics have sometimes complained that the plot of *A Christmas Carol* is childish and the writing is careless. But neither charge stands up. An examination of the manuscript pages is enough to prove that Dickens was a true artisan. He left nothing to chance, and in consequence produced a masterpiece. The original manuscript contained sixty-six pages. It was found that in six pages chosen at random there are 193 lines of script, and in those 193 lines there are 193 corrections of one kind or another. This is one correction per line; and in some cases words were changed not just once but two or three times.

The result, sentimental though it may be called, is a marvellous little story, one that has survived countless rewritings to turn it into stage or movie material. Not even Hollywood has managed to destroy the miracle that Dickens wrought in five and a half short weeks.

Letters from Anagnostes Solitarium,
April, 1971

Austin Tappan Wright

For thirty years I have been the willing captive and admirer of one book in particular. It was on a gray and rainy day in the spring of 1942 that I was browsing along the shelves of a lending library in a little Pennsylvania college town. One book seemed almost to push its way to attention as I glanced from title to title. Bound in a pleasant, heavy, white cloth, its title stood out obviously on its spine: *Islandia*. I took it home with me for a long weekend, and spent that entire weekend in a kind of daze of wonder as I read the book entirely through, and then went back to reread dozens of its passages. I have continued to reread *Islandia* at least once a year since that day of discovery. I have suggested it to a larger and larger circle of friends; have loaned my battered early copies dozens and dozens of times; have purchased used copies to give to friends; have gathered copies of each succeeding edition for myself, along with a great many copies of reviews and various other associated items. In all of the years of enjoying this single work, it is no exaggeration to say that on each rereading I have never failed to find something new, something which somehow had escaped me in earlier readings. There have been innumerable discoveries and rediscoveries of passages of special beauty, of wonder or miraculous perception. This continuing renewal of excitement over *Islandia* makes it difficult for me to write what I actually feel about this book, for somehow there is the feeling that my personal involvement with the work has become too personal and ought, in fact, to be kept to myself. Yet the urge to share this unusual and, indeed, classical volume with others is undeniable.

Islandia represents, to begin with, the almost total involvement of its author in a kind of dream world, a utopia created in his fertile mind and filled with so much richness of detail that it and its neighboring country, Karain, seem actually to exist. In the beginning, as I read voraciously through the novel it was enough that the legend itself was there to read. But the more intimately acquainted with the work I became, the more convinced I was that such a place could and did exist. It was only a year or so later, when I learned more of the circumstances under which the novel *Islandia* was created, that the full importance of this work became evident to me.

Wright was a successful corporation lawyer and a professor of law both at the University of Pennsylvania and the University of California. His court briefs were generally accepted as outstanding examples of legal scholarship, and his lectures, a few of them published in legal journals, were brilliant analyses of the legal problems to which he directed his attention. Upon retirement, all this was left behind, and Wright slipped away from his profession, his friends, and even his family, into a miraculous world which existed solely in his own mind. He conceived the country of Islandia as the southernmost portion of a small continent facing the Antarctic seas, somewhere to the east of Australia. He created an Islandian society, made up of three major classes: the Islar, the Tanar, who constituted a middle class group of land and farm owners; and the Denerir, who were their willing and contented dependents. The latter were not peasants, nor poor, but merely families who supplied the labor force in the almost feudal society that existed in Islandia.

Wright escaped one of the most serious hazards of the creators of utopian societies. Most earlier writers, from Plato to More to Bellamy, spent so much time explaining the utopian concepts of their mythical lands that little was left for demonstration of the actual workings of the societies they created. Wright surmounted this difficulty by creating a mass of background material entirely separate from the story of Islandia itself. He wrote a military history of Islandia; he created a literary form peculiar to Islandia, a kind of Islandian Aesop's fable; he produced an almanac which described climate, annual production on the farms, population changes, etc., etc.; he produced a carefully drawn series of maps in an atlas that indicates in marvellous detail the geography, geology and political divisions of the country; he developed an Islandian currency and an Islandian calendar, different entirely from our own; he detailed the political hierarchy of Islandia's rulers; and he even went so far as to outline in elementary form a religion peculiar to Islandia. And when all of this was done, Wright produced his novel, *Islandia*.

The novel is concerned with the happy meeting at Harvard of John Lang, an American, with Dorn, a powerful and thoughtful young man born of the domnant ruling family of Islandia. This acquaintance leads to Lang's growing interest in his friend's country and ultimate appointment as United States consul in Islandia. In Islandia Lang gradually adopts the way of life he finds there and eventually, after an exciting event in which he behaves heroically, he becomes an Islandian citizen.

The narrative is so clear and clean that the reader is swept along in its powerful, yet slow action. There is violence, but the violence is overlaid with the dignity and purposefulness of a great people. There is love, but love not inspired only by physical attraction. Instead it is the sort of love that lends credence to the notion that the life of an individual or a people is dependent upon the continuation of solid values from one generation to the next.

Islandia served Austin Tappan Wright as a sounding board to present his views on what he considered the shallow, materialistic concerns of America at the turn of the twentieth century. It is no tirade. It does not reject what Wright found objectionable in the society in which he lived, but holds up for comparison two ways of life, two manners of living, two social philosophies, and lets the reader make his own judgments.

Islandia is the greatest of the utopias of the twentieth century, and merits its place among the half dozen utopian masterpieces of all time. And while it is not a book for all readers, there is no doubt whatsoever that the reader who brings himself or herself to this work allows Wright's long, swinging prose sentences do their work, will be enthralled. Such a reader may at the same time become convinced that the world needs an Islandia.

Letters from Anagnostes Solitarium,
January, 1972

Charles Williams

It is C. S. Lewis who, convinced that the forces of evil were incarnate in a living, factual creature called the devil, finds it curious that the early and not-so-early church both made the mistake of postulating the existence of a serious contest between the forces of good and evil, between God and the devil. Lewis goes on to suggest that the mistake had to do with the drama implicit in such a contest. The suggestion appears in Lewis's writings that the hopelessness of the devil's position adds weight to this dramatic conflict and makes the devil somehow appealing to the modern age, which tends to support the underdog. This is of course a kind of secular nonsense, reducing the endless combat between right and wrong or good and evil to the stature of a mere stage play, with the crescendo of the drama coming, as in all good plays, at the end of the second act, just before the villain begins his rapid fall toward destruction. Strangely, but not so strangely perhaps, Lewis goes on to suggest that there does exist a physical devil, who has the temerity to challenge God.

This letter, however, is not intended to enter into a discussion of the rightness or wrongness of the C. S. Lewis schemata. Its purpose is to look briefly at a miraculous little group of novels which expresses many of the ideas found in the writings of Lewis, Tolkien, and most of the rest of the Oxonian group who referred to themselves quaintly and preciously as "The Inklings."

The novels of Charles Williams, written rather offhandedly during the course of an astonishingly complicated literary career, are so filled to overflowing with philosophical reflection and personal faith that they all but take the reader by storm. Edmund Fuller, in his excellent work, *Books with Men Behind Them*, asks the question, " . . . can [you] imagine grafting a Dorothy Sayers detective story onto the Apocalypse of St. John? The resulting fruit might be like a Charles Williams novel." Williams's seven remarkable tales are, as Fuller goes on, " . . . transcendental thrillers, supernatural melodramas. In them are loosed immeasurable powers, and terrifying events follow. The characters live, move, and have their beings in dimension which sometimes appall, but through which Williams shows us the full implications of creeds too much taken for granted."

Perhaps the most readable of Charles Williams's thrillers is *War in Heaven*. This novel gives the newcomer to Williams's astonishing literary world a sense of what he or she might expect to find ahead. That *War in Heaven* is more than a mere yarn must be understood, but Williams's skill as a storyteller is paramount. On the surface the story seems merely to tell of an effort on the part of a few vaguely cynical villains to gain possession of a lovely and valuable chalice owned by a local church. Out of such a plot have come numerous tales of stupid thievery. But as the reader slips more and more into the mood of Williams's story, an awareness is created of tremendous forces at work in the world Williams describes and in the reader's own mind. The chalice, it becomes clear, is in fact the Holy Grail, returned to England in modern times, and the cynical villains finally shed their cloak-and-dagger costumes to reveal themselves as the rulers of the kindgom of evil. The poor defenders of the grail are at first caught up in a tumult of violent action which leaves them stunned and in fear of the powers they sense swirling around them. But soon they become aware of other greater powers, which encourage them to press on, even against their own will or desire in the battle they are fighting. Williams's careful depiction of violent conflict is so graphic and bloodthirsty that the reader is left in doubt until the last moment as to the outcome of the story. Excitement is an understatement in describing the reader's experience. A kind of exhaustion overtakes the reader as Williams pursues his plot line, but in the end the reader shares in the victory that is attained.

No novel by Williams can be compared properly with any other. Each has its own peculiar quality and of course its own theme. Yet all seven of the novels are concerned in one way or another with the allegorical battle between good and evil. Williams clearly grasped the significance and tone of both the good and the evil worlds. Williams, too, was capable of understanding and believing in the efficacy and ultimate triumph of the forces of good.

These novels of Charles Williams are as much essays concerning his own Christian faith as they are powerful melodramas relating to faith in general. They can be read on several levels—read swiftly and solely for their melodramatic impact or in depth for the richness of their symbolism and for the challenges to faith they portray. The serious reader, whatever his religious persuasion, will find them highly meaningful and moving.

Letters from Anagnostes Solitarium,
January, 1976

Stephen R. Donaldson

A new Tolkien-like figure has appeared in the world of literary fantasy. This is Stephen R. Donaldson, a young man who has created not another Middle Earth, but a world so fantastic that it must stand out as one of the most remarkable creative works of the day. His work draws this comment from one who does not every day find the fantastic worlds of science fiction engrossing or even credible. But Donaldson has accomplished a *tour de force* that bears more than a single reading and demands those who enter his remote and often terrifying landscapes not merely that they suspend disbelief but also that they empathize closely with his hero in the long series of both shattering experiences and uplifting events that came along.

Lord Foul's Bane is the first volume of a trilogy covered by the conglomerate title *The Chronicles of Thomas Covenant the Unbeliever*. Following *Lord Foul's Bane*, the trilogy includes *The Illearth War* and *The Power That Preserves*.

The broad sweep of this narrative is almost overwhelming, moving as it does from a tragic beginning in our own times into a world so separate from ours and so replete with secret powers and magic that the reader is practically flummoxed by the turmoil into which he or she is led. Events occur in a maelstrom, and there are so many characters, all of them both believable and unbelievable, that only a few chapters can be read at a single sitting without encountering exhaustion. It is tempting to draw comparisons between Tolkien's mystical world and Donaldson's astounding landscapes and societies. It is tempting, but is not really a desirable thing to do. In Tolkien two elements come together to provide his utopia with verisimilitude. One is in the creation of his Hobbits, a population of people who are of tiny stature, and a condition that somehow makes them the right and proper defenders of the free world. The Hobbits are certainly not negative, in the sense that they are unimportant, but they are underdogs in their battle against the evil forces about them if for no reasons other than their diminutive size and pleasing nature. Donaldson's hero, Thomas Covenant, on the other hand, is in one sense an anti-hero, because he rejects all offers of friendship and assistance. He is the complete introvert, hugging to himself all his problems and triumphs, while at the same time driving himself relentlessly on a quest to deliver a message to the authorities in charge of a battle against time and evil.

To describe even a few of the remarkable characters that make their appearances in this tale is to indicate the variety and convincingness of Donaldson's work. First there is Trell, a giant of a man, a leader in his Mithil Stonedown, a kind of primitive, fortress city, a man who speaks seldom and acts with deliberation. There is Atiaran—Atiaran Trell-mate—wife to Trell the giant. It is she who starts Covenant off on his journey toward Lord's Keep. Atiaran is a most complex individual, driving herself on the journey to the point of self destruction, carrying Covenant along with her by sheer force of character. During the course of this journey through the mountains toward Lord's Keep, there are events so filled with tension as to deeply disturb the reader, and yet the desire to continue to follow these two people, Atiaran and Covenant, is not to be denied.

A second phase of Covenant's quest for Lord's Keep begins with a meeting with Foamfollower, another giant, whose roaring laughter thunders about Covenant's ears, but whose might and spirit are so powerful that he is capable of incomparable feats of strength and daring. In this relationship with Foamfollowers, Covenant comes in direct contact with one of the magical secrets of the strange world in which he finds himself. Foamfollowers is the possessor and pilot of a kind of enormous canoe made from the wood of a mysterious tree called Gildenlode. Foamfollower, through strength of will, draws a mysterious energy from the keel of his vessel that is sufficient to drive the vessel against the powerful current of the stream they must follow to reach Lord's Keep. Such magic seems preposterous in our pragmatic age, of course, but it is the stuff of fantasy, and as such Donaldson manages to make it real, understandable and convincing.

The sum total of the impact of this first part of the *Thomas Covenant Chronicle* is enormous. Donaldson's vocabulary is as sophisticated, as entirely mature, as could be desired. His imagination is given full and sweeping freedom. He has the capability of developing characters who, while grotesque, are still believable and real. Great pleasure is to be found in the descriptive passages which are written in a poetic prose that sings and echoes in the mind long afterwards. There are moments of tension and terror which, because of Donaldson's lyric and thought-swift narration, are all but unbearable. The reader is swept along in a torrent of action, only to come up against the hardness of Covenant's resistance to friendly assistance or offers of friendship. Much of the contrasting beauty and evil with which the tale concerns itself is made more acutely real by constant reminders that in his real life Covenant had been stricken with leprosy and rejected by his family and friends. Covenant's new world, however, is one where sickness, save for sickness of the spirit, is unknown.

Donaldson, born in 1947 in Cleveland, Ohio, lived in India from the time he was three years old until he was sixteen. His father, a doctor, worked with lepers, and out of his awareness of the tragedy of leprosy, Donaldson developed the idea of using a leper as the protagonist of his story. A graduate of Kent State University in Ohio, where he earned a Master of Arts degree, he also attended the College of Wooster. He has written a powerful and fascinating story with such skill as to allow hope that further tales of fantasy will come from his pen.

Letters from Anagnostes Solitarium,
August, 1978

His People, His Country

Only rarely does one have the opportunity to watch the growth and development of a true literary genius, and too often that opportunity is lost in a failure to recognize, at first hand, the characteristics of such a genius. In recent years, however, we have had an opportunity to witness the development of a Canadian author who has marched in long strides from the promise of his first work to the publication of his most recent offering, a novel that signals the full flowering of his greatness. Hugh MacLennan, scholar, essayist, philosopher, humanist and dedicated observer of humankind occupies a unique position in the literature of modern times. His new novel, *The Return of the Sphinx*, represents a high point in a career dedicated to keenly wrought studies of the Canadian world in which he has spent his life. One of the most exciting aspects of his career has been the parallel growth of his skill as a writer and his perception of the agonizing crisis which has for half a century crept up on Canada and her culturally divided citizenry.

Beginning in 1941, with the publication of his stunning first novel, *Barometer Rising*, it was apparent that MacLennan was possessed of skills that most novelists never acquire. The story—a swiftly moving, tense narrative concerned with the events of the three days in 1917 during which Halifax harbor is destroyed in the explosion of an ammunition ship—gave MacLennan an opportunity to demonstrate his outstanding capacity to write taut, exciting prose. The story begins with the arrival of the ammunition ship in the harbor. No warning is given of impending disaster, save that MacLennan's young hero is ridden by a murmuring premonition of danger. The blast, when it occurs, levels whole streets and drives the terrified residents of the dock area into a blind, self-destroying panic. The story is told with such energy and speed that the reader is carried along, page after page, in almost breathless excitement. The narration that follows of the emotional and physical impact of the explosion upon its helpless victims is in its way equally exciting, and constitutes a remarkable feat of narrative skill.

There are glimpses in this first book of the author's concern for the people of eastern Canada, though the Nova Scotian populace was not to represent his chief concern in the years of writing that were to follow. He turns to what is apparently a work of semi-autobiography in *The Precipice*, published in 1948, to tell the story of a Canadian student who goes to the United States to attend college and stays on for graduate study at Princeton. This situation provides MacLennan with an opportunity to examine his Canadian reactions to Americans and the careless unconcern with which they view their northern neighbors. He examines, too, the subtle, yet overbearing, influence of the American way of life upon his fellow countrymen, and sees for the first time the pale flickering fires of dissension in the eyes of his French-Canadian friends who have begun even then to resent the casual reactionary attitudes toward their French neighbors of *les anglais* who still dominate the politics of their sprawling young country without regard to the cultural and ethnic differences that exist in *la belle provence* of Quebec. The novel provides both a fine study of American academic life and a clear prediction of the future course of MacLennan's novels.

Two years before the appearance of *The Precipice*, MacLennan had turned his attention to the deeply disturbing conflict which had developed between the young French-Canadian generation and the Catholic Church. In *Two Solitudes*, a story of the slow-burning contest between the complacent ideologies of the Church establishment and the restless, unharnessed energies of young French-Canadians, is one of the first representations of the shattering challenge that was to threaten within a decade the whole unity of Canada. MacLennan, keenly aware of the implications of this early ideological revolt writes somberly of it, and uses his characters with deft skill to reveal some of the deep tragedy of the war of ideas and attitudes which was soon to create open, bitter enmities. For the first time, MacLennan revealed in this work his power to evoke character and conflict in a moving story that was almost too close to reality to be anything but disturbing to the reader.

In 1951 came the second volume of what was to become a loosely tied together tetralogy concerned with the agonizing inner conflict which would break Canada into two separate armed camps. *Each Man's Son*, a darkly-etched story of a young miner of eastern Nova Scotia who finds in the new scientific age following World War I that his only hope of making his way in the world was in a life of physical violence in the boxing ring. The physical and mental destruction of this man is as stark and tragic a tale as is to be encountered in the literature of the first half of the twentieth century. The contrast between the bitter, brutal existence of the underprivileged miners and the comfortable and opportunity-filled life of Ontario and western Quebec foreshadow indelibly the period of impending conflict that is to follow.

By 1959 MacLennan was fully aware of the political and social implications of such disparities and in that year he published *The Watch That Ends the Night*. This is a mature piece of writing in which the fire of MacLennan's anger is always present under the surface. This anger reveals itself in occasional flashes of condemnatory prose, as the story of the sharpening conflict between the French-Canadians and their English compatriots unrolls. MacLennan is acutely aware of the full tragedy inherent in the conflict. His sympathies are enlisted, but he is impatient with the idiocies of which both sides are guilty. *The Watch That Ends the Night* serves as a sharp warning of the dangers that lie in a separated Canada to the peace and stability of Canada itself and of the whole of the North American continent.

The final work in the group of novels by MacLennan is *The Return of the Spinx*, a work in which the author highlights the Canadian conflict through the dramatic confrontation of a father and son, one born of a generation whose passions were drained by the brutal futility of World War II, the other born into a world of violence and revolution in which the standards of the past lack meaning and definition. It is a tragic encounter in which the protagonists are lost in the failure to communicate. And this personal conflict MacLennan has placed in the context of the confusion and invidious political maneuvering taking place within the national government of Canada.

At first glance the impression created as a whole by this group of novels, which was produced over a period of twenty years' time, is not overwhelming. But compared with the grand total of Canadian literary production having to do with this most violent crisis in Canadian history, MacLennan's five novels stand out as a fine achievement. MacLennan's acute dissection of the strands of the English/French conflict is alone sufficient to delineate the issues. It surprises a little that MacLennan has chosen to reflect most of this conflict in the quiet lives of fictional characters, but the reader cannot fail to be impressed by the depth of his insights into what is a highly troubling Canadian problem. His characters stand neither as Canadian archetypes nor as symbols of the dissension rocking their country, but instead are ordinary Canadians caught up in events that are at explosion point.

It is interesting that MacLennan is perhaps more revered in the United States than he is in his native Canada. This may in some measure be accounted for by the fact that part of his education was gained here, a circumstance that gave him a new perspective on the Canadian scene and enabled him to regard with detachment the events embroiling his countrymen. Beyond this, MacLennan has the ability to marvel in the strength and beauty of his sprawling homeland. His works offer an abundance of rewards, not the least of which is a new sense of the greatness of the giant to the north.

Letters from Anagnostes Solitarium,
May, 1980

Edwin Way Teale

The recent death of Edwin Way Teale, the author of countless articles and books in natural history, brings sadness and a sense of loss to thousands of his readers. Americans were fortunate to have had this thoughtful, keenly observant and generous man among them. Teale's greatest contributions lay in a profound appreciation of nature and eagerness to share his adventures with friends and his host of readers here and elsewhere.

Natural history, happily, is one of those marvelous fields of scientific inquiry that are amenable to enjoyment by both ordinary persons and those professionally trained in the area. And America has been fortunate to produce over the last century a dozen or more writers in the natural history area who were blessed with high literary skills. Led by John Muir, ably seconded by such authors as Ernest Seton Thompson, Joseph Wood Krutch, Hal Borland, this group of writers has provided both pleasure and information to generations of bird watchers and other observers of the natural scene. Teale offered over the years a long series of familiar essays, in which he recounts a lifetime of encounters with the wonders of nature. He describes vividly the excitement, beauty and frequent sadness of these encounters, and in doing so shows himself to have been a man of gentleness, compassion and considerable knowledge. His description of the tensions between the world of men and animals and of the ways in which these tensions are eased or made to benefit people and animals together, constitute some of the loveliest examples of the literature of natural history. He and his colleagues were the quiet "clerks of the woods," whose painstaking reporting of what they saw, whose thoughtful investigation of the meanings that lay behind the natural wonders they reported on, stand as proof of their humility and of their genuine and eager willingness to serve as interpreters of the natural world.

Teale wrote in a simple, straightforward style, but at the same time he was able to produce passages that were miracles of precise and elegant observation. In *Autumn Across America*, he describes the imprisonment of insects in the crystal amber of another age, and almost in the next paragraph comments on the everyday excitement of watching a field mouse carry her young to safety after her nest is destroyed by a late plowing. In *North With the Spring* he speaks with delight of the "vertical migration" of certain warblers, up and down the mountains of the southern Appalachians, then describes the beauty of great skeins of Canada geese hurrying south along the Atlantic flyway. His interests were as varied as the seasons through which he moved, and his curiosity about nature enabled him to investigate with pleasure to himself and the reader the many facets of the hidden world of nature in the meadows of his beloved Connecticut farm.

It is interesting to note that his writings about people lack the warmth of those that deal with nature. In consequence, his descriptions of the people who lived in the close-knit community near his farm retreat are less convincing in some ways than his revelations about the lives of the tiny creatures living on the edges of his private lake. His enthusiasm for single events of nature or, say, the discovery in a nearby wood of an unusual and hard-to-identify moss catches the fancy of the reader more readily than his amused comments on the man-of-all-work who helped rebuild his farmhouse in the early years of his ownership. In short, he was an historian of natural rather than human events. To him the life of a damsel fly was more significant than the life of many a person. He was not of a cold nature, but he had his priorities.

Armchair naturalists have lost a great companion. Teale knew the joys of learning about nature as a boy and as a young man. He set about, as a youth, teaching others in the best way that he knew. He wrote of everyday common things, explaining them. He wrote of events which bear on the lives of all of us, expressed wonder at the miracles of which daily life is made up. But more than merely recording those miracles, he sought to make them understandable. His essays on natural history are not sugar-coated stories, but are careful descriptions and explications of natural happenings. Teale reveled in the explorations of his youth, and never lost the sense of wonder and the excitement that nature brought him. As long as he lived, he did all he could in his writings to transmit these feelings to his readers.

Letters from Anagnostes Solitarium,
November, 1980

SECTION IV
BOOK COLLECTING

To know where books are and who is collecting them is part of the responsibility of the collection development librarian. The history of libraries abounds in examples of how the acquisition of a fine private collection made a good library great. It is probably true that the best collection development is done by private collectors, and librarians neglect this source at their peril.

Disreputable Scholarship

The world of books has produced so much of beauty and value that one is apt to forget that the world of print has attracted its own share of crooks and tawdry cheats.

One of the saddest and most despicable of bibliographical stories has once again in recent weeks been brought to attention in a pair of articles in *The New Yorker* and the *London Times Literary Supplement*, on Thomas J. Wise and his forgeries of nineteenth century pamphlets. *The New Yorker* article presents a readable and authentic account of Wise's doings; the *London Times* story identifies an until now unknown Wise forgery.

One must wonder what led Wise to become a forger. It is true that he was never a rich man, but he was sufficiently well off to have been able in the course of a relatively few years to build the spectacular Ashley Library. This collection of books, while less massive than the Huntington and Pierpont Morgan collections, was nevertheless notable in that it contained copies of most of the important first editions of the nineteenth century, and is even today considered auspicious. Wise's reputation at the time he began his forgeries was high. He was one of the most outstanding and highly regarded bibliographers and bookmen of his time. Wise had much to lose in turning forger and nothing to gain. The man's psychology is fascinating to contemplate. His compulsion was to forge unique "first" editions, and along the way was guilty of a form of blackmail in his treatment of the bookseller, Herbert Gorfin, who was at first an unwitting and later a rebellious agent in the sale of most of the Wise forgeries. Just what means Wise employed to draw the respectable printing firm of Richard Clay & Sons into his net is not clear, but draw them in he did and at tremendous financial gain to himself. Wise in fact made use with varying success of the talents of many others in the promoting of his forgeries, and these mostly guileless persons suffered badly in consequence.

I for one cannot forgive Wise for his shameless treatment of Edmund Gosse. Nor for the ruthlessness revealed in his besmirching of Buxton Forman's name, even after Forman's death made a defense on that man's part impossible. Moreover, it was despicable of Wise

193

to have bribed or blackmailed Forman's son into collusion in the matter. But more of my anger is concerned with what Wise did to Gosse.

Gosse was for me, as a young man, a much loved writer. I truly admired him, but pitied him a little, too. My first acquaintance with him was through his delightful and deeply moving autobiographical work, *Father and Son*. That book stands as a monument to the terrible unease that ensued in England (and in the world, for that matter) from publication of Charles Darwin's *Origin of Species*. Born the son of a fundamentalist theologian, Gosse was caught in the struggle between people of his father's mind and those whose minds were appealed to and liberated by the arrival of the age of scientific inquiry. Gosse tells of his having been taken to hear a preacher who denounced the whole concept of Darwin's thesis, arguing plainly and clearly that Darwin's evidence was based on fancies and false ideas. Gosse, educated at a time when Darwin's theories were being accorded credence, found himself in the uncomfortable spot of accepting either the fundamentalist ideas of his father or the new ideas being promulgated by the scientific community. He eventually chose the side of science. His account, in *Father and Son*, of the struggle between his father's world and his own, is a wonderfully human document, and one worth reading even today. As I say, I felt some affection for Gosse, and the fact that he was in his younger years a librarian at the British Museum Library only added to this affection.

Gosse was maneuvered into becoming an accomplice in the Wise forgeries when he was persuaded to publish in his volume of critical essays, *Critical Kit-Kats*, the spurious story of the manner in which Elizabeth Barrett Browning wrote her lovely *Sonnets from the Portuguese* for her husband. (Gosse later agreed with Wise that the *Sonnets* should be sent to Miss Mitford, who would supervise their publication in the notorious 1847 Reading edition.) Gosse was appealed to, I am sure, by Wise's assumed but flattering interest in his work. Gosse had been unfavorably reviewed in the public press, and he felt that publishing this choice little "inside story" would redeem him. The fact that Gosse allowed himself to be duped by Wise is not to his credit. There is little question that he was not a strong personality—he sought public acclaim and was easily beguiled by the most obvious flattery. Yet it was Wise who was the real villain of the piece.

Later, after Wise's forgeries had been revealed, Wise somehow persuaded the hapless Buxton Forman, Jr. to say that his father had misrepresented information to Wise and that Wise was the dupe and the elder Forman the forger or at least the one responsible for the sale and distribution of the forgeries. This last touch, hard to believe in its Mephistophelean cruelty, leaves little to be said for the character of Wise, who stands as a paradox in the field of English bibliographical scholarship, a man who had achieved fame as a bibliophile and scholar and who yet defamed his field by creating false first editions and attempting to sell them to unsuspecting amateurs on the strength of his own high reputation.

This story of Wise's forgeries is told in one of the most fascinating books of the last thirty years, a book with a stilted title but a plot like a detective story. This is John Carter and Graham Pollard's *An Enquiry into the Nature of Certain Nineteenth Century Pamphlets* which came out in 1934. The book, while never mentioning Wise's name, points an accusing finger at Wise. But few doubts were left in the minds of early readers of this remarkable piece of bibliographical detection. The Carter-Pollard work was a bombshell which exploded the myth of Wise's bibliographical integrity and left the book business reeling. The result was a series of other publications, some vituperative, some scholarly, either attacking the accusers as charlatans or denouncing Wise. One of the latter sort was Wilfrid Partington's vicious biography of Wise, rather too cleverly entitled *Forging Ahead*. Partington, who had himself been duped by Wise, wrote scornfully and bitterly of his former acquaintance. Unfortunately much of the usefulness of his work is diluted by the sharpness of his bias. Another more scholarly work was written by Fannie Ratchford, librarian of the Wrenn Library at the University of Texas which owns all of Wise's forgeries. Ratchford actually began her work as a defense of Wise, gathering the correspondence between John Henry Wrenn, a major American book collector, and Wise, who had taken delight in selling Wrenn his forged first editions. The Ratchford investigation only served to draw the rope tighter about Wise and made clearer the extent to which Wise had bilked his friends and customers. The work Ratchford produced, *The Letters of Thomas J. Wise and John Henry Wrenn*, was a clinching statement of Wise's duplicity, and makes for sad, if enlightening, reading.

Two other interesting sidelights were thrown on the matter with the publication of *Between the Lines*, letters and memoranda between the elder Forman and Wise, and D. F. Foxon's *Thomas J. Wise and the Pre-Restoration Drama*, a study in sophisticated duplicity and thievery. The revelations continue, until today there is a considerable literature concerning the methods and productions of the man who was too wise, if one can be excused for saying so, for his own good. A sad sidelight on Wise's activities, incidentally, is that Wise managed to destroy many fine books as he pursued his career as a forger. Even sadder of course are the lives he damaged. What he did was thoroughly reprehensible, and one can only regret that his unmasking did not occur until after his death.

If I may, I will add a related incident in which I myself played a small part. As a boy of twelve I lived in Lakewood, Ohio, near the corner of Detroit Avenue and Robinwood Avenue. In a large, yellow brick house on that corner lived Paul Lemperley, a lesser known but astute book collector of the period between 1912 and 1940. Lemperley used to invite me, whenever the occasion arose, to come into his library, a wonderful place full of mustiness and leather smells, and there I was permitted to handle the lovely works that crowded the shelves, and there I suspect gained a taste for the nineteenth century literature which has continued to give me pleasure over the years. I remember very well a rainy Saturday when I had spent a whole morning in a vast leather chair beside Lemperley's desk reading while he went about his correspondence. He sat back finally and spoke to me, holding in his hand a letter he had been poring over. Lemperley was a softspoken man, serious, seldom given to laughter but ready always to smile. This morning he was unsmiling, however, and sterner than I had ever seen him. "This is a letter," he said, "from a man in England, who is one of the great book collectors, and he is a scholar too. Look at his name here, and remember it." I looked, and there at the bottom of the letter was the signature, clear enough, "Tom Wise." "I've had a lot to do with this man," Lemperley went on. "He has written to me often, and tried to sell me some of his books. But I shall never buy a book from him. He is a liar, and his books are not true books."

This occurred in the mid-nineteen twenties. Wise's forgeries were not to be revealed for more than ten years. Lemperley was one of the few recognized collectors in whose hands were not found copies of the forgeries. His bibliographical acumen was sound indeed. I like to think of that morning, for it amuses me to think of Wise as industriously selling his flawed editions. But better than that, it makes me feel good that I knew someone who was not fooled by him.

The Printer's Mark,
November, 1962

Treasure Hunt

A friend and I have just returned from a treasure hunt. It was not the kind of hunt that ends on the sweeping, white sanded beach of some forgotten isle, but it had nevertheless its moments of elation and reward. It was the fourth such treasure hunt in recent months, and on each occasion the return journey was laden with treasure.

The two of us spent a happy couple of hours seeking this treasure at a used book sale held in behalf of some worthy cause at an armory in this eastern city. Long ranges of tables were piled with books of every description. These had been arranged in a sort of freewheeling order by type, subject and special appeal, and they had about them a kind of carefree heterogeneity that was a magnet to the buyer. Sitting companionably side by side on the tables were novels hardly a year old alongside hoary veterans of other centuries. I saw an 800-page giant, *Advise and Consent*, beside *Mrs. Miniver*, and next to *Mrs. Miniver* that tale of another century, *Richard Carvel*, by the Americo-Englishman Winston Churchill. I saw Jeffrey Farnol's *Money Moon* next to Helen Weston's *Dark Wood* and Marquand's *Wikford Point*. And there were the *Two Little Confederates* close beside Ian MacLaren's *Bonnie Briar Bush*. A handsome edition of Sasson's *Memoirs of a Fox Hunting Man* stood beside two stumpy volumes of an odd, nineteenth century Appleton edition of William Makepeace Thackeray's *The Luck of Barry Lyndon*. The latter sold in its heyday for fifty cents a volume, a scandalous price for what was almost certainly a pirated edition, but yesterday it was offered at forty cents a volume, a still scandalous price, incidentally. On a table of juveniles I saw Harry Castlemon's *Frank in the Woods*, a surprisingly clean copy of *Tom Swift and his Undersea Search*, and a much read but still sound copy of Henty's *By Pike and Dyke*, all eager to catch the reader's eye.

Now the half-humorous juxtaposition of some of the titles named above was both interesting and amusing, but there were other elements in the sale that were even more rewarding. There was a long table, carefully placed against a wall, over which a sign promised that here were "Nostalgic Books" for sale. It was a collection of titles which, in this particular context, seemed both amusing and sad.

I twice walked the length of that table picking up a volume here and there, more for old time's sake than with any purpose of purchase. One little cluster of books brought back the memory of a grandmother's bookshelf, where *Queechy, Queed, The Garden of Allah* and *The Woodcarver of 'Lympus* all stood for a good many years as her books for reading just before sleep. I found a copy of *The Mistress of Shenstone*, and one of *The Rosary*, both by Marclay and both blatantly sentimental, with their heartbroken young ladies, their tragic heroes going blind, their haunting gardens and tear-stained pillows. Although that grandmother often laughed over her own predilection for such teary-eyed romance she was in fact as sharp and strong-minded a critic as anyone I have ever known. I held these volumes, bound in lavender and mauve, and felt a momentary glow of affection for them overtake me.

What is important about a book sale of course is the fact that the books are there and for sale. To one who visits such sales with more or less regularity, there are fascinating ups and downs in the availability of certain types of books. If records could be gathered concerning the appearance at rummage sales of specific titles and types of works, they would provide the grist for a veritable history of taste. It is evident, for example, when one browses among the juvenile titles for sale this year that the great splurge of interest in the F. W. Dixon Hardy Boys series, so popular in the late '40s and early '50s, has now subsided. I counted nearly fifty Dixon titles on one table, and there seemed to be no interest in them. And despite the fact that among serious book collectors old Frank L. Baum Oz books are of continuing interest, I saw three such works, all in good condition, pass unnoticed. In all honesty, they were not first editions, yet almost any of the early editions of "Oz" can be expected to draw attention. It is a relief, incidentally, to report that the last of the Elsie books have apparently gone to some fate which they deserve, since ten years ago they seemed a glut at every book sale. This year I saw only one Elsie. It was battered and stained and it lay forlorn and untouched under a pile of other girls stories.

Book dealers often manage to sweep away the more interesting titles offered at these sales before the ordinary reader has an opportunity to find them. Still, good items remain. At this particular sale I noted, for example, that John Kendrick Bangs and James Whitcomb Riley were left untouched. A full set of the Rollo books was sitting apparently unnoticed and offered at a convenient price. John Galsworthy, too, was ignored, even though he is now moving back into his own and no doubt will soon become a matter of bidding interest in future marketplaces.

Continued interest and enthusiasm for some authors are apparent in the absence of their books at such sales as these. The wildfire interest among college students for fantasy may be observed in the failure to appear of such items by, among others, Tolkein, Charles Williams, C. S. Lewis, Mervyn Peake and Charles Eddison. Along this line, where a few years ago works by George MacDonald and such romantic fantasists as Lord Dunsany and the wilder Machen, all appeared with dismaying regularity in the book sales, today they are hardly to be found except in battered and tattered copies with broken spines and missing pages.

To the reader whose interests are limited to what is new, such sales as I have recently visited hold little enough interest. But to us omnivorous and eclectic readers who were unable to buy books when we were young, the opportunities provided in these accumulations of publications of the last half century or more are welcome indeed. I returned home last evening laden with such a parcel of books as, when I was young, would have seemed nothing short of miraculous. For a few quarters and a few dimes I upgraded three or four small collections that are of particular interest to me. I brought back with me at least two authors new to me, who appealed to me from the mobbed tables as I surreptitiously scanned a dozen pages or so, while other book hunters pushed around me. I took one of these discoveries to bed with me, and read for an hour or two. As I grew eye weary, my eyes caught a passage that has continued to haunt me. At the top of a page I read, "One of the truths of the play [Richard the Third] is a very sad one, that being certain is in itself a kind of sin, sure to be avenged by life." I paused to let that sentence sink in. Next I glanced out of the window at the foot of my bed, and saw the heaviest fog of the season gathering along the street below. Then I fell asleep.

Letters from Anagnostes Solitarium,
May, 1969

Books as Treasures

It is a paradox that there are books which are not really meant to be read. For what purpose, one may well ask, would a printer lay down his columns of type with such painstaking care if he did not intend the resulting work to be read. Yet a great many books have been issued not to be read rather as a means of honoring the work thus issued. Other books, especially those to be found in the class known as incunabula, doubtless were intended to be read, but now have become so rare or so honored as to make them unreadable.

Once, years ago, a breathtaking exhibition was mounted by the J. Pierpont Morgan Library to honor an anniversary of the art of printing and as a chance to display some of the Morgan Library's richest possessions. In that exhibition was a carefully guarded case containing two of the rarest volumes in the history of the book. Leaning close above the case, one's eyes were dazzled by the noble columns of a perfect copy of the Gutenberg Bible and close beside the Gutenberg lay the only known copy of the world's first book printed with movable type, the so-called Constance Missal. The latter's type face, obviously an earlier working of the more perfect Bible face, seemed crude and a little unfinished. Yet there was a dignity and power about the balanced lines of print, which made one feel sure the type used here had been the product of the same genius's hand. Now these two honored books are not certainly intended to be read. One's eyes, gazing down upon their pages, are not greatly tempted to decipher the print they contain but instead to contemplate them as sublime works of art.

In the Huntington Library in San Marino, California, one may see the lovely Ellesmere *Chaucer* manuscript. Here there is a somewhat different reaction in which a combination of the handsome script, the delicate illumination and marginalia and the music of Chaucer's lines all add up to something that takes the breath away. The manuscript need not be read, for its contents are available in common print, but it gives delight as an artifact and token of Chaucer's greatness.

Recently at Evergreen House, the Rare Book Library of Johns Hopkins University, a rich display was mounted which included some of the finest works of five centuries of printing. One case held an example of each of the four first folios of Shakespeare, all in splendid, tall copies. These are not to be read, except perhaps by scholars, and yet in the seeing they somehow give the visitor a feeling of being in direct touch with the Bard of Avon's own exciting times.

In another case there lay the ornately decorated pages of William Morris's Kelmscott Press edition of Chaucer's work. Its bold Chaucer type and intricately woven woodcuts make some pages painfully black, so black indeed that they make the book in a way unreadable. This work represents of course Morris's pre-Raphaelite notion of what the world of Chaucer was like. That it fails for some to do so is perhaps as much due to the boldness of the typeface as to the overly ornate woodcuts, with their long-lined figures and disturbing delicacy. Yet the Kelmscott *Chaucer* stands as one of the most beautiful books ever printed, admired for the completeness of its concept and the perfection of its printing.

There are, resting here beside me, two books, or rather, six, each a three-volume edition of Sir Walter Scott's works, one of *Ivanhoe* and the other of *Quentin Durward*. Plainly printed, in clear, readable type, these volumes were certainly intended to be read, and that they have been read is attested to by the poor battered spine of each and every one of them. But today they are not to be read. Rather they are to be seen as milestones in English literature—first editions to permit the observer to see what Scott works looked like when first offered to the world. These physically all but exhausted volumes stand bravely here, evidence in their broken bindings and with the slightly darkened edges of their pages, of the hours of joyous adventure and romance they have given for 150 years! This *Ivanhoe* was published in Edinburgh in 1820. Each three-volume set represents across a century and a half the legacy of one of the greatest of romancers of all time, and humbly offers him the kind of immortality that only the printed page seems truly capable of doing. One's fingers tremble a little, turning the lovely pages with their marching lines of print.

Across the room, standing sedately on a shelf is the three-volume first edition of Thomas Hardy's *The Dynasts*. Its print is undistinguished, its binding the common green buckram so often used by American publishers at the turn of the twentieth century. It is here on my library shelves for two reasons: first, because as a Hardy first edition it stands as a monument to its author's greatness, and, second, because its poetic drama sears the consciousness of every reader. Christopher Morley, it is to be remembered, caused Roger Mifflin in *The Haunted Bookshop* to say that, "If every man could be forced to read *The Dynasts* and made to comprehend its meaning, there would never be another war."

The praise accorded lovely books is always outweighed by their loveliness.

Letters from Anagnostes Solitarium,
January, 197

From Bibliomania to Bibliophobia

There is nothing particularly new in a predilection for the collecting of books. People in every age collected, sometimes compulsively, copies of the writings of others. These harvesters of the written and printed word are blessed with an almost limitless supply of material, and so it is no surprise that specialization flourishes. Some collectors, like the Duc de Bury, collect books for the beauty of their format. Others, like Duke Humphrey, whose gift of his library to Oxford University marked the beginning of its great Bodleian Library, collected "ideas" rather than books in the mere physical manifestations. Still others collect books that are, in one way or another, related to some person, place or time. I know a man who has set for himself the considerable task of acquiring all of the important books published in a single decade. Another seeks out every book mentioned in novels, a hobby requiring discretion, since many such books are themselves fictional.

It is both interesting and amusing to contemplate the vocabulary which has grown up about these varied collecting interests. It is noteworthy in this connection that book collectors are hard put to it to define some of the terms used to describe their activities and proclivities. A slender pamphlet came to my hand recently in which a sterling but unsuccessful attempt is made to distinguish between classes of book people. This is W. J. Van B. Pipp's collection of three essays that appeared in 1943 under the general title *The Atrocities of Book Collecting and Similar Afflictions*. Pipp says:

> The difference between Bibliographers, or Lovers of Books, and Bibliophagi, or Collectors of Books, is but one of degree and is seldom distinguished. Men may love books without collecting them, as they may love women without marrying them. However, in these days of slipshod thinking and loose terminology, the significance of Bibliophagi has been forgotten and we collectors are all designated as Bibliographers—and as such we are content to remain. Indeed few of us are fit to be called Bibliophagi—and I know not a single individual who is worth of the highest title of all (as indicating the greatest love of books)—a Bibliopegist.

Interesting, but Pipp has missed on three counts. At least a half dozen dictionaries agree that a bibliographer is an expert in bibliography, a compiler of bibliographies, a lister of books. A bibliographer is likely, thought not necessarily, a lover of books; there are other ways of defining the term "bibliographer." A bibliophage may indeed be a "collector of books," but is first and foremost an "ardent reader of books," in fact a bookworm. And finally, a bibliopegist, albeit often possessed of the "greatest love of books," is simply a bookbinder.

Even an abridged listing of the vocabulary of the world of the book collector convinces one of an astonishing spectrum of feeling among these often erudite people. The hero of *The Bondage of Ballinger*, whose life was literally destroyed by his passion for books, was a victim of bibliomania, an illness which turned him into a bibliolator, a man whose very soul was given to books. Another book collector's illness is described as bibliokleptomania, bringing to its victim the distinction of being a biblioklept, the compulsion to steal books (sadly a not uncommon disease). There have been cases, moreover, in which the biblioklept's difficulty assumes an extreme form called biblioclasm. In this the destruction or mutilation of books takes place. Practitioners, among them bookburners and such, are known as biblioclasts. Misers sometimes become bookpeople. There bibliotaphs tend to gather great numbers of books and lock them away, gloating, one imagines, over their beauty or monetary value. And then, of course, there is the bibliophobe, the person who hates and distrusts books and all that they represent.

A host of mouth-filling words are employed to describe others who are closely associated with books. The bibliograph is one who writes books; the bibliognost is one versed in the knowledge of books, which probably means that this person knows much about books as physical objects; the bibliosoph is one who simply knows about books; and another word for librarian is bibliothecary! If one has a friend who reads to the exclusion of all else, he might be called a bibliophagist, one who devours books.

A new kind of librarian has appeared in recent years. This person calls himself or herself a bibliotherapist, that is, one who looks upon the practice of reading as an ameliorative adjunct to other forms of therapy.

A final term describes an odd practice that perhaps is not truly a literary pursuit. It is bibliomancy, or divination by means of a book, a sort of semi-literary water-witching. In bibliomancy a book, especially the Bible, is opened at random to some verse or passage, which is then used to foretell the future, to determine a course of action or to judge as good or evil some particular act. Do you remember the pages in Hugh Lofting's *The Voyages of Doctor Dolittle* where the good doctor and his young assistant let an atlas fall open, and place at random the point of a pencil on the open page to determine that their voyage is to take them to Spidermonkey Island? I myself have taken part in an adult game in which in a similar manner a book would be opened three times and a pencil point placed on a random word, and when the three words have been thus chosen, they were to be combined, either into a single sentence or into a story in which they were crucial words.

Book collecting is, despite Pipp, scarcely an atrocity; the concocting of biblioterms may be.

Letters from Anagnostes Solitarium,
May, 1970

Book Shops

When I was young, my family had the pleasant custom of going at least once a year to Chicago, which in those days was to me a place of great excitement and pleasure. There was the Field Museum on the lakefront, where one could spend days and weeks exploring the past. There was the Rosenwald Museum, brooding in a park close to the University of Chicago's sprawling campus. There one could see a wide-angled picture of the world's technological development, explore a coal mine beneath the city's streets or see a grisly display of human anatomy in the medical section. But there was one palace of pleasure to which I was always most eager to go. On the fourth floor of the elegant Marshall Field store at the corner of Randolph Street and State Street was to be found what was called the bookstore which to my young heart represented a clear reflection of heaven. It is today, in this modern age, not quite the same, being a book department of much more mundane nature. But in those other days, it presented to the wide-eyed wonder of a young boy a vast and shining array of all the wisdom, all the literary graces, all the crescendos and nuances of the symphonies of reading that the world could supply. And this was not all. It was staffed by men and women who were blessed with a miraculous capacity for knowing when a person wanted only to be left alone to pore over the tables, to browse along the weighted shelves and for knowing, too, exactly when to come to the visitor's assistance. I got to know two or three of those bookish people very well, and on each visit would seek one of them out for a half-hour's joyous conversation, a half-hour from which I inevitably emerged with an armful of books.

I wonder where those book people have gone. The new people are fine, no doubt, but scarcely of the bookish nature of their predecessors. On the few recent occasions when I have found myself in that book department, I have been aware that the people there are not primarily book people, as formerly had been the case but in fact salespersons. The old staff took the time to share their knowledge and enthusiasms with the customer. They were people with a passion for reading and for sharing that passion with others. The new people, bookish or not, lack the time and energy perhaps to offer such attentions. The cash registers must ring, or the department is losing money.

It is a sadness to me to see books merchandized, to use a good commercial term, but evidently our day and age require this. It is old-fashioned of me, I am sure, but books in my opinion are too precious to be treated as a mere commodity. Ruskin expresses this view eloquently. In describing what a book is, he says:

> This is the place of true knowledge which his [the author's] share of sunshine and earth has permitted him to seize. He would fain set it down forever; engrave it on rock if he could; saying, "This is the best of me; for the rest I ate, drank and slept, loved and hated, like another; my life was the vapour, and is not; but this I saw and knew; this, if anything of mine, is worth your memory.

The significance of this statement is of course that a book is a reflection of the spirit that produced it. There are implications in that statement that ought to be heeded by book people. These are, first, that book people, librarians and booksellers, among them, ought to treat their books with the care that any precious item warrants. And, next, that placing a book in the hands of a reader, particularly a new or inexperienced reader, is a huge responsibility, as it has the potential of affecting the reader's life for good or ill. The game of putting the right book in the right hands at the right time is clearly not without its own peculiar dangers. The true book person is always willing to risk them.

Letters from Anagnostes Solitarium,
February, 1976

Book Hunting

There are times when, in the happily endless search for materials to enrich any given library, the librarian has an opportunity to visit a private collector's home and personal library. Such opportunities provide experiences that are usually exceedingly happy but sometimes touched with real sadness. I, for one, never am happy about finding myself face to face with a bookman who because of some misfortune is forced to dispose of his personal book collection. But there are other times when the opportunity to explore a book collector's private collection is provocative, rewarding and filled with real pleasure.

A friend who has notified me of more than a few private book collections recently found another for me. The experience that ensued was highly pleasant. This friend and I went to an ancient but well cared for house that was built against a mountainside and looked out across the Delaware River toward the little community of Frenchtown, New Jersey. The rooms were fine and high-ceilinged and the walls were for the most part lined floor to ceiling with shelves of books. The furnishings were simple, but charming in the nineteenth century style. But it was not the physical aspect of the rooms that made them impressive. It was that they were pervaded by a presence, despite the absence of the owners. These rooms were rooms where people had lived; these were rooms that were full of a warm and a cultivated atmosphere. It was when I had begun looking at the long rows of shelved books that the reason for my awareness of the presence inhabiting those rooms became apparent. On the shelves were books that had obviously been read, lovingly handled, gleaned of their ideas. They were books from all over the world. There were novels, biographies, histories. And in those I took down I invariably found notes in a neat handwriting that suggested "conversations" between these books and their owners. Left to myself, I wandered into what had been the library and stood quietly for a moment, looking about me, and there again I felt the presence of those people who lived there, enjoying the peace of the fine old house. Upstairs in a bedroom there were more shelves, and the books that were the bedside companions of the house's owners revealed again something of the kind of people they were. These people had not produced books, as writers or publishers; but they had lived with books throughout their lives, and this had somehow produced an aura of richness and culture that suffused their surroundings.

My friend had, a few years earlier, driven me to Princeton, to examine in another empty house a fascinating collection of books concerning world expositions that had taken place in the latter part of the nineteenth century and the early part of this era. I was struck during that afternoon's visit again with a sense of knowing something of the man who had brought these books together. Certainly it was his interest and spirit that had given point and unity to this collection of illustrated books. And there was something else. Was it simply that I knew the collector was seriously ill, or was it this compounded with sympathy that his need at this point in his life for money was greater than his ability to hold together his marvelous collection?

A different kind of experience came several years ago when an elderly farmer in the county where I lived invited me to come to his farm, which he was breaking up, to appraise and perhaps buy what he called his library. I arrived at what was a rickety old farmhouse and was shown a scramble of tattered and cheap editions that the farmer thought might have value because their title pages showed publication dates of 1895 and 1900. It was difficult for me to tell him that his library was not worth anything at all. Before I left, however, I noticed an untidy pile of newspapers and pamphlets in a corner of his kitchen, and asked if I might look at what was there. He agreed without enthusiasm. I picked up a handful, and out dropped a thin, twenty-page pamphlet, with a dirty, peach-colored paper cover. My hand shook as I picked it up, for I had seen one such pamphlet several years earlier. It turned out to be the fourth known copy of a booklet entitled *Memoirs of an Old Settler* by Christian Cackler. This is one of the rare, first-hand accounts of the earliest years of the pioneers in the Old Northwest. Cackler's pungent descriptions of his troubles with the Indians in northeastern Ohio are classic. His account of the leap across the Cuyahoga River by Brady at the head of pursuing Indians was the seed from which grew a whole family of accounts of escapes made good by leaping rivers. The farmer was disbelieving of the value of the little pamphlet that he had considered mere wastepaper. I was delighted of course to have been able to save from destruction a precious item of pioneer history.

Letters from Anagnostes Solitarium,
April, 1976

What Collectors Collect

Collectors, if not totally idiosyncratic in their collecting interests, nevertheless tend to develop idiosyncrasies. A lawyer of my acquaintance collects defense lawyers' winning statements that are unusually imaginative. Another lawyer collects admonitions to the jury by judges in trials. I have heard of a dentist who amassed a fine collection of "five point molars" that he himself had extracted. I know more than one professor who have collections of ingenious responses by students to examination questions. (I have a favorite student answer of my own. Asked to identify Assurbanipal, one of the earliest librarians, the student replied that Assurbanipal was an "association of urban and municipal libraries." He almost received credit.) But among bookmen and book collectors—and let us add librarians—idiosyncracies seem to reach new heights of both variety and imagination.

Book collectors especially appear given to bizarre ideas. I know a man who collects old books not for themselves but for objects he finds inside them. His finds have included letters, photographs, the occasional one or five dollar bill, locks of hair, ladies' handkerchiefs, a silk stocking, a news clipping telling of Lindbergh's flight and on and on. His collection contains several hundred volumes picked up in secondhand bookstores, auctions and public sales about the city where he lives.

Another collector friend collects books for the interest of their first paragraphs. This particular collection seems to me to have some merit in that it involves the collector in a small way in the business of critical evaluation. A friend of his, inspired by what the other was doing, has drawn together a delightful collection of novels and short stories in which the opening paragraphs tell of the arrival of the hero, always in the midst of a raging blizzard or pounding rainstorm, at the welcoming doorway of an inn or farmhouse. His collection is somewhat extended to include such yarns as *The Seven Keyes to Baldpate* and *The Sire de Maltroit's Door*.

Other collectors are interested in bindings. This interest can extend from trade of various sorts to those using rich leathers and other materials of high quality to highly specialized bindings that match the subject matter of the book or the nature of its production. There have been, sad to say, examples of books having been bound in human skin which, when used in this way, is apparently rather like high quality pigskin. I have just recently seen a book bound in zebra skin, quite a lovely thing in its way. Various woods, well polished and chosen especially for their beautiful grain, make splendid boards with which to cover books.

I know a collector whose interest is in mystery and detective stories, of both classic and non-classic quality. His collection is arranged according to the kind of instrument used to bring about death, and any special circumstance in which death occurs as, say, in a locked room, through the bite of a poisonous snake, by means of voodoo, etc. His large collection has given him information which, if he put it into practice, would make him a formidable opponent for such as Hercule Poirot or Lord Peter Wimsey.

Books of all sorts are of course collectible. I would suggest that an interesting sort of collection could be built round the sizable group of stories showing the evil influence of books upon their owners. Even as the Hope diamond has carried with it throughout its history a powerful curse, so have certain books seemingly created serious problems for their owners. There are those stories of people who have lost their souls in the business of gathering books. There are stories concerning ways people have used books to gain advantage over others. There are books in which coded letters and words result in death or loss of some kind. And so on, a hundred fold.

There is nothing really unusual or sinister in the concentrating of a collecting interest, whether the object collected is books or something else, into a narrow range. This is simply part of the game, and if it lends an added piquancy to the proceedings, that is all to the good. And book collecting of course is a great game. It produces for those who engage in it pleasure, excitement, competitive zest and sometimes outright acquisitiveness and greed. Books draw out the best in some people, and the worst in others. It is a paradigm of living. And it will endure.

Letters from Anagnostes Solitarium,
May, 1976

Disposing of Collections

"What shall I do with all the books I have gathered over the years?" This is a question often asked of librarians, and unfortunately the answer is not always as easy as it might seem to be. Some random comments, then, concerning this question. To begin with, not every collection of books has value, and not every collection is a welcome gift in a library or anywhere else. There are some things that can be said, however, about what might be done when one wishes to unburden oneself of one's books.

Despite the disclaimer just made, any gathering of books that represents an individual reader's special interest must be said to have value, if for no reason other than that the collection reflects the mind and spirit of the person who put it together. And the more complete a representation of that interest, the greater the value that attaches to the collection. Therefore, there is an advantage if the subject of the collection is not too large or scattered, as completeness is then attainable or at least within the realm of possibility. One's books may, for instance, form a collection that can be considered as relatively complete in terms of, say, their literary, historical, or critical contents. Or they may be complete in that they represent an author's total output or all of the first editions of a certain class of work. The possibilities are about endless. Collection, moreover, may have special value because of the rarity of certain of the items in it.

When the time comes to dispose of the collection, however, a number of matters must be noted. Having gathered the collection, and presumably read it in the process, the collector becomes an authority of sorts in that he or she has acquired along with the books some special knowledge concerning them. In preparing to dispose of the collection, this special knowledge should be put to use, and perhaps the best way to do this is in preparing a statement as to how the books were gathered, where they were obtained and what their purchase price was. The next step might be to determine a likely new home for the collection. There is a steady flow of private book collections into academic and public libraries, and so the possibility of sending it to a library should be considered. Book collections often wind up of course in the book market. Some go to bookstores, and some are sold at auctions. The private sale of books to a bookdealer makes possible the obtaining of a figure relatively near the market value of the books, as the dealer's offer, in the case of an important collection anyway, will not be too much below market price. Selling at auction, on the other hand, represents a risk as the price obtained in this way depends on several variable factors, among them the time of the sale, the presence at the auction of persons interested in the titles being offered and the skill and interest of the auctioneer. I have seen, for example, practically identical copies of the same book sold for $300 at one auction and for $50 at the next. And of course one has to realize that a percentage of the sale price is claimed by the auction house.

If the collection is to be given to a library, there are a few things to keep in mind. Very seldom is it possible for a library to maintain a gift collection intact, as this entails much expense and the setting up of special arrangements. In most instances in which maintenance of identity is desired, it is ordinarily sufficient to use a bookplate with the donor's name on it.

Another concern has to do with the appraising for tax purposes of gift books. It is not proper for a receiving library or its head to provide such an appraisal. It is, indeed, illegal to do so, although it may on occasion be permissible to suggest to a donor what the fair market price of his or her gift might be. The suitability to a library of a profferred collection must, as already suggested, be taken into account. It would be wasteful, of course, to give a specialized collection to a library where such material would not be used; and such a gift might, moreover, exceed the abilities of the staff to process it. On the other hand, even a deeply specialized collection might not contribute much to the holdings of a large research library, although the likelihood is that it would bring at least something that could be used. The point is that the donor should choose with great care the library to which his or her collection is offered.

The collecting of anything—books, paintings, coins or stamps—almost inevitably turns into an intensely personal concern, and so guidelines on how to proceed are for the most part by way of generalities. A few suggestions may, however, prove useful, especially if books are what one is collecting. It is useful in collecting books, for instance, to choose the subject or focus of the collection in such a way that completeness is an attainable goal. Next the books chosen should be in the best copy of the best edition one can locate. The added expense of opting for the best will more than be repaid in the long run. If the collection is an author collection, it might be rounded out with association material, that is, material relating to the author, including biographies, autographed copies, correspondence and so on. Another kind of collection is one in which all of the editions of a given title are gathered together. These suggestions are so obvious as to be banal but they are offered in the hope that they might keep the collector from wasting his or her money and time in irrelevancies.

I would like to suggest, finally, that one's collection ought to represent a personal reading interest or at least an intellectually appealing interest. Anyone can collect a roomful of books, buying them "by the yard," but the one thing that gives the collecting of books its special flavor and appeal is that the resulting collection embodies the collector's zest and enthusiasm for his or her subject.

Letters from Anagnostes Solitarium,
June, 1976

A Book Mystery

It is always an adventure for a librarian to be called upon to look into the possibility of purchasing a collection of books from an individual who has built a collection round some personal or professional interest. And at times the adventure assumes astonishing proportions. One such occasion came my way on a cold, blustery March day.

A phone call reached me from the executor of the estate of a prominent lawyer in a northern city. It was made clear to me that this lawyer's collection was first to be appraised, and then disposed of to the best possible advantage. A friend and I presented ourselves at the front door of a "doge's palace," a great pile of stone and brick, austere and imposing at the same time. We rang the bell and, after a long wait, found ourselves being peered at by somebody through a tiny door which had opened in the heavy oak door itself. We stated the reason for our call, and after more waiting, during which we heard chains being unhooked and locks being turned, were invited in by the servant who then stood before us full revealed at last. We entered to find ourselves in an entry hallway that opened into an imposing inner room. To our right was what appeared to be a sitting room, more like an empty museum display room than anything else. There was not a book in sight, and when we again stated the reason for our visit, the servant beckoned us to follow him to a shadowy corner of the sitting room. In that corner was a heavy iron circular staircase leading downward. As we reached the staircase, the silence of the room was shattered by hoarse screeching and an outpouring of epithets. We turned toward the sound and discovered at a balcony railing a woman with long, white hair streaming over her shoulders who pointed a scrawny finger at us and continued her abusive shouting. In a moment a nurse appeared beside her, and led her, protesting, out of sight.

Somewhat unnerved by this interruption, we descended the staircase as it curved downward into a half-darkened room as large and imposing as the one which we had left above. It was a room some fifty feet in length, and half as wide, lined floor to ceiling with shelves of books, save that separating each five or six sections of shelving were full-length, life-sized portraits of the lawyer who had built the collection. He apparently was interested only in life-sized portraits of himself, or reflections of himself in tall mirrors. We began to look over the shelves, and it became apparent almost immediately that this was no real collector's library. It was, in fact, the kind of decorator collection purchased by the yard. Sadly there were no titles worth even passing concern. At the end of an hour, we had determined that there was nothing of interest either for the collector or the casual buyer. I noticed, however, at the end of a shelf close to one of the portraits, a little book of poetry which I pulled off the shelf to examine more closely. I was about to return it to its place when I noticed in the wainscoting near the portrait an ivory button. I called it to the attention of my friend, and after a moment's discussion we decided to push the button.

There was a creaking sound, and very slowly the portrait and the wall behind it began to swing slowly outward, revealing, to our surprised eyes, a room perhaps twelve by fifteen feet, again lined entirely with bookshelves. A light switch close by the doorway lit the room dimly, and now our surprise became one of distaste, for we quickly discovered that the room contained a sizable collection of pornography—multiple copies of some of the classic works, many of them extra-illustrated. Our dilemma lay in the fact that we had no idea whether we were even supposed to have discovered this collection. It should be said that at the time such a collection would have been difficult to dispose of through regular book channels. We were in the 1950s, and the social attitudes of that time did not encourage a taste for literature of the sort. After some discussion, we decided that we would close the secret room again and wait to see what might occur.

We hardly closed it when we heard the circular iron staircase creaking as someone descended into the room where we stood. A huge man appeared, and almost stumbled across the carpeted floor toward us. He spoke in a deep, rumbling voice that was almost impossible to understand. He continued to mutter and gesture, but at last shrugged his shoulders and slowly moved back up the staircase, obviously drunk. We were to learn that he was the son of the lawyer whose books we had been examining, a recluse who had hardly left the house for fifteen years.

We talked for a moment, trying to determine what we should do, and my friend suggested that if there were one room, there might be another, and so we searched, and after some trouble located a second ivory button. When it was pushed, again one of the portraits moved outward and behind it was another secret room with another special collection of books in it. This time, however, the books were jewel-like rarities. There were fine copies of first editions, mostly of the nineteenth and early twentieth centuries; there were pleasant association copies, many autographed; there were spectacular bindings, at least half a dozen with jewels in them. We discovered more than a dozen books with fore-edge paintings and several volumes with gauffered edges. One volume was a late fifteenth century work, and there were two rows of Elzevir publications. In short, it was the sort of collection that we had been known as a bibliophile of distinction. But again we were puzzled as to whether we had been intended to find this secret cache of rare books.

That mystery was not solved, but instead was deepened. We made, between us, an appraisal based on all that we had seen, turned it over to the executor and waited to see what would happen. But nothing happened. That entire book collection was to disappear without a trace. It never arrived on the open market, either at sales or in any kind of auction. Ten years after our visit, the house itself was first abandoned, and then torn down, to be replaced by a small apartment building. No one that we knew was even aware of the removal of the household belongings or the books. The widow died shortly after our visit; and the son was taken to an asylum, where he lived only a short time. And the books have not been seen since the day we made our strange and fruitless visit. The executor, when questioned, claimed to know nothing about their disappearance. We were paid for our appraisal, but beyond that there is no evidence that there ever existed the collection we had seen.

Letters from Anagnostes Solitarium,
May, 1979

When Is a Book Not a Book?

When is a book not a book? It must be said right at the start that the word "book" has different meanings for different individuals. Is a vellum scroll on rollers really a book? Is a bundle of inscribed palm leaves a book? Were the great stone slabs upon which the early Chinese incised characters books? Were the children's hornbooks of yesterday books? Such questions are not easily answered.

One of the excitements in book collecting is that in general a collection has no bounds whatsoever. There is a tale of a nineteenth century Prussian king who left his son a bequest of a set of books. These volumes bore in German the inscription "Posthumous Memoirs of the King, for his Son Alone." The pages of these books were not, however, ordinary pages, but were actually sheets of banknotes, representing the monarch's private fortune. Whether the tale is true or not, is it proper to say that this trove was made up of books?

It can be pointed out that a book may indeed be a book even though it has not literally been written. One such, perhaps one of the very few valid unwritten books, is James Lordan's *Colloquies*, a book that treats of English poets and poetry. This book, which appeared in 1844, was never written down but composed directly at the type case of Lordan's small printing shop in old Olmney, England. Similarly, the great American editor, William Allen White, often composed his editorials for the *Emporia Gazette* while standing at his type case.

To suggest the variety of unorthodox forms in which publications have been offered, we need only turn to The Umbrella Globe. This curiosity of more than a hundred years ago, was in fact a portable terrestrial globe of the world, printed on silk, and skillfully made on the umbrella principle. When this "umbrella" was opened, it became a globe with a circumference of fifty inches. Folded, it fit in a wooden box thirty inches long. It was patented and published, if that is the word, by John Betts, 115 Strand, London, 1840. Another globe of the world printed on silk was published in 1898. This one was smaller. It had a diameter of eighteen inches.

Some years ago I was shown a book in cast iron binding ornamented and, one assumes, made lighter in weight with an open work design. This book was a treatise on British coinage. There is at the University of Edinburgh a volume consisting of three iron leaves of oriental script held together by iron links. Perhaps, if the suggestion is forgivable, not the lightest reading in the world.

Books sometimes contain unusual information, and sometimes assume unusual shapes. In 1916, for instance, a book called *Facts about Georgia*, which extolled the products of that southern state, appeared in covers shaped like the map of Georgia.

Of interest for a different reason is a book devoted to the subject of dementia that was written, printed and bound by the inmates of a mental hospital in Stockholm, Sweden. One might suppose that this work had an authoritative text.

The material used in the production of books, of course, determines in many cases the nature and format of the published volume. The ancient Chinese excelled in bone carving, and numerous examples exist of works published in China in which the writing was incised or carved on bones. In Sumatra inscriptions on ivory are too numerous to be counted. Horn has been used in many parts of the world for the transmission of messages. The Arabs in ancient times scratched inscriptions on the shoulder blades of sheep. In Central and South America, the great circular calendar stone of the Aztecs is a book of sorts. The Mayan-inscribed monoliths there can also be regarded as books. An equally exotic book was made by the Incas in Peru of knotted, colored strings. Ivory and sharkskin, the stomach lining of unborn calves and snakeskin, these and many other materials have been used in the making of books. There is at least one case in which recourse was had to a multiplicity of materials in the recording of a single event. The Arctic expedition of Sir John Franklin carried with it on board the Assistance a printing press; and when the ship's stock of paper was exhausted, the expedition's story was continued on chamois leather, on shirts and in one instance on a blanket. A question might well be raised here: When that blanket was neatly folded and laid away with its printed message, was it part of a book?

Finally, it matters very little what material is used in putting a book together. The thing that does matter is that the book is actually created. That this is true is confirmed by the fact that one of the most satisfactory methods for the storage and dissemination of information is the book, and this remains true despite the advent of computer and laser technology. We need not quibble over what a book is made of nor over the format in which it appears. The fact alone that it exists more than makes up for any idiosyncrasies or lapses in its manufacture.

Letters from Anagnostes Solitarium,
May, 1981

SECTION V
LIBRARIES, LIBRARIANSHIP, AND THE FREEDOM TO READ

It may be said that in the history of libraries, in the biographies of great librarians, and in the discussion of most aspects of librarianship are lessons to be learned about collection development. These final essays of tribute, opinion, history and admonition reflect on what has been done and on what we ought to be doing.

Information Retrieval

It is a puzzle to me that people call themselves librarians who spend all their time slogging through the electronic morass called information retrieval. This condition, describable as computeritis, has created mischief that is going to be hard to counteract. And, because I look at what is happening with mixed contempt and despair, I have set myself the task of discovering just what the difference is between the old and trusted librarianship and that in which canned and automated data is resorted to first and foremost.

Now, information retrieval, a genuine if untrustworthy electronic wonder, involves itself with tiny units of information stored in great banks of electronic impulses which, when tapped, will return all it contains in an orderly (usually) and logical (usually) fashion. In order to insert data into the electronic bank, it is necessary to translate them from their traditional form into a kind of formula, and in the translation all that resembles the force and loveliness of words is lost. The bank contains but shreds of language, neatly snipped into bits and pieces, thoroughly dried and deftly set in ordered rows of electrical dots and dashes. To retrieve the wonders thus stored, a still more delicate and tenuous translation must occur, and in this process some astounding events take place. There is the story of the computer that had been fed every imaginable bit of information relative to the possibility of a World War III. A general, determined to ascertain the computer's capabilities, then asked it, "What about World War III?" The computer immediately replied, "Yes." The general, annoyed, boomed out, "Yes, WHAT?" The computer crackled alertly, "Yes, SIR." Now, this tale may be amusing, but it is also symptomatic of the general's failure to speak to the computer in its own language.

We have heard a great deal, too, of the marvelous capacities of even the most modest computers for the storing of information. It is probably true that a computer, costing in the neighborhood of a million dollars, might be expected to gulp up five million bits of data, hold them contentedly until their retrieval becomes necessary and then spew them out, on command, in countless pages of printed information. And depending upon the accuracy with which these data have been inserted in the computer in the first place, the retrieved data would be accurate and usable.

Computer addicts have always stressed the economy of space which their great machines can claim in the storage of information. But can one truly imagine a more economical storage space than (a) a normal, octavo book with something in the neighborhood of 100,000 units or bits of information in it, all of which are held in a container 8 1/2 inches by 5 1/2 by 1 1/4 in size; or (b) an encyclopedia such as the *Britannica*, with literally millions and millions of bits of information stored in a twenty-four volume set of books that takes up less than four cubic feet; or (c) a research library, such as the one at Harvard, with its untold billions of bits of information stored in no bigger a space than would be needed to keep a dozen million dollar computers well and happy? All of this seems to be begging for a return to the past, but that is not in fact the point. I wish merely to suggest that while computers have a place in our technological world, to imply that they will make books obsolete is to fail to recognize the nature of scholarship and to deny the great pleasure that is found in books as books.

A book is a mysterious compound of many things. In a well-written novel is the reflection of a creative person's thought processes. In a similar vein, the report of a scientific discovery gives substance to the scientist's thoughts that are presumably meaningful and special. And books of poems and plays quicken the senses and bring perspective to everyday matters. The computer merely yields, upon demand, what has already been stored in its coils. A book, a novel, a research study, a poem all enlarge the reader's capacities in ways that are strong, provocative and unarguable.

It was Robert Louis Stevenson who complained, "Books are good enough in their own way, but they are a mighty bloodless substitute for life." Yet Stevenson gave us *Treasure Island* and the *Master of Ballantrae*! Thomas Carlyle wrote once, "May blessings be upon the head of Cadmus, or the Phoenecians, or whoever invented books." Do you suppose that some youngster, in the age of computers which stretches on ahead of us, will murmur, "May blessings be upon the head of Edison, or General Electric, or IBM or whoever invented recording devices"?

Books are meant to be held in the hand, to be savored by the mind, to be loved and cared for in gratitude for the wonders they have brought us. One remembers Lionel Cabot, the best friend of Ulysses Macauley in William Saroyan's *The Human Comedy*. It was

Lionel who, wandering in the stacks of a library, said to his good friend, "Look . . . all of these . . . and these . . . Here's a red one . . . here's a green one . . . all these books . . . and every letter's different . . . every word's different . . . Books all over the place . . . I wonder what they say?" Just think of his excitement in that moment of discovery of the world of books! It reminds one of the story of the young man who asked of the librarian if he might enter the book stacks, which were closed. "I'd like," he said, "to carouse among the books a while." The young man could well have been absolutely right in the choice of words he made. According to the dictionary "to carouse" means "to revel, delight, and enjoy." Can one imagine oneself reveling among the shelves of microfilm reels? Or before the keyboard of a computer? But in a library, with shelves of red and green and blue and brown and purple books at hand, the revelry seems somehow appropriate.

Letters from Anagnostes Solitarium,
October, 1970

Books in Unexpected Places

I remember an enthusiastic librarian in a suburb of Cleveland, Ohio, who astonished those attending a regional librarians' meeting by suggesting that one of the prime missions of the public librarian should be to see to it that books were available in unlikely places. Her thesis was, very simply, that the public library building was one very excellent reason for poor circulation. It was her suggestion (and this was what shocked her colleagues) that librarians should establish small collections of books in such places as drug stores, hardware stores, grocery stores and public bars. To these she added a list of other unlikely places where books might be expected to reach an audience: bake shops, furniture stores, haberdasheries and beauty parlors. The idea is intriguing, and the fact that it has not actually been used serves as a commentary on the traditional mind of the librarian more than on the idea's impracticality. This idea, incidentally, is akin to the suggestion made in the 1930s by Christopher Morley, who wrote in his pleasing *Christopher Morley's Briefcase*:

> The railroads are said to have done well with their bicycling specials, winter sports specials, etc. Occasionally we have thought how agreeable it would be to stock up a baggage car with books and run a train into a siding somewhere where the passengers could spend a peaceful day simply reading. There would be, of course, complete dining and club car service, and those socially inclined could pick out their own kinspirits by noticing what books were being read. (Books in plain wrappers supplied to those who did not wish to talk.)

What a typically Morleyian idea! Other versions suggest themselves. There might be a reading journey across the continent, from one side to the other and return, on which eight or nine days of uninterrupted reading comfort were assured. A Mediterranean cruise could be for readers only which would provide the opportunity to read a dozen or so of those titles which one has always meant to read, but never found the time to do it. There could be an air flight to some Pacific isle, with a stopover long enough to read Boswell's *Johnson*! There could be a book lover's journey in October to Spitzbergen, where comfortable lodgings, good books, blazing fireplaces, food and drink would be supplied for a long winter of reading. The travel people would do well to look into such an idea!

To return to books in unlikely places, some amusing specializations might occur. If, for example, the books placed in drug stores were to be associated with the commodities on sale therein, the shelves might be seen to bear such titles as *Confessions of an English Opium Eater* or the adventures of that famous addict Sherlock Holmes. A hardware store would without doubt find a brisk sale for how-to-do-it books and handyman repair guides. Grocery stores would be a happy market for cookbooks and perhaps such titles as *Stalking the Wild Asparagus* and *Stalking the Blue Eyed Scallop*. A neighborhood pub could well stock copies of *The Lost Weekend* or of *The Face on the Barroom Floor* along of course with books of drinking songs.

A bakeshop library might include *The Taste of Honey* or John Hay's *The Breadwinners*. Or, better yet, one might discover there a copy of Lawrence Stallings' *The Doughboys*. A library collection suitable for a beauty parlor would include obviously a copy of *Vanity Fair* and *Scarlet Sister Mary* side by side with *Black Beauty* and perhaps *The Crazy Ladies*. And at the haberdasher's one might find *Monsieur Beaucaire*, *Yankee Doodle Dandy* or even Michael Arlen's *Green Hat*. A visit to a furniture store might uncover such titles as *Mr. Blanding Builds His Dream House*, or *A House in the Country*, or *The Fall of the House of Usher* as well as *A Man of Property*.

All of this aside, the idea is one that might very well be given consideration. The use of unorthodox methods in the circulation of library books is, for that matter, not new, and has proven worthwhile in the past. Some of the earliest libraries in America were the "package" libraries sent into Maryland and Virginia by Thomas Bray in the eighteenth century. Bray's packet libraries contained titles which that man of the cloth felt both suitable and appropriate to the colonies. That they circulated heavily and were much appreciated as they found their way into such unlikely places as the American colonial frontier is a measure of the soundness of the idea. The "rotating book collections' of northern England in the eighteenth century were in many cases placed in pubs and inns, and there is ample evidence that they were read and appreciated.

In the world of the academic library, experiments have been tried in which books were placed in small dormitory libraries, in fraternity houses and—let me whisper it—even in classrooms and administrative offices. And especially in the last two surprising places, use has often been more than casual.

That public librarian was right, of course. Reading need not be confined to a particular time or place. It is something that offers pleasure whenever and wherever it happens, and should be promoted with more verve and imagination than it now is.

Letters from Anagnostes Solitarium,
June, 1972

Computers

There have been few men in any century who could claim that they knew everything that there was to know in their own time. Plato, Socrates, Aristotle, each in his own way, might have been said to have possessed global knowledge. And whether or not they knew all that there was to know in their time, Benjamin Franklin and Thomas Jefferson applied so well what they did know that they certainly can be said to have dominated the thinking of their own time. In our own time, in this last quarter of the twentieth century, few men can be thought of as even knowing most of what there is to know in their own specific field of endeavor. Buckminster Fuller assures us that he knows all there is to know that is worth bothering about, but some would argue with this assessment. Arnold Toynbee lays claim to an enormous command of the details of history and philosophy, a claim that, unlike Fuller's, does not seem excessive. A startling example of a man who has digested terrifying masses of data in widely differing fields is Immanuel Velikovsky, the author of *Worlds in Collision* and other provocative books. Nevertheless, polymaths are few and far between, if in fact there are any at all. It is evident certainly that almost no one in our own time matches the description.

The totality of the world's knowledge, one can reasonably assume, exists in the form of manuscripts and documents of one kind or another, and is more or less available to everybody who wishes it in our public and private library holdings. The rub comes in producing without undue delay any piece of that information needed at a particular time. Librarians have always sought the sort of fingertip control of knowledge that would allow this. A first step in the right direction was taken when the clay tablets of the great library of Assurbanipal were roughly indexed so that each tablet could be found as needed. And a catalog was constructed of the great collections of scrolls and manuscripts in the Alexandrian library. In more modern times, the publication of the first bibliographies by German, French and English scholars brought some order to a situation that with the rapid increase in the number of books was become chaotic. It was, of course, not enough. One thing that helped significantly was the development in American libraries of the author-subject-title book catalog. Again, however, more needed doing.

And now there is the computer. Scholars everywhere are turning in droves to the computer which allows them to organize their data and retrieve them with unexampled efficiency. Unfortunately, computers too have their limitations. They keep accurate counts, they organize enormous bodies of similar and dissimilar data, but the subtleties of philosophy, the esthetics of the creative arts, the ramifications of the social studies are beyond them. And so we often find ourselves forced back in the position of having to ignore this marvelous invention and rely, as heretofore, on human ingenuity and brain power.

Scholarly endeavor may be aided by the computer, or it may not. Relying upon people, on the other hand, presents hazards of its own. Two instances come to mind. There was a remarkable professor of the romance languages whose teaching of language skills was less important to his students than what he imparted on the philosophy of communication. This professor had, during a lengthy career, written little—it was suggested that at the time of his death only about ten percent of his research findings were down on paper. All else was lost. The second instance concerns a postage stamp dealer. This man had spent forty years studying Asian countries, and had attained a considerable reputation as an expert in this field. Then he was killed in a plane accident, and once again, as in the case of the professor, a huge and irreplaceable body of knowledge was lost. One presumes that data blanked out in a computer's memory can be restored; knowledge in a person's head is of another order, and once lost is gone forever.

Now what is all of this leading up to? It is simply the long preamble to a short plea that books continue to be given the place in our lives that they so richly merit. If we are to have even the faintest hope of gathering, protecting and making available for the future the masses of information needed to interpret our present world, this must be done through the instrumentality of books. When all is said and done, books, as we know them, are far and away the most efficient means for the storage and retrieval of information, and are likely to remain so despite the computer's competition.

Letters from Anagnostes Solitarium,
January, 197

Libraries and Technology

The year that I was born was some nine years after the December when the Wright brothers launched their first successful aeroplane flight at Kitty Hawk. For another twenty years the flight of a plane across the skies of the city where I lived continued to result in a rush from the houses to the yards and surrounding field to watch, as the splendid thing thrust its weight against the pull of gravity and gave its pilot an hour or so of bird-like freedom in the air. My grandchildren now hardly spare a glance into the sky as tremendous jet planes boom overhead on journeys to what far part of the world. These same children have even become blasé about the flights into outer space and the dispatch of insect-like machines on probes of Mars and Venus and beyond. Such is our capacity to accept as commonplace and unexceptional the miracles that technology produces. Very little merits a second look these days. Things once considered mere dreams have achieved reality, and the impossible becomes a challenge.

Technological advances have brought about fascinating changes in the world of the librarian. Within my own experience a series of developments has occurred which constitute, in themselves, small miracles. And the impact of these developments upon scholarship has been so great as to make one wonder how scholars of the past were able to do anything at all that mattered. What is of particular note is that the developments I refer to have come within the space of relatively few years, between 1930 and 1973. Let me give a single example.

In the mid-1930s I was engaged in gathering a bibliography of materials relating to the life and work of Robert E. Lee. Through diligent search and frustrating hours of blind hunting, I had compiled a list of some 900 items. As I was determined that my bibliography should be annotated, it was necessary for me to examine each item personally. Of the 900 or so items on my list, more than 700 were in libraries and personal book collections in the state of Virginia. But the last 200 were harder to locate. For each item that I sought I prepared a typed postcard and reproduced it in 100 copies. These 100 copies were sent to 100 libraries where there seemed some possibility that a copy might be located. I remember that I sought a four-year run of a little southern literary magazine entitled *The Rose.* As the first mailing brought not a single response, a second mailing of 100 was sent to a wider circle of libraries in somewhat more remote states. Still no response. Finally, after a third mailing and a total of waiting time of more than four months, a response came in, an interlibrary loan was arranged, and after more than five months I held the fragile little volumes in my hand. Today such a search could be accomplished in less than a week, and sometimes overnight, through use of the telephone and of the bibliographical services available everywhere.

In 1933 I saw my first bit of microfilm, a foggy and somewhat besmudged photograph of a single page of a manuscript. It was shown to me with not a little astonishment by one of my history professors who declared it a wonder of our age. Eleven years later I watched as two American scholar librarians argued the possibility or not of a new development, microprint, in which a page of type would be microfilmed and then printed, through a sort of inverted microscope, on a sheet of sensitized paper. This process, its inventor claimed, would make possible the reduction of sixty pages of print to a card three by five inches! It was suggested that this process would make it possible to store literally thousands of volumes in the cubic space occupied by a single drawer of catalog cards. I shall not comment here on the weaknesses of this process, nor the reasons for them. What is important is that the process represented a tremendous step forward in the reduction of space required to store information. In less than ten years, through advances in the technology of film, the first examples of microfiche—microscopic "bits," in rough translation—made the microworld of film publication come true. In the production of microfiche it was possible to reduce to a piece of film approximately three by five inches in size in the neighborhood of 120 pages of print. But we were not through yet. The next development brought us ultrafiche, which makes possible the reduction of a thousand pages of print to a piece of three-by-five film. Thus the entire run of the *Atlantic Monthly,* reduced to ultrafiche, may be easily held between the thumb and forefinger! Moreover, a laboratory demonstration has shown that an entire King James version Bible, which has more than 3,000 pages, may be reduced to a bit of film 17 inches square. And experimentation goes on. A new type of film, known as colloidal film, which is grainless, that is, not hindered by the grains of silver nitrate found in normal film, will make possible reduction of printed material beyond even this point. It is not beyond the realm of possibility that whole books might sometime be placed upon the head of a pin. One supposes that when that time comes, a scholar might carry in a thimble or waistcoat pocket all of the printed material relating to his or her field of scholarship.

This is not to say, of course, that the book as we know it will become extinct. Such microfiche wonders are intended for the storage of information. But it is information that comes from books, and the convenience, portability and attractiveness of books, among other things, ensure their continuance.

Letters from Anagnostes Solitarium,
July, 1973

Humor in the Library

Humor in the library is often directed at the librarians themselves. The stereotype of the librarian is lampooned widely, despite efforts by the profession to show the falsity of the stereotype. But there are also many "in" jokes in libraries that the general public seldom hears. Some of these professional jokes come from the mechanics of keeping a library in proper running order; some are in the nature of comments on what are regarded as the idiosyncrasies of librarians; and some arise from confrontations between an unwary public and the professionalism of the service desk.

One amusing exchange occurred in an academic library in Virginia. A lady of the town appeared at the circulation desk saying that a friend of hers had recommended a book entitled *No More Desire.* A search of the card catalog produced no such title in the library's holdings, but a check in the circulation records revealed that the book in question was Victoria Sackville West's *All Passion Spent.* The lady was satisfied.

In a great public library the story is told of a young man who requested something called *The Red Sailboat.* No such title could be located. He then suggested, in succession, that he might be looking for:

The Scarlet Schooner
The Carmine Canoe
The Crimson Catamaran
The Cerise Steamship
The Rose Rowboat

And finally it dawned on the frustrated library assistant that what he wanted was *The Rubaiyat of Omar Khayyam.* This tale doubtless has been embroidered by younger generations, but it remains a tale that once was true.

Even the card catalog has produced its moments of amusement. A few years ago, at Duke University, the great card catalog contained an almost musical sequence of cards or one at least that formed a rudimentary little story all by itself:

Look
Look Away
Look Before You Leap
Look Homeward Angel
Look Never Backward

And there is the much repeated story of the despair of the head of the classification division at the Library of Congress who discovered that somebody had neatly assigned St. Augustine's *City of God* to the classification JS344 (municipal government by city manager).

When the splendid *Dictionary of American English* first appeared, it came out in parts. One every two or three months. The editors inadvertantly created amusement in the labelling of the first four issues. Part I contained the entries for words from A to Baggage, and the contents of the following issues were given as follows:

>   Part II   Baggage man to Baggage sale
>   Part III Baggage smasher to Butterfly
>   Part IV   Butterfly net to Corn

This made the first bound volume run from A to Corn. In the case of the prestigious Bibliographie de la France, a similar labelling risibility occurs. One of the volumes in this set proceeds from "Rock" to "Roll."

Libraries usually have restricted areas in which books of great value and others, often of a pornographic nature, are placed for safekeeping. These areas often have distinctive and highly appropriate names. The Bibliothèque National in Paris, for instance, refers to its area of shelving as *L'Enfer*; and a midwestern library in the United States, which occupied what had previously been a nightclub building, materials needing sequestering were stored in "The Icebox," a vast walk-in refrigerator in the old kitchen of the club. A more common designation for such a storage place is simply "The Cage." Some librarians of course say when asked about sequestered materials that they are "in the boss's office."

At another midwestern library, a special file of cards was kept at the circulation desk, each card bearing the peculiar way in which various faculty members would refer to books their classes would be using in a particular semester or year. One such professor's card read, "That set of purple books." The librarians knew well the titles of the books but could not convince the professor that, because of his regular assignment of the books, they had had to be rebound and so were no longer purple but had passed through at least three varying colors in the course of time.

Still another professor, determined one January that his students would learn to use the library properly sent the members of two of his classes to locate certain titles in the reference room. The students were asked not only to give the call numbers of the books but also to indicate "the direction in which you were facing when you located the book." The assignment might have been a success, except for one thing. Over the Christmas holidays the entire reference room had been reshelved. The best laid plans of mice and professors aft gang agley.

The humor of librarians is for the most part of the "in" variety, but is no less entertaining for that. Most librarians would agree that it adds spice to a day that is sometimes demanding and full of detail.

Letters from Anagnostes Solitarium,
March, 1974

The Coonskin Library

At the turn of the nineteenth century, as New England settlers began making their way into the Old Northwest, one of the most significant elements in their move was that they took with them a conviction that their children needed to be adequately educated. Among the first buildings that went up in the Old Northwest were simple schoolhouses; and where such buildings were not possible, the settlers made certain that space was set aside in some wilderness home or other for school purposes.

Wilderness schools were usually under the direction of clergymen, and as most of these had been educated at Harvard, they brought with them to the wilderness small libraries, which were made available for the use of the students under their supervision.

Libraries, as we know them at least, were non-existent until sometime after 1800, when at least three libraries that can be thought of as public libraries, were established north of the Ohio River between Marietta, Ohio, and Cincinnati.

One of these libraries, known as "The Farmer's Library," reportedly existed at Bellaire, Ohio, just west of Marietta on the Ohio River. Its collection seems to have been made up largely of pamphlets and text books relating to the arts of agriculture and animal husbandry. This library is known to have existed for a period of nearly thirty years, although no actual evidence of its ever having been located in a particular spot or building has been discovered. Letters from settlers in the area about Bellaire during the first thirty years of the century mention its usefulness, however, and references to it appear in the 1850s in Old Northwest newspapers. Aside from this, however, nothing is known. The Cincinnati Library appears to have catered largely to lawyers and clergymen, but since it was burned and its building and entire bookstock destroyed, including its records, nothing is known for certain about its purpose or use.

The most romantic and obviously the most successful of the three early libraries west of the mountains was founded in the little hamlet of Ames, Ohio, in 1802, and this one came to be known among librarians long after its closing as "The Coonskin Library." It seems that in the fall of 1801 a group of young men learned that a college or university was going to be founded at Athens, Ohio, possibly in 1803. These young men, eager to further their education, met one night in a log cabin in the great forest just east of Ames, Ohio. At that meeting they not only determined to apply for entrance to the newly proposed college, but they also discussed the need they had for books even before they went to college. And so was founded The Western Library Association of Ames, Ohio. Officers were elected, and a proposal made and agreed upon, that during the succeeding winter their group would hunt as usual to supply their families' needs, and that animal skins over and beyond those used by their families would be sold in common to acquire money for the purchase of books for the Western Library Association of Ames.

In the early spring, just before the breakup of ice in the rivers, members of the Association met once more and each young man tossed onto a heap of furs and pelts his contribution to the Association. Tom Ewing, one of the youngest of the members, was one of the last to appear. His contribution to the cause consisted of fifteen coonskin pelts. Hence the name eventually applied to the Association's collection of books.

The skins were packed carefully in watertight packages and turned over to Samuel Brown, who took them by pirogue and horseback to Pittsburgh, where they were sold for the sum of $75.65. Brown then continued on his way by canal boat and horseback to Boston where, after consultation with the Reverend Cutler, a library of seventy-five volumes was purchased. This library consisted of volumes of history, some literature, most of a religious nature, a half dozen biographies, some language texts, Latin, Greek, Hebrew and French, some grammars and a few geographies. An examination of the titles reveals that it was a formidable collection to expect teenaged boys to read, let alone enjoy. But it was to form the nucleus of a library that included several hundred titles before the middle of the century arrived. The records of the Association show that the books were read, not by one or two, but by most of the members.

Ten years after the founding of the Association, several of its original members had moved west to the old town of Dover, Ohio (its name was changed to West Dover in mid-century). These members took with them their share of the library's holdings, and with these books established the second public library (more properly proprietary library), known as the Library Association of Dover,

Ohio. This truly first library west of the mountains continued in existence until late in the 1850s, when the books were turned over to the son of one of this new Association's founders. This man, Cutler by name, took the little collection to Philadelphia in 1876, where it was displayed during the Centennial Celebration of the United States at the first meeting of the American Library Association.

Letters from Anagnostes Solitarium,
September, 1974

Edwin W. Willoughby

A good many years ago, during one of the interesting winter conferences of the American Library Association at the fine old Drake Hotel in Chicago, I attended a formal dinner where my companion and I found ourselves at a table with Edwin W. Willoughby, the famous bibliographer of the Folger Library in Washington. Willoughby was a congenial dinner companion and my companion and I spent the rest of the evening in conversation with him. Willoughby was a short, rather heavy set man, his ruddy face surmounted by a mane of steel gray hair and his eyebrows dark and lowering above bright blue eyes. He told us countless stories of his adventures in seeking out and acquiring for the Folger Library some of the treasures that make up its priceless holdings. One such story had to do with his rescuing of a somewhat battered copy of a Shakespeare first folio that he found being used in a London tavern as a dartboard. He paid for it on the spot, out of his own pocket, and carried it away with him into a rainy night, hugging it to himself under his overcoat. He told of other discoveries of Shakespeare-related materials as he mined the rich warehouses of London's booksellers down on the waterfront of the Thames. He was strangely prophetic, that evening in the late 1930s, saying that the vast riches of the city's used book trade were in perilous danger if there should truly be a war, and London should suffer the kind of air raids Germany was carrying out to the east of its own borders. I saw Willoughby a few years after the fire raids of the Battle of Britain, and he reminded me of our earlier conversation, and informed me of the total destruction of three of his favorite book lofts on the river. He mentioned also the death of Thomas Heffer, who had been a lifelong friend, killed as he struggled with a single hose to keep the roof of his warehouse from burning.

But my recollections of Willoughby are chiefly of pleasant times. I visited him more than once at the Folger, and his delight in showing off his treasures was one of the things that made the Folger come alive for me. He turned the Folger's cathedral-like atmosphere into that of a warm and inviting personal library, where the host was happy to pull breathtaking editions and manuscripts from the shelves and cupboards and speak in a quiet, casual way of their significance. On one occasion that I visited him there, he asked, after showing me a sheaf of Renaissance manuscripts he had just found in England, if I could not return the following day, promising that he would show me something then that would delight me. I agreed with alacrity, and the next day, on my return, he took me to a nearby study room where he had laid out on the long tables each and every one of the Folger's ninety or more first folios. He handled them lovingly, and pointed out many of their special points, turning the leaves with care, but obviously with excited pride, for he had been responsible for gathering the majority of this largest of all collections of first folios. It was an adventure for me unlike any other I have ever experienced in a lifetime devoted to libraries and books.

Willoughby did not limit his interests solely to Shakespeare, however. He had two other special interests. One had to do with a particular aspect of life in Shakespearean times. He would invite himself to colleges and universities to deliver an address that he took chuckling and inveterate delight in giving. This was a carefully prepared and documented talk on the medicine and surgery of Shakespeare's time. It was replete with every conceivable gory detail, which Willoughby dwelt on with relish. His audiences, however, shuddered as he drew out his descriptions of agonizing pain, but this only encouraged the speaker to produce further instances of the primitive state of medicine as practiced then.

His other big interest was in murder—not the genteel stylized kind of murder found in mystery novels, but in the real thing. In both Chicago and New York, and particularly in Chicago, he had visited the scene of every violent killing reported on in the press. At another Library Association dinner, on a bitter cold night in December, he appeared at our table dressed as we all were in a tuxedo, but wearing under his dinner jacket a disreputable gray wool sweater. He was utterly unconscious, or seemed to be, of the amused glances which were turned his way as he took his seat among us. But his conversation soon made us forget his appearance that evening, for he announced that he was going to take three of us afterwards on a tour of Chicago's murder scenes.

With the dinner over, we bundled into warm clothing and met him at the front door of the Drake Hotel, where he commandeered a taxi, and for the next four hours he directed the driver to street corners, back alleys, garages on side streets, and buildings, which we entered to inspect second or third floor rooms in which murders had occurred. He recounted in astonishing detail the numbers killed in three mass murders, described more varieties of death than we had ever known to exist, expounded upon the success of various "rides" upon which gangdom's enemies were taken. He knew every name, knew each murderer's specialty (and there were many, ranging from stabbing to garroting). He later told me that he had researched each of these murder scenes as thoroughly as he did any Shakespearean document, and his extensive knowledge was abundantly evident that evening, as we followed his lead, shivering partly from the cold and partly from the gruesome subject matter with which we were being regaled.

There is no way in which one can completely describe the richness of Edwin Willoughby's knowledge. His murder stories and his renaissance medicine were only sidelines, of course, and one of the great experiences for any librarian or scholar was to find himself with this great man, especially when he was in the mood to display his erudition and wit. With his death, the world of Shakespearean scholarship lost one of its greatest, most lively and endearing characters.

Letters from Anagnostes Solitarium,
October, 1974

The Pierpont Morgan Library

In the mid-1930s two or three of us who were graduate students in the School of Library Service at Columbia University amused ourselves by walking down the block off Madison Avenue to catch a glimpse of the Irish guards who were responsible for the security of the Pierpont Morgan Library. Those guards, easily identified by their black suits and bowler hats, marched solemnly round and round the building apparently without letup. The building itself was formidable, and in those days it was very difficult for any but a chosen few to use its hallowed reading rooms, or even to visit the marbled hall where stunning displays were shown of the riches that Morgan had accumulated in the throes of an unparalleled collecting career.

Then one day a librarian friend called to ask if I would like to see Morgan's reading rooms and perhaps also some of the behind-the-scenes activity. It was with an almost unbelievable anticipation that we rang the bell at the ornate bronze doors facing 36th Street, saw them swing open, and were met by one of the guards, without his bowler derby but still looking the part he played. Inside the entrance, we presented the credentials my librarian friend had obtained for us. These were examined and checked against a master file. A telephone call summoned the man who had invited us to the Morgan. His footsteps echoed as he crossed the rear entrance hall. His greetings were in hushed tones, and our replies in kind. The fact that we were in a great library-museum was evidenced by rich hangings adorning the walls and portraits and other works of art everywhere.

We were first led into the silent display room where we were shown cases filled with medieval manuscripts, each a perfect example of the period it represented, each richly illuminated and adorned with great colored initial letters and marginalia. Viewers bent over the cases like genuflecting worshipers. The silence of the room, the spectacular displays of manuscripts from all over Europe, the omnipresence of the guards, all bore down upon the amateur observer, and in a way made it difficult, if not impossible, to savor the wonders laid out there for one's appreciation. Three quarters of an hour of poring over these splendors of the past left one spiritually drained and incapable of any kind of intelligent response to what had been seen. It was rather like being forced to enjoy a half-dozen desserts at a sitting.

Next we were led into the great hall where every available piece of wall space was covered with screened shelves, reaching from the floor to an ornate ceiling that arched two mezzanine balconies. Half a wall was lined with great Bibles and four alcoves contained association copies of works by English and continental authors. Great atlases, tall and weighty, tiny duodecimo and sextodecimos sat quietly in their places. The whole of the high, arched hall was permeated with the scent of leather and the soft mustiness that old books give off.

Finally we were led by our host into one of the workrooms where scholar-catalogers delved into the provenance of the library's riches, where books in need of care and attention were seen to by silent, master craftsmen. We were left for a few moments in our host's office alone while he went into one of the vaults to bring back things he was sure would be of interest to us. A copy of *The Gold Bug*, bearing an inscription by E. A. Poe, was opened gently on the table before us, and a Poe letter, tipped in facing the title page, was read aloud. A black-letter Caston *Chaucer* was displayed for my own benefit for I had only just completed an advanced degree in medieval literature. But then the crowning piece, for me certainly, was laid out on the table before us. There before our eyes lay the manuscript of Keats's *Endymion*. For the first time in my life I suddenly caught a true vision of genius at work. The lovely, smooth flowing lines of the poem are deceptive in their grace and swift, powerful movement. The manuscript showed the agony of creation: whole lines and phrases, pairs of line and long passages were crossed out and replaced by something new, and more to the poet's liking. It was an experience that I have never forgotten and never shall.

Looking back, trying to sort out my first impressions of that great library, I find that now, forty years later, it was one in which appeared an admixture of delight, awe and resentment. The fact that one man, who may not have known precisely what he was creating, had been able to acquire for himself so many of the world's great literary treasures left me with an equivocal sense of the fitness of such a happening. I could not then, and I cannot even yet, feel that those books should not be more readily available for viewing and use by the public.

Letters from Anagnostes Solitarium,
April, 1975

Conversations and the Freedom to Read

In the somewhat questionable intellectual atmosphere of these times, one of the arts that has all but disappeared is that of conversation. It is rare nowadays to find oneself taking part in the kind of conversation that alerts and sharpens the mind. Good conversation is lost in the cacophony of modern-day chitchat. An example of what I am trying to suggest occurred a few days ago when three of us over luncheon were attempting to dissect some of the underlying causes of the low spirit of modern comedy. The discussion started out energetically enough, but it was apparent in only a matter of moments that this was no conversation at all but instead a mere three-part series of unrelated remarks. Sad to relate, none of us was listening to what the others were saying. Each wanted only to score a point, whether or not it was sensible or relevant.

As a young man, when it occurred to me that I was going to spend my life in the academic world, that living in that world would mean long winter evenings, with feet close to a cheerful fire, and good friends with whom to converse, argue, debate. Such intimate meetings, I was sure, would be spontaneous things, in which a question or a moment would be followed by contented responses and careful evaluations of one another's ideas. That dream, alas, was short-lived. I discovered early on that academe is full of divisive elements. One of the biggest is the confusing rigamarole of academic specialization, which draws one into the closely defined circle of his or her own discipline, where informal, desultory talk is seldom engaged in, and in fact is often regarded as a frivolous waste of time. The academic world, then, is in some respects an oddly lonely place in which it is the exception rather than the rule for, say, physicists and literature specialists to find themselves conversing together freely.

The academic who devotes himself or herself wholly to the demands of a single discipline tends to lose the benefits that come from cross-pollenization, the testing and proving of his or her findings against those in other fields. The generalist, on the other hand, is looked upon as a time-waster.

Another impediment to the free exchange of conversation in the academic world is that the people there use jargon and buzz words almost as though these were what they grew up on, and ordinary, standard English a foreign language. It is conceivable that academics from different parts of a campus can converse for ten minutes without any real understanding on anybody's part of what has been said beyond the opening and parting remarks that are offered.

The academic life has its privileges, of course. One is the absolute freedom to investigate any subject one chooses to investigate and to express one's opinions, however outrageous or inimical to popular sentiment, in print.

Printed works, of course, allow readers an opportunity to converse in a sense with their authors. The reader can agree or disagree with an author. He or she may accept or reject the author's thesis. And he or she may even respond to ideas found in a book with a book of his or her own.

Such conversations, if they can be called this, are filled with richness. Yet they have some troubling aspects. The success of the confrontation between two minds, the author's and the reader's, is dependent upon a tacit agreement on the part of each to make the most of a shared experience by listening closely and suspending judgement until each has had his or her say. The reader must give full attention to the page before him or her; the author must do whatever is possible to present his or her ideas clearly and forcefully.

There is no substitute for the pleasures and other benefits gained in the free exchange of information and opinion. And it is in this free exchange that our thoughts, beliefs and instincts find their fullest play.

Letters from Anagnostes Solitarium,
November, 1975

Blanche McCrum

In the course of more than forty years of service in academic libraries, it has been my privilege to know personally a few of the leading figures on the national library scene. And it occurs to me that it might not be amiss to pay them tribute now and then. With this in mind, I would pay honor first of all to a lady who was without question one of the truly great librarians of this century. Blanche P. McCrum served our profession for nearly half a century with great distinction, but so quietly and unobtrusively that often what she was doing almost escaped notice.

I first met McCrum when I was a freshman at Washington and Lee University in the early 1930s. Before I met her I had had some notion of following librarianship as a career, but it was McCrum who crystallized that notion and turned it from fancy to reality. And gradually, under the demanding but gentle teaching of this remarkable woman, I made my way into the profession.

I was, for instance, introduced to the mysteries of cataloging and classification by a method which I think was unique but entirely plausible. It was Blanche McCrum's idea that one way to provoke interest in the business of cataloging books was to introduce the student by having him or her tackle such impossibly difficult materials as *incunabula,* and sixteenth century volumes, of which Washington and Lee had a fair number. The challenge of handling a rare book, deciphering a complicated colophon, doing the research to identify printer, author and place of publication, turned the matter of cataloging into an exciting, if difficult, game.

Another aspect of McCrum's teaching that deserves mention was her method of introducing her students to reference work. She had a file of reference questions which she herself had found difficult to answer, and she turned these over to her students, demanding that they find the answers to each, and maintain a log of the reference works in their search and the order in which they were used. Once the problem had been solved, McCrum's keen analysis of the logic of one's search invariably brought to light shortcuts that might have expedited the process. After a year or two of this sound practical work, of course, the student knew about all there was to know about the use of reference books, and quite a bit, too, about the happy way of life that librarianship portended.

McCrum left Washington and Lee in 1936 to become librarian at Wellesley College in Massachusetts, and she served that great woman's college until the mid-1950s. Her capacity for developing a strong staff and her awareness of the power of books as servants to scholarship were truly outstanding. Her annual reports to Wellesley's president were models of professional acumen. They were full of administrative wisdom, and beyond this, were works of literary art that were read by all who saw them with benefit and pleasure.

I have spoken of McCrum's truly remarkable professional capabilities, but she had other qualities and attainments. Her mind was keen, perceptive, sharply critical, and wise. Her talk was of the kind that made one hope she would never end. And she had a boundless stock of book lore, for she devoured books with a kind of omnivorous joy. And when she spoke of books, it was to place each book she mentioned in its proper perspective in the world of literature. In the years I knew her she was never content to let me grow lazy in my reading. She was forever introducing me to some new author, some new literary line, some fresh critical evaluation of the literature of an era or the literature of another country. To take a question to her concerning a book, author, or literary school or group was to enter into a warm world where an acute critical sense and vast reading experience were brought to bear without fuss or ostentation. She did not dominate a conversation, but she surely was in command, and seemed to enjoy leading her companions into fresh, brightly-lit avenues of talk. Her sense of humor which was always kindly and her ability to talk to younger and less knowledgeable persons without condescension made her a delightful companion.

McCrum would have been bothered by such praise as this, for she was a modest person. Yet, such praise proceeds from the fact that she was never content with anything but optimum performance. If her standards were strict, it has to be said that they were applied not only in the work she supervised but also in her own. She was a great lady of librarianship.

Letters from Anagnostes Solitarium,
October, 1976

Carnegie Libraries

It is interesting that one man, almost by accident, and with all good intentions, did so much to stereotype, indeed to freeze, librarianship into a pattern from which it has not yet entirely escaped. Andrew Carnegie, a Pittsburgh steel baron of Scottish descent, literally gave millions of dollars to construct library buildings so that every community that wanted one could have one. He employed architects who, in the interests of economy, developed a standard building design, or rather seven designs, which permitted the sort of assembly-line production of library structures that took place in the first part of the century. Paradoxically, the Carnegie design also produced a condition in which library activities were confined to a space that was seldom entirely appropriate to them. The Carnegie design, while useful, did much to stultify the development of imaginative library service before World War II.

Those seven designs were, in fact, merely the original design and six variations on this. The intention was to provide a dignified, efficient oblong building, eighty feet long and thirty-five feet deep. It had a handsome entrance way, at the top of a short series of steps, which brought the library user immediately into a small central room. Here was the circulation desk, behind which most of the library's professional activities were carried on. To the right of this central hall was another oblong room, which contained the reading materials for adults and whatever reference materials were available. To the left of this hall was another oblong room that was used for children's activities. It was not for more than thirty years that it was seen that there might be a use for a room to serve young adults. As an aside, this failure might well have been an important factor in the loss of many persons in this category as readers.

A somewhat larger community was served by the second library building plan. The basic pattern remained the same, but the first floor plan was somewhat enlarged. The depth of the building was increased to fifty feet, while the breadth of the building became either one hundred or 125 feet. A variation on this second plan appeared, when a second floor was added. The second floor was, in fact, identical to the first, with a stairway leading up from entrance hall to a central room that had, again, a room on either side. These rooms were used for library activities and for public meetings. The essential physical structure of the larger building remained unchanged.

Five more times the basic structural plan was enlarged as the complexities of library service made more and more demands on space. The ultimate Carnegie building is that of the New York Public Library at 42nd Street and Fifth Avenue.

The Carnegie pattern was of course fine for its day, but it is unfortunate that the pattern continued to be used, after its usefulness had been outgrown in public libraries and even academic libraries. The Carnegie library architectural plan was, over more than seventy years, the fashionable plan, and architects accepted it unquestioningly. The splendid Cleveland Public Library building, while adopting minor variations on the Carnegie plan, was still built more or less according to Carnegie's number 6 plan. The Chicago Public Library is another in which that plan, with minor variations incorporated into it, was used. More than fifty structures in large cities about the country are essentially Carnegie structures.

These structures forced libraries into unbelievably frozen patterns of service. And the consequences were predictably unfortunate. The primary building separated adult services from juvenile services. Children were usually forbidden to enter the adult reading rooms, unless accompanied by their parents. Young adults were disenfranchised, since they considered themselves above being seen in the juvenile reading areas and were not welcome in the adult areas. Territorial cleavages appeared in library staffs. Reference librarians claimed the adult reading areas as their own, and childrens' librarians retreated into the juvenile area. The catalogers disappeared into the shallow work space provided for them behind the circulation desk in the central hall and, the circulation people barricaded themselves behind the semi-circular circulation desk. Communications between these embattled and defensive groups became less and less a matter of practice, and service to the public suffered.

All of these restrictive factors were, to be truthful, brought about by the well-intentioned, if ill-advised, use of a building plan that was predicated on production-line economies rather than, as it might have been, on service-oriented requirements. A conjecture may be raised as to how library service would have been affected if Carnegie, in his generosity, demanded more skill and variety in the designing of his libraries.

Letters from Anagnostes Solitarium,
August, 1979

The Bookish Empire

Christopher Morley, certainly a great lover of books and libraries, wrote in his delightful *John Mistletoe,* "The book store is one of humanity's great engines, and one that we use very imperfectly. It is a queer fact that most of us still have the primitive habit of visiting bookshops chiefly to ask for some definite title. . . ." Now Morley was speaking here in the vein of his redoubtable character Roger Mifflin who expressed the belief in *The Haunted Bookshop* that everything needed to cure the world's ills can in fact be found in bookshops. He might as well have been speaking of libraries, however, as the same can be said of them.

It is odd that we so often go to a library to get some specific book or some specific piece of information. This purely utilitarian concept of the way in which a library should be used entirely overlooks one of the most important aspects of a library's reason for existence and, at the same time, some of its most commendable features. What a pity that in our hurried efforts to thrust as many happenings and successes as possible into the confines of a single day, we deny ourselves many of the pleasures and opportunities that the library offers. Morley echoes this sentiment in the amusing sign which he claimed immediately caught the eye of every visitor who entered the doorway of Roger Mifflin's establishment. It was a sign that held out open arms to the visitor, urged him or her to browse to heart's content, hinted that on entering this dusty, book-lined sanctuary an encounter was likely with the ghosts that haunted its dim aisles, and finally suggested: "We have what you want, though you may not know you want it."

This is a straightforward expression of the philosophy of at least one librarian who lived while Morley was still present. It tells of the purpose behind the immense amount of work that always goes into the gathering and processing of a book collection, whether it be for the scholar or researcher, the casual reader or anybody else. Enter this library, it suggests, and take the risk that you will yourself be changed. Move up and down these ranges of books, at pain of being caught up in some new idea that will expand your mind or even damage some one of your favorite prejudices.

Yes, as Morley said, a bookstore or a library is an engine. It is in fact a Trojan horse ready to move within the walls of one's preconceptions and break them down. Our great difficulty is that too few of us are willing to invite the impact of ideas that a library is forever offering to provide. Morley said that we use these engines most inexpertly. Worse than this, we are often afraid of the engine and so unable to have it work for us.

Has any reader of these lines ever had the peculiar experience that comes to one on being alone in a library when its doors have been locked and its visitors gone home? It is one of the most remarkable sensations that a reader of any sensitivity whatever can know. Entering into a building where great dynamos are to be found, spinning in endless rotation is somehow comparable. There, the visitor senses, almost with fear, the great rush of power issuing from those machines. In similar fashion, one is somehow aware in a closed and darkened library of a murmuring silence generated by the energy lying waiting to be tapped in all the rows of books. Books do possess power. Let us not deny it. Who knows what will happen when the measured lines of type on any page of any book touch the quickening thoughts of a reader? Who knows into what magic form an idea found in a book, years old perhaps, can be transformed by a reader of genius? Who knows when someone's mind will be nourished and enlightened by a book that comes to hand? The atmosphere of libraries is unquestionably and palpably electric. Yet too often these great reservoirs of information are left untapped, lie quiet and unused. Or, if they are used, they are not used as fully as they might be. They have a thousand uses: to provide pleasure; to encourage and assist in scientific discovery; to bring about social and political reform; to cure ignorance; and simply to inspire.

It certainly is no mere romantic notion to attribute such powers to books. Books, aligned in their rows on the shelves, are the building blocks of past achievements and upon which the future depends.

Letters from Anagnostes Solitarium,
January, 1980

The Freedom to Read

Censorship of books, urged or practiced by volunteer arbiters of morals or political opinion and by organizations that would establish a coercive concept of Americanism, must be challenged by libraries as part of their responsibility to provide public information and enlightenment through the printed word. (Library Bill of Rights. Adopted by Council of A.L.A., at Atlantic City on June 18, 1948.)

A freedom taken by most Americans almost as a matter of course is the freedom to read whatever they choose. Yet this freedom is fenced in by numerous limitations and controls, some of them intentional, some not.

Censorship is something for which most American readers and scholars hold a marked distaste. The control of ideas is, in popular opinion, totally un-American. The freedom to seek truth wherever it is found and to make whatever use one wishes of that truth, once found, is considered by most an indispensable concomitant of the American ideal.

The university librarian very often feels pressures to limit in one way or another this basic freedom. Almost never a month goes by during which some individual does not step into the librarian's office to raise a question concerning the propriety or advisability of keeping some particular book on the library's shelves. The points of view represented by such persons have ranged from extreme conservatism to extreme liberalism, from soundly critical comment on the inadequacy of a given author or researcher to irrational anger against a book that expresses a point of view different from that of the critic. A student recently announced in the librarian's office that he was certain the librarian was a Communist, because, "the only magazines you subscribe to are the 'leftish' ones." The same student was only moderately chastened, and could not see how he could have missed them, when he was shown sitting on the library's shelves not only a considerable number of "rightish" journals but also a considerable number of "non-partisan" periodicals. On another occasion the librarian was accused by a second student of being "ridiculously conservative" in the choice of periodicals purchased for the library. A faculty member once suggested in all seriousness that students should not be permitted to read books of a controversial political nature unless the student could demonstrate that he or she had taken that professor's course in the rudiments of political science. Another faculty member demanded that "propaganda" material placed on the library's shelves should be labelled "propaganda." On numerous occasions students and faculty members have asked that particular titles be removed from the library's shelves because they were "dangerous" or "improper" or "anti-American."

Two aspects of the problem are reflected in the above examples of the pressures brought to bear on the library because of controversial materials. First, as in the case of the students who thought the library purchased too many periodicals that were either left or right of center in their orientation, the students' actions were based on lack of information. Professionally trained librarians, charged with the responsibility of developing an adequate and useful library, are wholly aware of the need to make available to the reader works representing all points of view and every category of opinion. Second, some interesting issues arise when an individual requests that a book be withdrawn from the shelves or specially marked in some way because it differs with a particular point of view. These can be expressed in the form of questions. Why should any individual set himself or herself up as a judge of what another individual or a group of readers, should read? If a book is specially marked to indicate its point of view, or bias, is it possible for a reader, having seen this special marking to read the book with any degree of objectivity?

Any librarian worth his or her salt would fight for the right of an individual to disagree with an idea or a bookful of ideas. Any librarian would encourage an individual who had such a conflict to express himself or herself either publicly or privately concerning a book or the ideas in it that the individual considered offensive. And no librarian with any awareness of his or her trust to bring people into contact with books and ideas would accept the notion that disagreement with the point of view of a book gives any individual the right to withhold that book from other readers. This sub rosa censorship is in direct opposition to the principle of the right to read, a principal for which American librarians have stood for nearly a hundred years.

Any librarian should be willing to admit, however, that a kind of censorship is practiced every time a book is ordered for his or her library. In selecting books, the librarian always tries to do two things: first, to choose the best possible book on any subject, and, second, to provide as many points of view as possible for the library's users, particularly on subjects that are more or less controversial. The first of these is, as a matter of fact, a form of economy urged on the library by limited funds. The second is a matter of policy which cannot help but make the library's book collection more useful, since individuals of widely varying opinion must always make up the library's group of users, and each user, regardless of his or her opinion, has the right to find information supporting that opinion.

A policy, therefore, that permits the library to adopt a tenable and defensible position with respect to its acquisitions will ensure that books are provided to meet all needs. In maintaining such a policy the library must occasionally make a decision as to the propriety of obtaining a controversial book and making that book available on its shelves. Such decisions are necessary more often in the field of fiction than in other fields. Probably the most important criterion applied in such cases is the one of intention. That is to say that if a book is controversial, and the point of controversy has to do with the moral tone of the work, a reasonable criterion to apply is that of intention. Was this book written in good faith, and is it true to its intention? Or are its questionable passages presented solely for their sensational value? Several years ago, for example, a library refused to purchase Kathleen Winsor's *Forever Amber*. When questioned, the librarians who had made the decision claimed that had the book contained only the superb passage on the plague years in London, it would have been acceptable, but that the repetitious passages concerned with Amber's passionate voyage through life contributed nothing to the significance of the work and destroyed the validity of the author's presentation. Employing the same criterion, and the same line of reasoning, this same library felt no compunction about the purchase of another controversial novel, D. H. Lawrence's *Lady Chatterly's Lover*. If censorship is the policy, then let us make the most of it. But so long as books are purchased under sound policy and for sound reasons, let us make certain that they are all available under identical conditions for all who wish to read them.

Letters from Anagnostes Solitarium,
January, 1981

Index

Adams, Henry. *Education of Henry Adams, The* 24-25,54
Adventures of Huckleberry Finn, The (Twain) 28
Adventures of Tom Sawyer, The (Twain) 63,67
Advice and Consent (Drury) 197
Aesop 176
African Queen, The (Forester) 38
"Aldine Folio Murders, The" (Blochman) 85
Aldrich, Thomas Bailey. *Story of a Bad Boy, The* 67,79-80
Alice's Adventures in Wonderland (Carroll) 50-51
All Passion Spent (Sackville-West) 245
"Allegash and East Branch" (Thoreau) 35-36
Allingham, Margery 159
Alone (Byrd) 81
Along the Road (Huxley) 102
America At Last (White) 92-94
American Boy, The 39
American Tragedy, An (Dreiser) 63
"Antiseptic Baby and the Prophylactic Pup, The" (Guiterman) 18
Appleton, Victor. *Tom Swift and His Undersea Search* 197
Areopagitica (Milton) 11-12
Ariosto, Ludovico 103
Aristotle 239
Arithmetick (Cocker) 102
Arlen, Michael. *Green Hat, The* 236
Arthur, King 21
Astoria (Irving) 25
At the Back of the North Wind (Macdonald) 166
Atlantic Monthly, The 49,242
Atrocities of Book Collecting and Kindred Afflictions (Pipp) 205-207
Augustine, St. *City of God* 246
Austen, Jane 150
Autumn Across America (Teale) 189-190
Awakening (Galsworthy) 89

Babbit (Lewis) 63,65-66
Bach, Johann Sebastian 160,161
Bacon, Francis, Sir. *De Augmentis scientiarum* 103

Bangs, John Kendrick 198
Barbour, Ralph Henry 39
Barclay, Florence Louisa. *Mistress of Shenstone, The* 198, *Rosary, The* 198
Barfield, Owen 123,133
Barometer Rising (MacLennan) 185-186
Barren Ground of Northern Canada, The (Pike) 74,123
Baum, Frank Lyman 198
"Baxter's Procrustes" (Chesnutt) 49
Beebe, Charles William. *Galapagos, World's End* 71, *Jungle Days* 71, *Nonsuch, Land of Water* 71
Bellamy, Edward 176, *Looking Backward, 2000-1887* 129
Benet, William Rose 118
Berry, Jean de France, duc de 205
Beston, Henry. *Outermost House, The* 81-82
Betts, John, firm, London. "Umbrella Globe, The" 225
Between the Lines (Forman) 195
Bible 135,201
Bitter Lemons (Durrell) 36
Black Beauty (Sewell) 236
Blackstone, William, Sir 13
Blackwood's Magazine 118
Bleak House (Dickens) 66
Blochman, Lawrence G. "Aldine Folio Murders, The" 85
Bondage of Ballinger, The (Field) 84, 206
Bonnie Briar Bush, The (Maclaren) 197
Book of the American Spirit (Pyle) 71
Books With Men Behind Them (Fuller) 179
Borland, Hal 189
Boswell, James 44,102,135-136 *Life of Samuel Johnson, LL.D., The* 102, 236
Boy With the Secret Service, The (Rolt-Wheeler) 71
Boy With the U. S. Weather Service, The (Rolt-Wheeler) 71
Boy's Life 39
Bread-Winners, The (Hay) 236
Brown, Samuel 250

© 1986 by The Haworth Press, Inc. All rights reserved.

Browning, Elizabeth Barrett. *Sonnets From the Portuguese* 194
Buchan, John, Sir. *Castle Gay* 41,154, *Dancing Floor, The* 154,155, *Gap In the Curtain, The* 154, *Greenmantle* 40, 141, 153-155, *House of the Four Winds, The* 40,154, *Huntingtower* 40,154, *John Macnab* 154,155, *Man From the Norlands, The* 154, *Memory Hold-the-Door* 156, *Mr. Standfast* 40,154,155, *Montrose* 25,156, *Mountain Meadow* 154, 156-157, *Pilgrim's Way* 156, *Power-House, The* 154,157, *Sick Heart River* 156, *Sing a Song of Sixpence* 154, *Sir Walter Scott* 156, *Thirty-Nine Steps, The* 40, 154-155, *Three Hostages, The* 40, 154,155
Burney, Fanny. *Camilla* 102
Burroughs, John. *Signs and Seasons* 51
Busman's Honeymoon (Sayers) 28,161
Butler, Pierce. *Introduction to Library Science, An* 4
By Pike and Dyke (Henty) 197
Byrd, Richard E. *Alone* 81 *Little America* 51-52

Cackler, Christian. *Recollections of an Old Settler* 212-213
Caesar, Julius. *Commentaries* 103
Caesar, Julius, Sir 101
Camilla (Burney) 102
Canby, Henry Seidel 118
Cape Cod (Thoreau) 97
Captains Courageous (Kipling) 37-38,71, 168
Carnegie, Andrew 265-266
Carroll, Lewis 134 *Alice's Adventures in Wonderland* 50-51
Carter, John 195
Carter, John and Pollard, Graham. *An Enquiry Into the Nature of Certain Nineteenth Century Pamphlets* 195
Castle Gay (Buchan) 40,154
Castlemon, Harry, *Frank In the Woods* 197
Cather, Willa 28
Caxton, William 258
Cerf, Bennett 152
Cervantes, Miguel de. *Don Quixote de la Mancha* 22,103,111
Charlemagne 21-22

Charles Waddell Chesnutt (Chesnutt) 50
Chaucer, Geoffrey 4,12,79,201,202,258, Ellesmere manuscript 201
Chesnutt, Charles Waddell 49-50, "Baxter's Procrustes" 49, *Conjure Woman, The* 49, *Wife of His Youth, The* 49
Chesnutt, Helen. *Charles Waddell Chesnutt* 50
Christie, Agatha 159
Christmas Carol, A (Dickens) 129,171, 172,173
Christopher Morley's Briefcase (Morley) 235-236
Churchill, Winston. *Richard Carvel* 197
Churchill, Winston, Sir 165
Cicero, Marcus Tullius. *Pro Archia* 102
City of God (Augustine, St.) 246
Clemens, Samuel Langhorne see Twain, Mark
Clerk of the Woods, The (Torrey) 97
Clouds of Witness (Sayers) 159
Cocker, Edward. *Arithmetick* 102
Cohan, George M. "Seven Keys to Baldpate" 215
Collequies (Lordan) 225
Commentaries (Caesar) 103
Confessions of an English Opium-Eater (DeQuincey) 236
Conjure Woman, The (Chesnutt) 49
Conover, David. *Once Upon an Island* 125-126
Constance Missal 201
Cook, Edward, Sir 102-103
"Coonskin Library, The" 249-251
Country of the Pointed Firs, The (Jewett) 28,60
Coyle, William. *Ohio Authors and Their Books* 50
Crazy Ladies, The (Elbert) 236
Critical Kit-Kats (Gosse) 194
Crusoe of Lonesome Lake (Stowe) 126
Cutler, Manasseh 250

Dancing Floor, The (Buchan) 154,155
Dante Alighieri 103,161, *Inferno* 12
Dark Wood (Weston) 197
Darwin, Charles. *Origin of Species, The* 17,61,194
David Copperfield (Dickens) 66
Day's Work, A (Kipling) 168
De Augmentis Scientiarum (Bacon) 103
Death In the Afternoon (Hemingway) 64
Decline and Fall of the Roman Empire (Gibbon) 103

Delaney, Shelagh. *A Taste of Honey* 236
DeLa Roche, Mazo 87
DeQuincey, Thomas. *Confessions of an English Opium-Eater* 236
Dickens, Charles 66,136, *Bleak House* 66, *Christmas Carol, A* 129,171, 172,173, *David Copperfield* 66, *Dombey and Son* 66, *Great Expectations* 66, *Martin Chuzzlewit* 172, *Old Curiosity Shop, The* 66, 172, *Oliver Twist* 66, *Our Mutual Friend* 131, *Pickwick Papers, The* 171,173 *Tale of Two Cities, A* 63,66
Dictionary of American English, A 246
Dixon, Franklin W. Hardy Boys series 198
Dodgson, Charles Lutwidge *see* Carroll, Lewis
Dolbier, Morris. *Magic Shop, The* 140
Dolphin, The 83
Dombey and Son (Dickens) 66
Don Quixote de la Mancha (Cervantes) 22,103,111
Donaldson, Stephen R. 181-183, *Illearth War, The* 181, *Lord Foul's Bane* 181, *Power That Preserves, The* 181
Donne, John 12,160
Doughboys: A History of the A.E.F., 1917-1918, The (Stallings) 236
Douglas, Lloyd C. *Magnificent Obsession, The* 63,64
Dreamthorp, A Book of Essays Written in the Country (Smith) 139
Dreiser, Theodore. *American Tragedy, An* 63
Drinkwater, John 36, *Robinson of England* 17,41,59-60,91-92,151
Drury, Allen. *Advice and Consent* 197
Dryden, John 13
Dunsany, Edward J. M. D. P., Lord 199
Durrell, Lawrence. *Bitter Lemons* 36
Dynasts, The (Hardy) 202-203

Each Man's Son (MacLennan) 186
Eddison, Charles 199
Edinburgh Review, The 118
Education of Henry Adams, The (Adams) 24-25,54
Elbert, Joyce. *The Crazy Ladies* 236
Ellesmere manuscript (Chaucer) 201
Elsie Dinsmore (Finley) 198
Elzevir family (printers) 223
Emerson, Ralph Waldo 12-13,23

Encyclopedia Britannica 102,103,232
Endymion (Keats) 258
England Have My Bones (White) 76,151
Enquiry Into the Nature of Certain Nineteenth Century Pamphlets, An (Carter and Pollard) 195
Essay on Criticism, An (Pope) 18
Estimate of Standards for a College Library, An (McCrum) 4
European Discovery of America: The Northern Voyages (Morison) 44
Eustace Diamonds, The (Trollope) 29, 131
Ewing, Thomas 250

Face On the Barroom Floor, The (Titus) 236
Facts About Georgia 226
Fadiman, Clifton 117
Fairbrother, Nan. *House In the Country, The* 236
Falkner, John Meade. *Lost Stradavarius, The* 61, *Nebuly Coat, The* 60-61
"Fall of the House of Usher, The" (Poe) 236
Farewell to Arms, A (Hemingway) 65
Farmer Takes a Wife (Gould) 80
Farnol, Jeffery. *Money Moon, The* 197
Father and Son (Gosse) 17,61,194
Faulkner, William 130
Fear of Books, The (Jackson) 4
Fellowship of the Ring, The (Tolkein) 165
Femmes Savantes, Les (Moliere) 8
Field, Roswell. *Bondage of Ballinger, The* 84,206
Finley, Martha. *Elsie Dinsmore* 198
Fitzhugh, Percy Keese 39
Ford, Collin *see* Pipp, W.J. Van B.
Forester, C. S. *African Queen, The* 38
Forever Amber (Winsor) 271
Forging Ahead (Partington) 195
Forman, Harry Buxton 193-195, *Between the Lines* 195
Forman, Harry Buxton, Jr. 194
Forsyte Saga, The (Galsworthy) 40, 87-90,131
Fosdick, Charles Austin *see* Castlemon, H.
Foxon, David F. *Thomas J. Wise and the Pre-Restoration Drama* 195
Frank In the Woods (Castlemon) 197
Franklin, Benjamin 239
Franklin, John, Sir 226
Frost, Robert 32-33,72

Fuller, Buckminster 239
Fuller, Edmund 15, *Books With Men Behind Them* 179

Galapagos, World's End (Beebe) 71
Galsworthy, John. *Awakening* 89, *Forsyte Saga, The* 40,87-90,131 *Indian Summer of A Forsyte* 89, *Man of Property, The* 236, *On Forsyte 'Change* 89, *Swan Song* 90
Gap In the Curtain, The (Buchan) 154
Garden of Allah, The (Hichens) 198
Gaudy Night (Sayers) 161
Gautier, Theophile 9
Georgian Scene, The (Swinnerton) 152
Gerard, John. *Herball or Generall Historie of Plantes, The* 109
Gibbon, Edward. *Decline and Fall of the Roman Empire, The* 103
Gibbons, Euell. *Stalking the Blue-Eyed Scallop* 97,236, *Stalking the Wild Asparagus* 97,236
"Gold Bug, The" (Poe) 258
Gone With the Wind (Mitchell) 119
Gorfin, Herbert 193
Gosse, Edmund, Sir. *Critical Kit-Kats* 194, *Father and Son* 17,61,194
Gould, John. *Farmer Takes a Wife* 80
Grahame, Kenneth. *Wind In the Willows, The* 63,65
Grapes of Wrath, The (Steinbeck) 63,66
Great Divorce, The (Lewis) 165
Great Expectations (Dickens) 66
Green Hat, The (Arlen) 236
Greene, Anne Bosworth. *Lone Winter, The* 80-81
Greene, Robert 66
Greenmantle (Buchan) 40,141,153-155
Guiterman, Arthur. "Antiseptic Baby and the Prophylactic Pup, The" 18
Gutenberg, Johannes 201

Habitation Enforced, An (Kipling) 168
Halliburton, Richard. *Royal Road to Romance, The* 71
Handbuch der bibliographie (Schneider) 4
Hardy, Thomas 91,136-137, 151, *Dynasts, The* 202-203
Hardy Boys series (Dixon) 198
Harrison. Henry Syndor. *Queed* 198
Haunted Bookshop, The (Morley) 28,59, 84,110,139,203,267
Hay, John. *Bread-Winners, The* 236

Hazard, Thomas Robinson. *Johnny-Cake Papers* 51
He-Who-Came? (Holme) 151
Heffer, Thomas 253
Hemingway, Ernest. *Death In the Afternoon* 64, *Farewell To Arms, A* 65, *Old Man and the Sea, The* 63,64-65
Henty, George A. *By Pike and Dyke* 197
Herball or Generall Historie of Plantes, The (Gerard) 109
Hichens, Robert S. *Garden of Allah, The* 198
History of British India, The (Mill) 103
History of France (Simonde de Sismondi) 103
History of Pendennis, The (Thackeray) 19-20,66
Hodgins, Eric. *Mr. Blandings Builds His Dream House* 236
Holme, Constance 149-152, *He-Who-Came?* 151, *Lonely Plough, The* 151, *Old Road From Spain, The* 149,150-151,
Holmes, Oliver Wendell 114-115
Holmes, Oliver Wendell, Jr. 24-25
Holtby, Winifred. *South Riding* 151
Homer. *Iliad* 103, *Odyssey* 103
Hood, Thomas 110
Horace 103
House In the Country, The (Fairbrother) 236
House of the Four Winds, The (Buchan) 40,154
Howells, William Dean 50
Human Comedy, The (Saroyan) 232-233
Humphrey, Duke of Gloucester 205
Hunter, Dard. *Papermaking in Indo-China* 76
Huntingtower (Buchan) 40,154
Huxley, Aldous. *Along the Road* 102

Iliad (Homer) 103
Illearth War, The (Donaldson) 181
Indian Summer of a Forsyte (Galsworthy) 89
Inferno (Dante Alighieri) 12
Introduction To Library Science, An (Butler) 4
Irving, Washington. *Astoria* 25
Islandia (Wright) 27,109-110,134, 175-177
Ivanhoe (Scott) 63,66,202

Jackson, Charles *Lost Weekend, The* 236
Jackson, Holbrook. *Fear of Books, The* 4

James, Will. *Smoky* 71
Jaques, Florence. *Snowshoe Country* 51
Jefferson, Thomas 239
Jeffries, Richard 9
Jewett, Sarah Orne. *Country of the Pointed Firs, The* 27-28,60
John Macnab (Buchan) 154,155
John Mistletoe (Morley) 267
Johnson, Owen. *Skippy Bedelle* 71, *Varmint, The* 71
Johnson, Samuel 102,135-136
Johnny-Cake Papers (Hazard) 51
Jungle Book, The (Kipling) 168,169
Jungle Days (Beebe) 71

Keats, John 118, *Endymion* 258
Kelland, Clarence Budington 39
Kennedy, John F. 93
Kipling, John Lockwood 169
Kipling, Rudyard 167-169, *Captains Courageous* 37-38,71,168, *Day's Work, A* 168, *Habitation Enforced, An* 168, *Jungle Book, The* 168,169, *Puck of Pook's Hill* 17,140, *Seven Seas, The* 168, *Something of Myself* 140, *Walking Delegate, A* 168
Krutch, Joseph Wood 97,189

Lady Chatterly's Lover (Lawrence) 271
Lamb, Charles 97
Landor, Walter Savage 54
La Rouchefoucauld, Francois 102
Lawrence, D. H. 8, *Lady Chatterly's Lover* 271
Lee, Robert E. 92,241
Lemperley, Paul 196
Lenski, Lois. *Little Farm, The* 67, *Little Fire Engine, The* 67, *Letters of Thomas J. Wise and John Henry Wrenn, The* (Ratchford) 195
Lewis, C. S. 123,133-134,163-166,199 *Great Divorce, The* 165, *Out of the Silent Planet* 164, *Perelandra* 164, *Screwtape Letters, The* 46, 163, *Surprised by Joy* 45, *That Hideous Strength* 165
Lewis, Sinclair. *Babbitt* 63,65-66
Life of Samuel Johnson, LL.D., The (Boswell) 102,236
Little America (Byrd) 51-52
Little Farm, The (Lenski) 67
Little Fire Engine, The (Lenski) 67
Locke, John 13

Lofting, Hugh. *Voyages of Doctor Dolittle, The* 207
London Times Literary Supplement 193
Lone Winter, The (Greene) 80-81
Lonely Plough, The (Holme) 151
Looking Backward, 2000-1887 (Bellamy) 129
Lord Foul's Bane (Donaldson) 181
Lordan, James. *Collequies* 225
Lost Stradavarius, The (Falkner) 61
Lost Weekend, The (Jackson) 236
Lost Woods, The (Teale) 51
Loveman, Amy 118
Lucas, E. V. *Over Bemerton's* 84-85
Luck of Barry Lyndon, The (Thackeray) 197

Macaulay, Thomas Babington 103
McCrum, Blanche P. 263-264, *Estimate of Standards for a College Library, An* 4
Macdonald, George 166,199, *At the Back of the North Wind* 166
Machen, Arthur 199
Maclaren, Ian. *Bonnie Briar Bush, The* 197
MacLennan, Hugh 185-188, *Barometer Rising* 185-186, *Each Man's Son* 186, *Precipice, The* 186, *Return of the Sphinx, The* 185,187, *Two Solitudes* 186, *Watch That Ends the Night, The* 187
Magic Shop, The (Dolbier) 140
Magnificent Obsession, The (Douglas) 63,64
Maine Woods, The (Thoreau) 35,36,97
Man From the Norlands, The (Buchan) 154
Man of Property, The (Galsworthy) 236
Marquand, John P. *Wickford Point* 197
Martin Chuzzlewit (Dickens) 172
Master of Ballantrae, The (Stevenson) 232
Melville, Herman. *Moby-Dick* 133
Memoirs of a Fox-Hunting Man (Sassoon) 197
Memory Hold-the-Door (Buchan) 156
Midsummer-Night's Dream, A (Shakespeare) 140
Mill, James. *History of British India, The* 103
Millay, Edna St. Vincent 72
Milne, A. A. 65
Milton, John. *Areopagitica* 11-12
Mr. Blandings Builds His Dream House (Hodgins) 236

Mr. Standfast (Buchan) 40,154,155
Mistress Masham's Repose (White) 92
Mrs. Miniver (Struther) 197
Mistress of Shenstone, The (Barclay) 198
Mitchell, Margaret. Gone With the Wind 119
Mitford, Mary Russell 194
Moby-Dick (Melville) 133
Moliere. Femmes Savantes, Les 8
Money Moon, The (Farnol) 197
Monsieur Beaucaire (Tarkington) 236
Montesquieu 13
Montrose (Buchan) 25,156
More, Thomas, Sir 134,176
Morgan, John Pierpont 257-259
Morison, Samuel Eliot. European Discovery of America: The Northern Voyages 44
Morley, Christopher. Christopher Morley's Briefcase 235-236, Haunted Bookshop, The 28,59,84,110,139, 203,267, John Mistletoe 267, Parnassus on Wheels 5,28,52,59, 85-86,110,139
Morris, William 54,91-92,131,202, News From Nowhere 36,60
Mountain Meadow (Buchan) 154,156-157
Muir, John 189, Yosemite, The 5
Murder Must Advertise (Sayers) 28
Mysteries of Udolpho, The (Radcliffe) 61

Napoleon I, 102
National Cyclopedia of American Biography 111
Natural History and Antiquities of Selborne, The (White) 17,51,59
Nebuly Coat, The (Falkner) 60-61
New York Times Book Review, The 118
New Yorker, The 118,193
Newcomes, The (Thackeray) 66
News From Nowhere (Morris) 36,60
Nine Tailors, The (Sayers) 29,161
Nonsuch, Land of Water (Beebe) 71
North With the Spring (Teale) 97,190

Odyssey (Homer) 103
Ohio Authors and Their Books (Coyle) 50
Old Curiosity Shop, The (Dickens) 66, 172
Old Man and the Sea, The (Hemingway) 63,64-65

Old Road From Spain, The (Holme) 149, 150-151
Oliver Twist (Dickens) 66
Olson, Sigurd F. Runes of the North 123
Omar Khayyam. Rubaiyat, The 245
On Forsyte 'Change (Galsworthy) 89
Once and Future King, The (White) 92
Once Upon an Island (Conover) 125-126
One Man's Meat (White) 106
Origin of Species, The (Darwin) 17,61, 194
Osler, William, Sir 17
Orczy, Baroness. Scarlet Pimpernel, The 159
Our Mutual Friend (Dickens) 131
Out of the Silent Planet (Lewis) 164
Outermost House, The (Beston) 81-82
Over Bemerton's (Lucas) 84-85

Page, Thomas Nelson. Two Little Confederates 197
Papermaking in Indo-China (Hunter) 76
Parnassus on Wheels (Morley) 5,28,52, 59,85-86,110,139
Partington, Wilfred. Forging Ahead 195
Pascal, Blaise 13
Peake, Mervyn 199
Pepys, Samuel 44
Perelandra (Lewis) 164
Peterkin, Julia Scarlet Sister Mary 236
Petrarch 103
Petzholdt, Julius 109
Pickwick Papers, The (Dickens) 171,173
Pigafetta, Antonio 44
Pike, Warburton. Barren Ground of Northern Canada, The 74,123
Pilgrim's Way (Buchan) 156
Pinkerton, Kathrene. Wilderness Wife 126
Pipp, W. J. Van B. Atrocities of Book Collecting and Kindred Afflictions, The 205-207
Plato. 54,134,176,239
Plutarch 23
Poe, Edgar Allan. "Fall of the House of Usher, The" 236, "Gold Bug, The" 258
Pollard, Graham 195
Pope, Alexander 13, Essay on Criticism, An 18
Power-House, The (Buchan) 154,157
Power That Preserves, The (Donaldson) 181
Precipice, The (MacLennan) 186

Pro Archia (Cicero) 102
Puck of Pook's Hill (Kipling) 17,140
Pyle, Howard. *Book of the American Spirit* 71

Queechy (Warner) 198
Queed (Harrison) 198
Quentin Durward (Scott) 202

Rackham, Arthur 65
Radcliffe, Ann. *Mysteries of Udolpho, The* 61
Ratchford, Fannie. *Letters of Thomas J. Wise and John Henry Wrenn, The* 195
Recollections of an Old Settler (Cackler) 212-213
Redding, Jay Saunders. *To Make a Poet Black* 50
Reilly, Robert James. *Romantic Religion* 133
Return of the Sphinx, The (MacLennan) 185,187
Richard Carvel (Churchill) 197
Riley, James Whitcomb 198
Robinson of England (Drinkwater) 17, 41,59-60,91-92,151
Rollo books 198
Rolt-Wheeler, Francis. *Boy With the Secret Service, The* 71, *Boy With the Weather Service, The* 71
Romantic Religion (Reilly) 133
Room of One's Own, A (Woolf) 125,133
Rosary, The (Barclay) 198
Rose, The 242
Royal Road to Romance, The (Halliburton) 71
Rubaiyat of Omar Khayyam, The 245
Runes of the North (Olson) 123
Ruskin, John 210

Sackville-West, Victoria. *All Passion Spent* 245
St. Nicolas Magazine 39,69
Saroyan, William. *Human Comedy, The* 232-233
Sassoon, Siegfried. *Memoirs of a Fox-Hunting Man* 197
Saturday Review of Literature, The 118, 152
Sayers, Dorothy 159-162, *Busman's Honeymoon* 28,161, *Clouds of Witness* 159, *Gaudy Night* 161, *Murder Must Advertise* 28, *Nine Tailors, The* 29,161, *Suspicious Characters* 161, *Whose Body?* 159,161
Scarlet Pimpernel, The (Orczy) 159
Scarlet Sister Mary (Peterkin) 236
Schneider, George. *Handbuch der bibliographie* 4
Scott, Walter, Sir 71,118,129, *Ivanhoe* 63,66,202, *Quentin Durward* 202
Screwtape Letters, The (Lewis) 46,163
Seaman, Augusta Huiell 39
Seton Thompson, Ernest 189
"Seven Keys to Baldpate" (Cohan) 215
Seven Seas, The (Kipling) 168
Sewell, Anna. *Black Beauty* 236
Shakespeare, William 134,136,202, 253-255, *Midsummer-Night's Dream, A* 140, *Tragedy of King Richard the Third, The* 199
Shelley, Mary 61
Sick Heart River (Buchan) 156
Sigismond Inheritance, The (Uzanne) 83-84
Signs and Seasons (Burroughs) 51
Simonde de Sismondi, Jean Charles Leonard. *History of France* 103
Sing a Song of Sixpence (Buchan) 154
Sir Walter Scott (Buchan) 156
Sire de Maletroit's Door, The (Stevenson) 215
Sismondi, Jean Claude Leonard de *see* Simonde de Sismondi, Jean Charles Leonard
Skippy Bedelle (Johnson) 71
Smith, Alexander. *Dreamthorp, A Book of Essays Written In the Country* 139
Smoky (James) 71
Snowshoe Country (Jaques) 51
Socrates 239
Something of Myself (Kipling) 140
Song of Roland 21
Sonnets From the Portuguese (Browning) 194
South Riding (Holtby) 151
Stalking the Blue-Eyed Scallop (Gibbons) 97,236
Stalking the Wild Asparagus (Gibbons) 97,236
Stallings, Laurence. *Doughboys: A History of the A.E.F., 1917-1918, The* 236
Steinbeck, John. *Grapes of Wrath, The* 63,66, *Travels With Charley* 93

Steiner, Rudolf 133
Stevenson, Robert Louis 95,232, *Master of Ballantrae, The* 232, *Sire de Maletroit's Door, The* 215, *Treasure Island* 40,232
Stockton, Frank 131
Story of a Bad Boy, The (Aldrich) 67, 79-80
Stowe, Harriet Beecher. *Uncle Tom's Cabin* 11,129
Stowe, Leland. *Crusoe of Lonesome Lake* 126
Struther, Jan. *Mrs. Miniver* 197
Surprised by Joy (Lewis) 45
Suspicious Characters (Sayers) 161
Swan Song (Galsworthy) 90
Swift, Jonathan 134
Swinnerton, Frank Arthur. *Georgian Scene, The* 152

Tale of Two Cities, A (Dickens) 63,66
Tarkington, Booth. *Monsieur Beaucaire* 236
Tasso, Torquato 103
Taste of Honey, A (Delaney) 236
Tatler, The 97
Teale, Edwin Way 189-190, *Autumn Across America* 189-190, *Lost Woods, The* 51, *North With the Spring* 97,190, *Wandering Through Winter* 51,97
Teasdale, Sara 72
Thackeray, William Makepeace 131, *History of Pendinnis, The* 19-20, 66, *Luck of Barry Lyndon, The* 197, *Newcomes, The* 66, *Vanity Fair* 63,66,236
That Hideous Strength (Lewis) 165
Thirty-Nine Steps, The (Buchan) 40, 154-155
Thomas, the Norman. *Tristan* 161
Thomas J. Wise and the Pre-Restoration Drama (Foxon) 195
Thoreau, Henry David. "Allegash and East Branch" 35-36, *Cape Cod* 97, *Maine Woods, The* 35,36,97, *Walden* 25,29,35, *Week on the Concord and Merrimack Rivers, A* 25,29,51,75,97,98,121
Three Hostages, The (Buchan) 40,154, 155
Titus, John Henry. *Face On the Barroom Floor, The* 236
To Make a Poet Black (Redding) 50

Tolkein, J. R. R. 123,133,166,179,181, 199, *Fellowship of the Ring, The* 165
Tom Swift and His Undersea Search (Appleton) 197
Torrey, Bradford. *Clerk of the Woods, The* 97
Toynbee, Arnold 155,239
Tragedy of King Richard the Third, The (Shakespeare) 199
Travels With Charley (Steinbeck) 93
Treasure Island (Stevenson) 40,232
Trevelyan, George Macaulay 103
Tristan (Thomas, the Norman) 161
Trollope, Anthony 118,151, *Eustace Diamonds, The* 29,131
Twain, Mark 129, *Adventures of Huckleberry Finn, The* 28, *Adventures of Tom Sawyer, The* 63,67
Two Little Confederates (Page) 197
Two Solitudes (MacLennan) 186

"Umbrella Globe, The" (Betts, John, firm, London) 225
Uncle Tom's Cabin (Stowe) 11,129
Uzanne, Louis Octave. *Sigismond Inheritance, The* 83-84

Vanity Fair (Thackeray) 63,66,236
Varmint, The (Johnson) 71
Velikovsky, Immanuel. *Worlds in Collision* 239
Virgil 103
Voltaire 13,103
Voyages of Doctor Dolittle, The (Lofting) 207

Walden (Thoreau) 25,29,35
Walking Delegate, A (Kipling) 168
Waller, Mary E. *Woodcarver of 'Lympus, The* 198
Wandering Through Winter (Teale) 51,97
War In Heaven (Williams) 180
Warner, Susan. *Queechy* 198
Watch That Ends the Night, The (MacLennan) 187
Watson, John *see* Maclaren, Ian
Week On the Concord and Merrimack Rivers, A (Thoreau) 25,29,51,75, 97,98,121
Weston, Christine. *Dark Wood* 197
White, E. B. *One Man's Meat* 106

White, Gilbert. *Natural History and Antiquities of Selbourne, The* 17, 51,59
White, T. H. 92-94, *America At Last* 92-94, *England Have My Bones* 76,151, *Mistress Masham's Repose* 92, *Once and Future King* 92
Whose Body? (Sayers) 159,161
Wickford Point (Marquand) 197
Wife of His Youth, The (Chesnutt) 49
Wilderness Wife (Pinkerton) 126
Williams, Charles 123,133,166,179-180, 199, *War In Heaven* 180
Willoughby, Edwin E. 253-255
Wilson, Edmund. 117
Wind In the Willows, The (Grahame) 63,65

Winsor, Kathleen. *Forever Amber* 271
Wise, Thomas J. 193-196
Wolfe, Thomas 119, 130
Woodcarver of 'Lympus, The (Waller) 198
Woolf, Virginia. *Room of One's Own, A* 125,133
Wordsworth, William 77,92
Worlds In Collision (Velikovsky) 239
Wrenn, John Henry 195
Wright, Orville 241
Wright, Wilbur 241
Wright, Austin Tappan. *Islandia* 27, 109-110,134,175-177

Yankee Doodle Dandy 236
Yosemite, The (Muir) 5

For Product Safety Concerns and Information please contact our EU representative GPSR@taylorandfrancis.com
Taylor & Francis Verlag GmbH, Kaufingerstraße 24, 80331 München, Germany